The Shakespeare Guide *to* ITALY

Retracing the Bard's Unknown Travels

Richard Paul Roe

HARPER PERENNIAL

NEW YORK • LONDON • TORONTO • SYDNEY • NEW DELHI • AUCKLAND

HARPER ● PERENNIAL

HarperCollins books may be purchased for educational, business, or sales promotional use. For information please write: Special Markets Department, HarperCollins Publishers, 10 East 53rd Street, New York, NY 10022.

Photoshop work on author's photographs by Stephanie Hopkins.

FIRST EDITION

Library of Congress Cataloging-in-Publication Data is available upon request.

ISBN 978-0-06-207426-3 (pbk.)

11 12 13 14 15   SCP   10 9 8 7 6 5 4 3 2 1

Contents

MAPS

All maps by Francis Sheehan

ACKNOWLEDGMENTS

The writing of this book would not have been possible without the encouragement and assistance of the numerous individuals in America, Italy, and England who selflessly contributed their time, impressions, advice, and expertise over the years—the number of which I hesitate to count.

Foremost among them is Jeanice Uhrich Lott, who, as my manuscript editor, has exercised her indispensable skills upon prose.

In addition to my gratitude to the many Italian archivists, curators, museum directors, translators, and assistants who shepherded my work along its unusual path, I am especially indebted to those Italian scholars and professors whose insights were invaluable. Their names are stated in the applicable chapters of this book.

Hilary Roe Metternich, my daughter, has been both my research and business aide throughout the period of writing this book.

Finally, for my wife, Jane, here is the story we have both been living.

RICHARD PAUL ROE

FOREWORD

One of the great satisfactions of life is to embark on a long, leisurely journey—especially an absorbing intellectual adventure filled with mystery and promise.

The book you are holding in your hands is the result of such a journey, undertaken by Richard Paul Roe, my father, who passed away on December 1, 2010. By the time Dad arrived at his desk to set down *The Shakespeare Guide to Italy: Retracing the Bard's Unknown Travels*, he knew, as a seasoned lawyer, that tangible evidence was probably the best source for getting to the heart of things. He would applaud the prosecutor who interrupted one witness's byzantine account of the murder with a laconic: "Just the facts, Ma'am."

My father focused on a question that had puzzled him for years: how could someone clearly as intelligent as William Shakespeare repeatedly say things about Italy in his plays that, as was commonly assumed, were so inaccurate? Was it because Shakespeare never left England and referred, therefore, to an Italy he couldn't possibly know? Could this be true? Dad didn't think so.

Armed with his deep knowledge of medieval and Renaissance history and literature, his law practice at an end, my father set out on his quest: investigating for himself whether Shakespeare's reference to localities on the ground in his plays set in Italy—which Dad called the Italian Plays—were mistaken at all. As the astonishing results of his search across the length and breadth of Italy revealed themselves one by one—much like an archaeologist excavating artifacts after centuries of buried silence—the only conclusion possible was that the descriptive references uttered by the characters in Shakespeare's Italian Plays reflected, to a surprising degree, realities on the ground. It never ceased to amaze my father that almost everything mentioned in the Italian Plays can still be visited now—and this, after four hundred years.

It was a great satisfaction for my father to experience the interest of others in the results of his quest. His book can be read on several levels: as a supplement to understanding more about each Italian Play; as a knowledgeable traveling companion of places in Italy where the plays are set; as a window into the politics and culture of the sixteenth-century Mediterranean; or, not least, as a serious forensic revisiting of the accepted belief that the writer of the Italian Plays never set foot out of Jolly Old England.

My father's fundamental goal in bringing into being *The Shakespeare Guide to Italy* has been to present, in an accessible manner, enough evidence to support the view that whoever wrote the Italian Plays must have, unlike William Shakespeare of Stratford-on-Avon, ventured out of England and onto the Continent. As my father has meticulously demonstrated between the covers of this volume, the only possible conclusion one can come to—throwing one's hands up in the air—is that whoever wrote the Shakespearean plays set in Italy, plays we have loved for centuries, could only have seen Italy with his very own eyes.

HILARY ROE METTERNICH

INTRODUCTION

*I*n revered Italian Shakespeare scholar Ernesto Grillo's acclaimed *Shakespeare and Italy*—a posthumous 1949 publication of his lectures—Grillo declares that far from being ossified Tradition's "unlearned actor . . . ignorant in the rules of prosody," Shakespeare was, instead, a masterful, erudite, multilingual artist whose compositional achievements were "in reality derived from a profound study of poetic art . . . such as [is] frequently found . . . in those writers who are most versed in the works of the Greeks and Romans." Shakespeare, Grillo protests, was "no unlearned genius . . . fallen meteor-like from heaven."

In subsequent years, scholars such as Andrew Werth ("Shakespeare's 'Lesse Greek'" [2002]) and Earl Showerman ("Mythopoesis of Resurrection: Hesiod to Shakespeare" [2009]) have extensively corroborated Grillo's observation that in Shakespeare's lifetime "some of the books to which he was indebted for his material had not been translated into English." Shakespeare himself, they confirm, translated much theretofore untranslated material that the great poet-playwright wished to use in his plays and poems: "Frequently," observes Grillo, "[in Shakespeare's plays] we find whole lines translated literally from Italian without the slightest alteration. . . . [O]ur poet," he concludes, "must undoubtedly have had recourse to MSS. in Italian." Grillo's statement is supported by such academicians across the generations as J. Churton Collins (*Studies in Shakespeare* [1904]) and Jason Lawrence of the University of Hull ("'The story is extant, and writ in very choice Italian': Shakespeare's dramatizations of Cinthio" [2004]).

But Shakespeare was more than just an enthusiastic reader and translator of Italian literature. In the company of scholars such as Violet Jeffrey ("Shakespeare's Venice" [1932]) and Lewis Einstein (*The Italian Renaissance in England* [1902]), Grillo is assured by the playwright's exhaustive knowledge of life on the peninsula that not only "must Shakespeare have visited Italy," but "[he] must have visited Milan, Verona, Venice, Padua and Mantua." Grillo points out that Italy would beckon irresistibly to "a man of Shakespeare's culture and intellect . . . because to the literary and artistic world of his day Italy was . . . the mother of learning and classical culture." Grillo's conclusion ought to be of no surprise, for as Murray Levith puts it in *Shakespeare's Italian Settings and Plays* [1989]: "In almost all the dramas set in Italy, learning and education are major themes."

Now comes Richard Paul Roe's *The Shakespeare Guide to Italy* to demonstrate Grillo's point. In response, for example, to Grillo's statement that *The Taming of the Shrew* "displays such an intimate acquaintance not only with the manners and customs of Italy but also with the minutest details of domestic life that it cannot have been gleaned from books or acquired in the course of conversations with travelers returned from Padua," Roe expresses hearty agreement. Himself a celebrated writer, scholar, and lawyer, Roe once quoted Ray Bradbury to me: "The good writers touch life often. The mediocre ones run a quick hand over her." And if ever there were an author of Elizabethan England who was immersed in Italian literature and life, Roe argued, it was Shakespeare.

After all, apart from thirteen plays that selectively chronicle and imaginatively recount the history of England, Shakespeare sets the majority of his plays in *Italy*. This is a remarkable commitment to the exploration and exposition of a foreign culture by one who many still believe was an insular Cotswolds merchant, an English "homebody" more interested in the bourgeois pursuit of making money in Stratford and London than in a cerebral life devoted to the mastery of ancient languages, the poetic arts, history, politics, law, and the literature of classical antiquity—a life crowned by the experience of travel to such cities of historic import as Florence and Messina; Venice, a *machina theatralis*; and Padua, a renowned intellectual capital.

The measure of Shakespeare's dedication in his life's art to all things Italian should not be trivialized or overlooked. Such zealous, almost single-minded attention to a foreign country invites investigative inquiry rather than the easy wave-of-the-hand dismissal offered by many who believe the playwright's preoccupation is of negligible concern. After all, no reader would think it unworthy of investigation were Chaucer, the great court poet, to have set much of his work in fourteenth-century Scandinavia, or were Edith Wharton to have peopled her books with a superfluity of characters from the nineteenth-century Yucatán. And if Laura Ingalls Wilder had written not of pioneer life in the American Midwest but of life on the plantations of Mississippi, Alabama, or Georgia, scholars would be plundering the territory of the old Confederacy for footprints of the author's life and associations. After all, writers write of what they *know*. As Dee Stiffler puts it, they "cannibalize" their lives.

Hence the importance of Roe's groundbreaking achievement in *The Shakespeare Guide to Italy*, the product of decades of voluminous reading and study, nurtured by years of protracted on-site research in Italy. In his landmark contribution to Shakespeare studies, Roe has responded to the challenge posed by Shakespeare's obsession with Italy and has produced a work which, with unimpeachable authority, demonstrates that, like other great writers, Shakespeare wrote knowingly of a world within which he had lived and from which he drew much of his inspirational fire. Italy was his adopted world, and it was Shakespeare's experience there that he cannibalized, if you will, to create some of his, and history's, most accomplished literary achievements: the "Italian Plays" of the Shakespeare canon.

Can anyone doubt it? Well, some do. But *why*? Why does it distress so many that Shakespeare was in Italy? What are the implications of this discovery?

Why and what, indeed.

Most discerning readers know—quite apart from any discussion of Shakespeare in Italy—of the many questions that have arisen over the years due to the anomalies between the substance of the Shakespeare texts (composed by an unrivalled craftsman who, as *Oregonian* editor Harvey Scott has acknowledged, "gathered unto himself the intellectual wealth of an era") and the largely suppositious, nondescript life of Will Shakspere of provincial Warwickshire, to whom the authorship of those works is conventionally attributed. These readers know that Shakspere of Stratford, the long-serving candidate of Tradition—the butcher's-apprentice-turned-businessman of little more than anecdotal legacy—is an unconvincing recipient of the honor that has been bestowed on him. The "disconnect" underscoring the importance of Roe's book therefore occurs when Shakespeare the adventurer in Italy is compared with the Shakespeare we have been offered for generations by the fierce partisans of Shakespeare orthodoxy—those pious, unquestioning adherents to the legend of Shakespeare the bellowing butcher and mischievous deer-poacher who kept his Midlands feet firmly planted, like his mythic mulberry tree, in England. Fidelity to Tradition's fantastic description of Shakespeare as an unaccountable genius who could write knowingly of distant worlds to which he had never traveled almost necessarily requires that those solemn defenders of the Shakespeare Tradition disclaim and ridicule any argument that their man studied Italian and sojourned in Europe among the well- and nobly-born.

Roe helps us recognize that if we are to pursue a better understanding of Shakespeare, we cannot probe the life of a dull and almost assuredly illiterate man (Shakspere of Stratford neither wrote nor received so much as a single letter in his lifetime, and none of his children could write either). There is, after all, *nothing to probe*. Roe knows that the proper course to revealing his or her author in an authentic light, particularly in the absence of a credible biography, is through an examination of the writer's *works*—his or her literary fingerprints. Therein and thereby the life (and, as fingerprints also invariably provide, the identity!) of Shakespeare will be disclosed—not by an attempt to force irregular pieces into a literary puzzle in a misguided effort to reconcile the origin of these works with the life of a man who patently had none of the requisite preparation and experience to create them.

That such an investigative pursuit to clear the air of the smoke that has been blown up the noses of readers by the Shakespeare Establishment should be undertaken by Roe is in accord with the best principles of literary and historical scholarship, as well as standard biocritical practice. After all, we rely on plays like *The Importance of Being Earnest* to help us better understand the conflicted double life of a "Bunburying" Oscar Wilde ("Give a man a mask and he will tell you the truth," Wilde once, revealingly, said). Plays like *Long Day's Journey into Night* and *The Iceman Cometh* prove incomparable aides in helping us gain insight into the alcohol-soaked hell that tormented Eugene O'Neill. The cover of drama is a thin veil indeed, and Roe's *The Shakespeare Guide to Italy* parts of one of the more important veils in literary history—a veil that has hidden Shakespeare from our view for centuries.

With the publication of Roe's book one might say, "How timely!" or "At last!"—particularly given that such would-be guides to Shakespeare as Emma Jones and Rhiannon Guy dejectedly admit in their recent book, *The Shakespeare Companion* [2005], that "the hard facts we know about Shakespeare do not amount to much more than a rhyming couplet." Their mournfulness joins a chorus of lament that we have heard for generations, as Jones and Guy join illustrious company in their frustration. Authors such as Mark Twain (*Is Shakespeare Dead?* [1909]), Sir George Greenwood (*Is There a Shakespeare Problem?* [1916]), and Diana Price (*Shakespeare's Unorthodox Biography: New Evidence of an Authorship Problem* [2000]), as well as distinguished thespians Mark Rylance (the first Artistic Director of Shakespeare's Globe), Orson Welles, Michael York, Jeremy Irons, and the incomparable Sir Derek Jacobi are only several among thousands of Shakespeare aficionados who have long proclaimed what many others have been too timid to say: the thesis positing Will Shakspere of Stratford-upon-Avon as history's most formidable wordsmith, master dramatist, and ageless poet is simply untenable, for it is a faith-based conviction established not on evidence, logic, and commitment to the scientific method, but on sentimental legend, airy rumor, romantic fable, hearsay, and rank nonsense.

"Home-keeping youth have ever homely wits," Shakespeare writes in *The Two Gentlemen of Verona*, one of his lesser-known Italian plays. One can hardly imagine a writer with such a perspective on the illumination that awaits the sojourner of life in foreign climes to have arisen from a man who was rarely known to leave his house except to transact business. Many lesser dramatists of the Elizabethan and Jacobean eras such as Chapman, Marlowe, Lodge, Munday, Sackville, and Jonson were worldly travelers. It is impossible to imagine that the writer we have come to know as Shakespeare was not. Happily, given the work of Richard Paul Roe, we no longer have to guess. Now, we know.

DANIEL L. WRIGHT, DIRECTOR
THE SHAKESPEARE AUTHORSHIP RESEARCH CENTRE
CONCORDIA UNIVERSITY
PORTLAND, OREGON

PREFACE

T here is a secret Italy hidden in the plays of Shakespeare. It is an ingeniously described Italy that has neither been recognized, nor even suspected — not in four hundred years — save by a curious few. It is exact; it is detailed; and it is brilliant. It ranges across territories in Lombardy and the Venetian Republic, leaps over the Apennine Mountains to Tuscany, soars southward to span the great island of Sicily; and, not incidentally, makes a visit to a magical dot in the Tyrrhenian Sea, just off the Sicilian shore.

These descriptions are in challenging detail, and nearly all their locations can still be found in Italy today. It is an Italy that has never before been acknowledged because of a widely accepted dogma that negated its existence, dampening any motive to leave home and go in search of it. Of the few things about Italy that critics admit the playwright got right, they say he must have learned them from a source right there in England, especially since the proclaimed playwright, William Shakespeare of Stratford-upon-Avon, had never been in Italy — a consistently asserted fact used to explain why the author of the plays set in Italy made repeated mistakes about that country.

In truth, as will be demonstrated, the precise and abundant allusions in those plays to places and things the length of that country are so unique to it that they attest to the playwright's personal travels there. By journeying in Italy today, with the Italian plays in hand, reading them as though they were books of instruction, the playwright's vast erudition about that exciting country and its civilization is revealed.

The plays in the Shakespeare *First Folio* are organized under the subject headings *Comedies*, *Histories*, and *Tragedies*. However, if arranged differently, according to their principal geographies, it demonstrates that whoever wrote the plays set in Italy had a personal interest in that country equal to the interest in his own.

Thirteen plays are set in the playwright's own geography. These include the "History" plays, largely based on Raphael Holinshed's 1578 *Chronicles of England, Scotland and Ireland*, whose principal scenes are necessarily set in England; and, on its more antique soil, *King Lear* in ancient Britain and *Cymbeline* in ancient Wales. Yet when free to choose any locale in the world for a fiction play, the author has set *only one* of his plays in his own England: *The Merry Wives of Windsor*.

For Italy, there are also thirteen plays. Ten are set during the Medieval or Renaissance era, while the remaining three, *Coriolanus*, *Titus Andronicus*, and *Julius Caesar*, are set well in the past, on the soil of ancient Rome, in times and places which also exhibit the author's erudition.

There are ten additional plays, of course, and the playwright has chosen to set each one of them in a separate foreign place, such as his famous *Hamlet* in Denmark and his *Antony and Cleopatra* in Egypt.

To summarize: there are *ten* plays of fiction set in Italy, *one* fiction play set in England, and *one* play set in ten other places in the world. Why this ten-to-one ratio? Why has this most creative of writers, when free to choose a setting for a play, chosen Italy *ten times more often* than other places, *including* his own England?

A number of critics have suggested that the models for the author's Italian settings were actually places in England, to which he merely applied Italian names. On examining what henceforth will be referred to as the "Italian Plays" while in Italy, however, the places and things alluded to or described by the playwright reveal themselves to be singularly unique to that one country. How can this be?

～

THE PRINCIPAL GEOGRAPHIES OF THE SHAKESPEARE FIRST FOLIO PLAYS

There are *ten* plays of fiction set in Italy, *one* fiction play set in England, and *one* play set in ten other places in the world. Why this ten-to-one ratio?

ITALY

Romeo and Juliet
The Two Gentlemen of Verona
The Taming of the Shrew
The Merchant of Venice
Othello: Act I only
A Midsummer Night's Dream*
All's Well That Ends Well**
Much Ado About Nothing
The Winter's Tale
The Tempest*   *10 plays*

* Adduced
** Also France

ENGLAND

King John
Richard II
Henry IV, Part I
Henry IV, Part II
Henry V
Henry VI, Part I
Henry VI, Part II
Henry VI, Part III
Richard III
Henry VIII   *10 plays*

The Merry Wives
of Windsor   *1 play*

ANCIENT ROME

Coriolanus
Titus Andronicus
Julius Caesar

ANCIENT BRITAIN/WALES

King Lear
Cymbeline

OTHER FOREIGN PLACES

Measure for Measure	Vienna (Paris?)
As You Like It	France
The Comedy of Errors	Ephesus
Love's Labours Lost	Navarre
Twelfth Night	Illyria (Ragusa)
Troilus and Cressida	Troy
Timon of Athens	Athens
Macbeth	Scotland
Hamlet	Denmark
Antony and Cleopatra	Egypt *1 play each locale*

The Italy
in Shakespeare

Milan ○Bergamo   Padua
Freetown/Villa Franca○   *   Venice
Sabbionetta/"Athens"* Verona   Fusina / "Tranect"
                    Mantua   Malcontenta / "Belmont"

Pisa   ●Florence
Livorno○×
       ○Siena

*ADRIATIC
SEA*

CORSICA

ITALY

SARDINIA

○Naples

*TYRRHENIAN
SEA*

*IONIAN
SEA*

Vulcano*

Segesta *   Palermo   Messina

SICILY

● scene places specifically named
* scene places unnamed
○ places referred to by name
× places referred to but unnamed

0   100   200 km
0   100   200 mi

N

Disputes about the authorship of the *First Folio* plays are now widespread. Numerous books have been published in a number of countries — many very recently with undoubtedly more to come — arguing that some person other than William Shakespeare was the real author of the words which now bear that name.

All such publications, including the multitude declaring William of Stratford to be the "true author," have the same shortcoming: their arguments are only conjectural. They insist that their candidate "could have" known, "would have" known, or "surely" knew from other people — or from some then-existing book or books (none ever identified) — the many unusual features that he wove into his plays. The dispute has given rise to what is widely known as the "Shakespeare Authorship Controversy."

No book or article addressing the identity issue has provided a forensic examination of the unique references that the author has specifically disclosed in his plays. Indeed, his familiarity with Italy, its sites and sights, specific details, history, geography, unique cultural aspects, places and things, practices and propensities, etc. — is, quite simply, astonishing.

To enhance objectivity, this book shuns all existing arguments about the identity of the playwright, simply calling him "the playwright" or "the author." In only a few passages is the study conjectural, and I have clearly stated the rationale upon which each conjecture — my opinion — has been based. Apart from these few conjectures, all matters in this book rely on hard facts and report where those facts are to be found. Pictures, photographs, drawings, and maps are provided to illustrate those matters.

What then, did the real author of the Italian Plays, whoever he was, know about Italy? What information does he reveal that was not available in the media of his day? And what does his body of unique and personal knowledge disclose about this man of actual travel and wide-ranging awareness of the affairs of state?

Let us begin with *Romeo and Juliet*, commonly said to be the first play the author wrote. It could also be considered the first in another way, since Verona is the first Italian city a sensible traveler from England would reach, having successfully crossed the Alps and come down through the Brenner Pass.

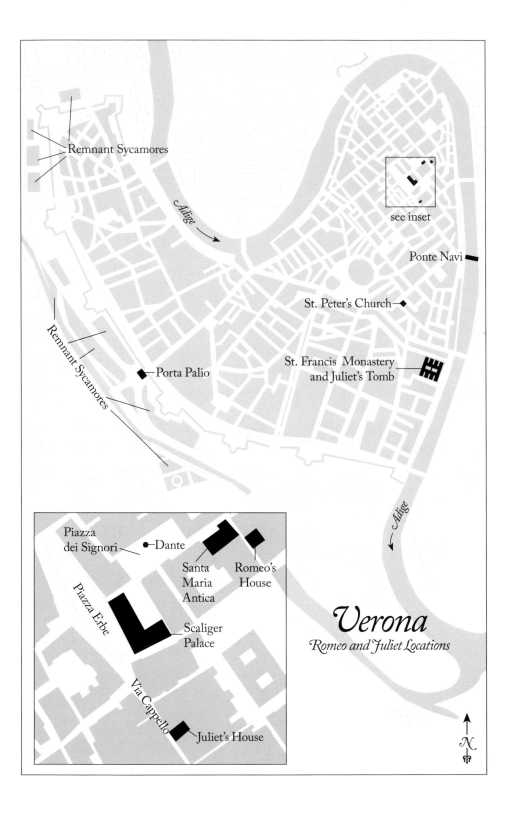

Remnant Sycamores

Adige

Remnant Sycamores

see inset

Ponte Navi

St. Peter's Church

St. Francis Monastery
and Juliet's Tomb

Porta Palio

Adige

Piazza
dei Signori ●Dante

Santa
Maria
Antica

Piazza Erbe

Romeo's
House

Scaliger
Palace

Via Cappello

Juliet's House

Verona
Romeo and Juliet Locations

N

Romeo and Juliet
"Devoted Love in Verona"

I had not admitted to anyone why I was going to Italy this time. My friends knew that I went there whenever I could, a reputation that gave me the cover that I wanted for my fool's errand in Verona. But was it so foolish? Had I deluded myself in what I had come to suspect? Only by going back to Verona would I ever know. Of that much I was certain.

Then I arrived, and stepping outside my hotel, glad I had come, conflicting emotions began to make my blood race. I was half excited with the beginning quest, and half dreading a ridiculous failure, but obsessed with the idea of discovering what no one had discovered — had even looked for — in four hundred years.

My start would be — was planned to be — absurdly simple. I would search for sycamore trees. Not anywhere in Verona but in one place alone, just outside the western wall. Native sycamore trees, remnants of a grove that had flourished in that one place for centuries.

In the first act, the very first scene, of *Romeo and Juliet* the trees are described; and no one has ever thought that the English genius who wrote the play could have been telling the truth: that there were such trees, growing exactly where he said in Verona. In that first scene, Romeo's mother, Lady Montague, encounters her nephew on the street. His name is Benvolio; he is Romeo's best friend. She asks Benvolio where her son might be. Listen to Benvolio's answer:

> Madam, an hour before the worshipp'd sun
> Peer'd forth the golden window of the East,
> A troubled mind drave me to walk abroad,
> Where, *underneath the grove of sycamore*
> *That westward rooteth from the city's side,*
> So early walking did I see your son.   (Emphasis mine)

∽

The author who wrote those lines did not invent the story of this immortal play. Many think that he did, but he didn't. He borrowed it. It was an old Italian tale. The man who recorded it for its first printing in 1535 reported that this was so. He was Luigi da Porto, and he said that he had heard the story told many times. Da Porto did not mention any sycamore trees. But after all, he was not a native of Verona; he was a nobleman of Vicenza.

When da Porto's story was published in 1535, it was soon borrowed and embellished by another Italian, a great storyteller named Matteo Bandello. Bandello did not give us any sycamore trees either. Then a French writer, Pierre Boaistuau, took over Bandello's rendition and put it into French, adding whimsies of his own and some goofy descriptions about Italy; but he did not include any sycamore trees.

Boaistuau's narrative soon arrived in England, where it underwent more transformations. One Englishman, named William Painter (or Paynter), wrote a modest prose version; but another, a lad named Arthur Brooke, got carried away. Brooke wrote the story as a tedious poem that he filled with fantasies, asides, and moralizations. It took him 3,020 lines to finish the job. Brooke claimed that he used Bandello, but he didn't; he really used Boiastuau. You can tell, because his poem has Boiastuau's embellishments. Brooke had plenty of room for some sycamore trees, but there aren't any. No one pays much attention to Painter, but just for the record, there are no sycamores in Painter's prose either.

All of this evolution happened before the *Romeo and Juliet* of the playwright was composed. Shakespeare scholars insist that he got his material for *Romeo and Juliet* from Brooke's enormous poem and that the celebrated playwright had never been in Italy; therefore, he could be expected to make mistakes about its topographic realities. They say he invented a peculiar Italy of his own, with colorful nonsense about what was there. But (and here is the inexplicable thing) alone in the playwright's *Romeo and Juliet* — there and nowhere else, not in any other Italian or French or English version — has it been set down that at Verona, just outside its western walls, was a grove of sycamore trees.

~

My driver took me across the city, then to its edge on the Viale Cristoforo Colombo. Turning south onto the Viale Colonnello Galliano, he began to slow. This was the boulevard where, long before and rushing to the airport at Milan, I had glimpsed trees but had no idea what kind.

Creeping along the Viale then coming to a halt, the driver, with a proud sweep of his hand exclaimed: "Ecco, Signore! There they are! It is truly here, outside the western wall that our sycamores grow." And there they were indeed. Holding my breath for fear they might be mere green tricks of the sunlight, I leapt from the car to get a closer look at the broad-lobed leaves and mottled pastel trunks, to make absolutely certain that it was true; that the playwright had known, and had told the truth. Benvolio was right. And I was not a fool.

The Porta Palio, one of Verona's three western gates. Sycamore trees can be seen through the archway. *(Author's photo)*

Now the trees are in separated stands, the ancient grove cut and hacked away by boulevards and crossings, by building blocks and all the ruthless quirks of urbanization. But the descendants of Romeo's woodland are still growing where they grew in Romeo's day. Rejoined in the mind's eye, erasing the modern incursions, those stands form again the grove that once, four and far more centuries ago, was the great green refuge of a young man sick with love.

The playwright knew this, this unnoted and unimportant but literal truth about the lay of the city. He had deliberately dropped an odd little stone about a real grove of trees into the pool of his powerful drama. But concerned with great concepts, and the crises of a suspenseful love story, no one has noticed this small stone, the author's odd little fact: the westward sycamores of Verona.

This is the playwright who is said to be ignorant of Italy. But truth is revealed in trifles, not in the great words that sweep. Truth hides in the words that are overlooked — the dull words, odd words, the words that are dismissed as cluttering, inconsequential, irrelevant. These are the words, not the soaring ones, that tell what a person knows. But one must listen.

Place names will do it, too. They can give away who the ignorant and who the traveled are. Such is the case with "villafranca."

All of the playwright's predecessors — except Luigi da Porto — invoke the name of a place outside the city of Verona when they recount the story of Romeo and Juliet. The name, "Villafranca," appears in the early versions, such as when Lord Capulet is having his problems with Juliet. She is fussing about getting married, especially about getting married to Count Paris. She has never seen this fellow; how could she possibly be interested in him? And so, at a crucial place in the earlier versions of the story, Juliet is ordered by her father to go to Villafranca. He tells her Paris will come to see her there. When Bandello told the story, he used Villafranca too, but only to say that Paris was there, without further elaboration. It was after Bandello that the storytellers got creative — and wrong — about this place.

A "villafranca" is a "free town," a place where, under the aegis of its ruler, markets, trades, and fairs could be conducted under favorable advantages, with some or perhaps all the transactions free of taxation. Otherwise, there was nothing extraordinary about a villafranca; not a villafranca as such, that is. But there was something significant about the playwright's villafranca in his version of *Romeo and Juliet*. Like the sycamore trees, there was something different the playwright would weave into his play that is not found in any previous version of the story.

When Arthur Brooke finally arrived at the 1,974th line of his poem — that poem that is supposed to be the source of the playwright's material — Brooke introduced his villafranca to his English readers. He put its Italian name into English, "freetown," and had Capulet describe it as his, saying "our castle cald Free towne," which was located outside the city.

The playwright did not copy, did not borrow from Brooke's description, or, for that matter, from any description of freetown as ever written by anyone before him. Brooke's freetown may have been romantic for England, but to any northern Italian, or anyone who had come to Verona to delve into its history and explore its sites, the idea of a Capulet castle at Villafranca (freetown) outside Verona was just silly.

The playwright does not delay for 1,974 lines to invoke his own freetown. In his *Romeo and Juliet*, in that same first scene of the same first act, almost immediately — even before he tells about the syca-more grove — we hear of freetown. "Old Freetown," it is called. And what we hear from him about this place has nothing to do with an imaginary Capulet castle or noble's country retreat; it has to do with things far more serious: infeudation and the medieval powers of princes.

❧

This first scene of the play begins with dangerous men of hos-tile allegiances out on a city street looking for a nice chance to spill blood. They are the bravoes of enemy houses, the Montagues and the Capulets. They meet; they draw steel to do murder; and next, their ac-tual lords enter the fray. They are the blustering Capulet and the ar-rogant Montague, old fools who are not there to put down the brawl, as might be hoped, but to make the encounter still worse. And then there is hell to pay. Here, enraged, comes the great prince of Verona's domains, Escalus, their overlord prince. His fury freezes everyone, and the outrage upon the city's peace is halted.

Escalus' ringing words seize all attention. So much so that they can overshadow the puzzling commands to the lawless nobles that ar-rive at the end of his speech:

> You, Capulet, shall go along with me;
> And, Montague, come you this afternoon,
> To know our farther pleasure in this case,
> *To old Freetown, our common judgment place.*
> (Emphasis mine)

And there it is: Freetown, only as described in this play. Nothing is said about Juliet, nothing about Paris. Just Freetown. And whatever else Freetown might be, this much we have now learned: it is old, and it is the place where Prince Escalus pronounces his common judg-ments. "Common" does not mean "ordinary" here; it means "public." We are told nothing else. But why is Freetown mentioned in this early way, and what of those differing commands?

Capulet is to forthwith accompany Escalus down a Verona street; the Prince has no apprehensions about this old scoundrel. But Montague is ordered to appear before the Prince at a public hearing, at some other time and place, at old Freetown. From the Prologue of the play, we know that these two nobles are heads of houses "both alike in dignity." Yet here these equals are, in the same breath, assigned widely different commands. There is no clue as to why. Not only does the playwright fail to elaborate, he changes the subject abruptly, while almost completely emptying the stage. Escalus exits as suddenly as he appears, and we turn to Benvolio, who tells his aunt about the sycamore grove.

F reetown. And the playwright has called it "old." But old in what way? Old of long-standing practices, or physically old, or venerable otherwise? Or all of these? No other teller of this story had called it old or mentioned anything about public judgments. This town on the banks of the Tartaro River had been there since the Dark Ages, at least. It may well have been a village in Roman times. And here at the beginning of the play its author departs from antecedents: he makes Freetown "old," pointedly so; and the place of princely public judgments.

What's all this about? Is this nonsense? Neither has the question been asked nor does it seem that any curiosity has arisen over the pointed commands of Escalus — or about where, exactly, he directed Montague to go that afternoon or why.

It might seem that the playwright didn't need to write those lines for Escalus at the opening of his play. The other tellers of Romeo and Juliet gave their Villafranca allusion to Capulet, later in the tale. Our author, however, promptly gave the reference to Escalus, in an approach that is his alone. Why had he written these four perplexing lines?

There was only one way to settle the matter: I had to go to Villafranca di Verona in person, to see for myself what no one had taken the trouble to investigate. And this time as I left my hotel in Verona, I had no mixed emotions. I had firmed myself to be detached, to be clinical and objective, to go forward in that resolute and professional way in which surprises are to be expected and complications and blind alleys are normal realities. I had the questions; it was time for the answers. With maps and books and papers and camera, and two "emergency" apples, I drove away from Verona's walls to find this old Freetown, most especially, to find a place there with some singular stature for princely judgments.

Villafranca di Verona is about sixteen kilometers — ten miles — or an easy two- or three-hour ride for Montague — southwest of Verona on the vast and fertile plain of northern Italy. It is a rare tourist that ever goes there, even though it is near the highway to the popular Mantua. It is not a big city but is more than a country town. I drove easily into its center, ready for what I had told myself would be a dispassionate investigation, but what I spied through the windshield straight ahead made all of my resolutions wobble. I was stunned. Rising before me I saw, and knew immediately, what "old Freetown," that "common judgment place," was. It wasn't the city at all, but what was *in* that city. The city's name was just a simple way to identify it for contemporaries and long after. This was sort of an "emergency," so I reached for my apples.

Villafranca, old Freetown, is a brick colossus resting on massive earthworks. The whole is a formidable medieval castle with tall towers, gates around of every size, forbidding walls and ramparts, and high planes and harsh edges set in stern terra cotta masonry. Now, separated by centuries of intervening strife, old Freetown's strategic walls are rent and its interior keep and halls razed, but there the great stronghold endures, no longer in fact but forever in symbol, the unmistakable seat, just here, of the della Scala power in the Italian feudal world.

Spread out before its commanding gate that faces toward the modern town, there still remains, these centuries later, an open quarter of wide, flat acres. It was even wider at one time, though it's still there, ready to receive again the stalls and tents and booths and stacks of merchandise that were once displayed for sale, age after age under the brooding walls and venerated and venerable assurances — the old assurances, the old decencies — that were at the heart of that castle's honorable rulers. And who were those rulers? Was there such a man in history as the play's Prince Escalus?

When Luigi da Porto wrote the story of Romeo Montecchio and Giulietta Cappelletti, he quoted a man he called Peregrino, a man from Verona, whose version of the story was the one he chose to set down. Peregrino informed da Porto that the sad events had happened "during the time when the amiable and humane Prince Bartolomeo della Scala reigned over my most beautiful country." Della Scala. Escalus. The same Italian family. Escalus is a sort of Latin form for della Scala, a form that has been used for a very long time, and which has been used by other tellers of this tale. There are other forms of this family name as well. Perhaps the one most widely used in Italy is Scaligero, whose englished form is Scaliger.

The power of this della Scala–Scaliger family reached its first great expanse in the thirteenth century, with conquests of the wide territories all about Verona. Many of the conquests were carried out by Mastino I della Scala, whose domains eventually came to include Verona itself in 1260. This Mastino, of long life and high honor, died in 1301; and the next della Scala in line was his nephew, Bartolomeo. So popular was his succession that it was ratified by public acclaim. But Bartolomeo would not endure. He died in 1304; and thus Peregrino had not only identified Bartolomeo as the storied Escalus, he had narrowed the time for the story of Romeo and Juliet to one of three medieval years. But the Veronese — ask anyone there even now — are more precise: "It happened in 1302"; and it is always said without hesitation. This exact year is an important part of the Veronese unwavering tradition.

Italian road maps that show Villafranca di Verona usually carry an added notation: "Castello Scaligero." It means only that there is a castle at that spot on the map that was a Scaliger property. The Scaligers built many castles; and such maps will note many of their locations by that same undiscriminating label. Cartographers do not write history. They draw the maps and leave the history to others. The castle at Villafranca di Verona was not just another Castello Scaligero: only this one was the site of their princely court, the seat of Scaliger authority, and the venue for their public judgments.

It was built in 1202 and endured as the central Scaliger seat until 1354, when Cangrande II della Scala had the great Castelvecchio built inside Verona's walls. It was Cangrande who moved the Scaliger court away from "Old Freetown." But when Bartolomeo ruled in 1302, the Castello Scaligero was already a century old: old in tradition, old in family, old in power, and old in medieval protocol. Montague had no doubt where to present himself on that designated afternoon. And

"Old Freetown,"
the great medieval
Scaliger castle
at Villafranca
di Verona. The
market area is in
the foreground of
the photo above.
(Author's photos)

if the Montague in *Romeo and Juliet* knew, then its playwright knew, and knew as well that Escalus could properly call Freetown "old."

But there is more that the playwright indicated in Escalus' command. It was something that would be of concern to every Englishman — indeed every European — not only in the medieval ages but into the Renaissance, and well beyond. A feudal code should have been honored by Escalus when he separated the bloodthirsty

Capulets and Montagues. But he violates that code, and worse, he does it on a public street. He does not tender "equal dignity" to the noblemen. His commands to them are radically different.

At the start of the twenty-first century, I could only guess why, but for a sixteenth-century audience, Escalus clearly established the state of affairs in this opening scene. Through his ruling, Escalus disclosed — whether true in real life or not — that here was a ruling prince who was not just, and who was about to violate the ancient protocols between a ruler and nobles who were of "equal dignity." This injustice would signal to the audience that doom was on the way. We will see the Capulets favored again and witness Romeo Montague banished without a hearing. We will witness for ourselves the tragic result of bias, hatred, and injustice.

∽

What else might the playwright have told us about Verona in the pages of his play that was an unknown truth rather than the invention of an untraveled writer? There was one more pointed allusion that kept bothering me, more complex than the sycamore grove, and more hidden than the meaning of "old Freetown." It was an allusion to a minor place name that is always skipped over, ever-considered to be yet another of the playwright's fanciful inventions. It is "Saint Peter's Church," mentioned late in Act III. To discover whatever truth it might involve, I would need to explore Verona again. I would need to investigate its ancient parish patterns and fix firmly in mind the locations of the places in their city where the Veronese still say the story happened: the streets, the squares, the churches, and the important secular buildings that existed in 1302. Though I had not yet understood why, the arrangement of those places would become far more important than I expected when I began my exploratory walks.

∽

The story of Romeo and Juliet is known intimately to the Veronese. It is their story and a proud local tradition that has been handed from generation to generation. Their story is a true story, and far older than all the written versions of the tragic tale. Even today, the Veronese can point to the places in Verona where the events took place, many of which have been described in guidebooks, in every possible language, for visitors on a pilgrimage to the city of mortal love.

I knew from the words of the play's Prince Escalus, when he spoke of "old Freetown," that the playwright knew the truth of the Veronese tradition; and I suspected from his sycamore grove — though it's not part of the local recounting of the tale — that the author had been here, in Verona, himself.

I was intrigued. I needed to compare, with my own eyes, the Veronese tradition with the words of the playwright; but knowing what I knew about his methods, I felt almost certain that everything the author "sneaks into" his Italian Plays can be found on the ground.

My ultimate goal was to find that very Saint Peter's Church clearly named by the playwright. Although none of his scenes would be set there (only its name used to threaten Juliet), it had to be the Capulet parish church, and it would have to fit seamlessly into the Veronese version of the heartbreaking tale. Why our author would insist on such accuracy demonstrates not just respect for that Veronese tradition but, more important, a keen knowledge of the layout of Verona itself.

Before setting out on my comparative investigations, I sat in the lobby of my hotel with my paperback copy of *Romeo and Juliet* and systematically crossed off the headnote descriptions editors have provided for the play. I wanted a completely fresh approach. I didn't want to be influenced by what had been added later by someone who, very likely, had never been in Italy. I underlined *only* what I could glean about the settings from the words spoken by the playwright's characters — as Benvolio had done with the sycamore trees.

I kept firmly in mind the admonition in *The Reader's Encyclopedia of Shakespeare*:

> Modern editions of Elizabethan plays are generally misleading in their indications of act and scene divisions and in their identification of location.

With underlined paperback in one pocket, and dog-eared Verona guide in the other — and an opened umbrella above my head — I set out on the streets of the city under a drizzling rain, convinced I was about to confirm what I already suspected to be true.

*I*n *Romeo and Juliet* there are several scenes that take place in "public places" because the dialogue of the characters makes the identifications clear. Two of these public places are especially famous, and both make tempting identification traps.

Bartolomeo had his great palazzo in Piazza dei Signori; the building is still there. The other of these two prominent places is Piazza Erbe, just through a broad archway from Piazza dei Signori. While the former is where herbs — and fruits and vegetables — were sold, the other was and, in many ways still is, a place of municipal government. The challenge these squares offer can be in guessing whether either of them might have been the place for a scene or two, or maybe more, in *Romeo and Juliet*.

In one of my earlier sojourns to Verona, when I asked a native of the city whether one of these public squares might have been the site of the confrontations between the enemy families, I was promptly given an education in words much like these:

"The Capulet and Montague ruffians may have been ignorant, but they were not stupid. They would never have chosen a place to fight that was under the nose of Bartolomeo and the municipal authorities. The places where they fought were out at the end of Via Cappello, at Stradone San Fermo, when the Stradone was called 'il Corso.'"

When I asked how this was known, without hesitation, the response was: "We have always known." The Veronese tradition.

By walking from one place to the next accompanied by my paperback and guide, I saw that every site the Veronese identify in their own story lies easterly and southerly of those adjacent piazze. The area is contained on the east side by the southbound course of the Adige River. I could perceive no contradictions between the play's scenes and the specific sites described in my guidebook. The single oddity was the playwright's inclusion of that sycamore grove, far to the west of everything else.

Although I was now satisfied that no brawl had taken place between the Capulets and Montagues beneath a window of Bartolomeo della Scala — in either the Piazza dei Signori or the Piazza Erbe — I loitered for a time in dei Signori to admire once more the statue of Dante Alighieri that has been placed there. Verona memories are very long; it was not set up in that spot until 1865, but it commemorates an event of civic pride that happened in that same memorable year in

Piazza dei Signori.
The brick building
is still the seat
of Verona's
government and
police headquarters.
Through the arch
one can make out
the "Arche Scaligeri"
where the tombs and
family church of the
Scaliger family are
located. (Postcard:
Author's collection)

which Romeo discovered Juliet: 1302. When Dante was sentenced to death in his native Florence, he was given his first refuge in Verona by Bartolomeo della Scala, our "Prince Escalus," and Verona became his home for a number of years. This may be why da Porto's friend Peregrino said that the prince was "amiable and humane," although the playwright makes him less so.

We wouldn't know from any tales about the Capulets and Montagues about the coincidence of Dante's presence in the city. He would have been there — despite the academic fussing about dates — at the very time that the events between the Montagues and the Capulets had reached their climax. Indeed, it seems as though he might even have witnessed some of the story in person. In his *Purgatorio*, when he came to Canto VI, Dante wrote this admonition to the ruling German king, Albrecht I (1298–1308):

> Vieni a veder Montecchi e Cappelletti,
> … uom sanza cura …
>
> Come — you who pay no heed — do come and see
> Montecchi, Cappelletti, sad already …
>
> (Allen Mandelbaum, trans.)

Across the Piazza dei Signori to its far corner, the little medieval church of Santa Maria Antica, the family church of the Scaligers, still stands. It is a place where it might be guessed that Dante would have also heard mass recited. There, rarely noticed because it is inside the high wrought iron enclosure of the Scaliger monuments, is the sarcophagus of Bartolomeo della Scala resting in its indentation, as it has been since the time of Romeo and Juliet, in the exterior of the church's wall.

Turning down the corner street, and eastward for just a few steps, is the documented townhouse of the Montecchi, the Montagues, hence the city home of Romeo. Everything about it fits the story: the date of its age, the medieval design, the whole arrangement.

Returning back through the Piazza dei Signori, through the arch and into Piazza Erbe, then a turn to the left, the space of the piazza narrows to form the beginning of two different streets. The one on the right, Via Mazzini, has been an important street of shops since Roman times and leads south to the Roman arena. But the one on the left,

Left: **The statue of Dante** *was erected in the Piazza dei Signori in 1865.*

Right: **Tomb of Bartolomeo della Scala**, *"Prince Escalus." The tomb is on the exterior wall of Santa Maria Antica, the Scaliger family church, located in one corner of the Piazza dei Signori. (To gain entrance, apply to the rector, since this sarcophagus is well inside the outdoor wrought iron enclosure of the famous elevated della Scala tombs known as the "Arche Scaligeri." The iron fence decoration incorporates the ladder emblem of the family name — "of the steps" — della Scala.) (Author's photos)*

Scaliger Palace *in the Piazza dei Signori with the soaring Lamberti Tower.* (Verona: Inside & Out, *Storti Edizioni, 1966, p. 67)*

Romeo's house. *The townhouse of the Montague-Montecchi family in Verona. (Postcard: Author's collection)*

which runs eastward toward the Adige River, is Via Cappello. Down that street, not far from the piazza at No. 23, is the most important place of pilgrimage in Verona: the home of legendary Juliet.

Seldom is there a time when there isn't a crowd of visitors at Juliet's house, and this is to be expected, for it is one of the world's great shrines to mortal love. There is nothing quite like it anywhere, and the timid will cheat themselves if they do not make their way through the courtyard, enter, and mount the stairs.

This house, unlike the Montague-Montecchi house, has no documented history as the Capulet house. It depends on Veronese tradition for its authenticity. Some point to the ancient name of its street, Via Cappello, a variant of the family name, which is variable itself, such as Cappelletti, Capuletti, Capelletto, Cappello,

and so on, since streets were often named — or re-named — for important residents; but that alone is not proof that a young beauty named Giulietta Cappello, or Capuletti, ever lived here in 1302, even though the house is medieval and seems remarkably suited for the story.

Piazza Erbe showing the southern side of the Scaliger Palace. (Postcard: Author's collection)

Spoofers say this house was only an inn mere-ly named for the street, but the response to this is swift: many a great old house be-came a "bed-and-breakfast" at one time or another in its history, and this house has undergone seven centuries of changing uses. One hundred years ago it was a tenement slum, its rooms divided with

Juliet's house at 23 Via Cappello. The balcony was added in the 1930s. (Postcard: Author's collection)

wretched partitions, its courtyard jammed with rubbish; and this, too, is proof of nothing.

But there are some things that can be learned here. The house was rescued from deterioration in the early twentieth century by the Italian government. It has a perfect main room — or Great Room, call it what you will — on its "first floor," the floor which Americans call the second floor and Italians call the *piano nobile* — exactly right for the festive event where Romeo first sets eyes on Juliet. The room has been delightfully restored. But there is one glaring feature of the house that is a direct contradiction of the playwright's dialogue, a contradiction rarely noticed.

The celebrated balcony of Juliet that everyone admires is on the façade of the Capulet house above the entry door, overlooking the entry court. But inside the house, and strangely so, the balcony is an adjunct to the Great Room. In performances of *Romeo and Juliet* we are accustomed to a balcony that overlooks an orchard. From the lines of Act II Scene 2, it is clear that Romeo climbed over a wall into the Capulet *orchard* — not into an entry court — to woo Juliet up above. Where was the orchard overlooked by a balcony here at Juliet's house? Did the playwright make a mistake? Did he depart from reality for convenience?

Orchard? Balcony? There was something wrong here, but the entry court of Juliet's house was too noisy and crowded for me to concentrate. I needed to go over the play in quiet and with care.

∾

There are three scenes in *Romeo and Juliet* that have the same arrangement, with Romeo in the orchard and Juliet above. If there had once been an orchard at Juliet's house in centuries past, the crowding of city buildings and walls have since erased it. Intense urbanization over the years would easily have removed whatever orchard there might have been in 1302. A small orchard, however, had always been an important adjunct to the townhouse of a wealthy family in Italy. Presently there is only a small paved courtyard between the street gate and its front door. I was forced to let go of the orchard.

But the balcony? Far more disturbing is that balcony above the door. There is no "balcony" in *Romeo and Juliet*. None whatsoever. Not only is the word absent from the play, it isn't a word to be found

The Great Room in the Capulets' house *where Romeo would have seen Juliet for the first time. (Photo courtesy of Sylvia Holmes)*

in any other play, Italian or not, by the same playwright. For that matter, the word "balcony" is not found in any of the poetry ascribed to the playwright either.

The playwright's descriptions in *Romeo and Juliet* are clear: Juliet appears in every case, by the author's own words, at her "window." The playwright did not give Juliet a balcony, and it seemed to me that it would have been a careless father who would give his pretty daughter a bedroom that had a convenient balcony. While the existing balcony is indeed an authentic relic of medieval times, it was taken from some other building somewhere and attached to its present location at 23 Via Cappello in a spasm of touristic promotion in the 1930s. Juliet's balcony, admired by tourists the world over today, was not there originally; not in that spot, anyway.

❧

Two more quests remained. One of them was to revisit Juliet's revered resting place at the ancient former Monastery of Saint Francis — San Francesco al Corso — just beyond Verona's southerly medieval wall and near the Adige on the Via del Pontiere. The other was to look for a medieval church called "Saint Peter," another place name, like villafranca, that the playwright inserted into his story.

The St. Francis Monastery (San Francesco al Corso). This is where Friar Laurence married Romeo and Juliet. (Author's photo)

When I left Juliet's house at 23 Via Cappello, I made my way to the Monastery by walking to the end of the street and turning to the right onto Stradone San Fermo. In the medieval period this street led to the old southern city wall, where it ended. That wall is now broken open, and the street continues beyond the line of the former protective barrier. As it continues, its path takes it progressively further away from my objective, the Monastery where Juliet's confessor, Friar Laurence — Fra Lorenzo — had his cell.

When preparing for this walk, I had learned at the police office in Piazza dei Signori that the easiest way to reach the Monastery on foot was to leave Via Stradone after a short distance, at any convenient corner, and turn left until coming to the river's edge, then turn right along the river and follow my nose along the embankment to the Monastery. I followed the officer's instructions. He had said that if I wanted to go on foot from Juliet's house to the Monastery, just as she did when she went to see her confessor, Friar Laurence, this would duplicate the shortest and safest route that a woman would have taken in 1302.

The former Franciscan Monastery, San Francesco al Corso, is just where it might be for a plausible story, outside the ancient city wall but not too far, and within the walking reach of a proper noble maiden wanting to make her confession. It has not been a monastery for a long time. Disused and idle, it was taken over in the nineteenth century as a base for the Italian cavalry. The cloister at the Monastery had been filled with graves and gravestones — all of which were removed. The cells and halls became quarters and barracks and the Monastery grounds put to use for drills and parades. But these changes have not deterred the more determined visitors wanting to see where Juliet and Count Paris and Romeo died, near the vault which is still there, reached from steps down in the arcaded cloister. If it can be granted that an Englishman who wrote for a country where monasteries had long since been disestablished might call a cloister a "churchyard," then the dialogue in the play closely fits both the cloister and its large adjacent burial vault at San Francesco al Corso.

The place the playwright calls "Capel's monument" is large enough to be "pack'd" with the bones of any number of Juliet's ancestors. It is below ground level, and consists of two vacant connected chambers with only a heavy pink marble sarcophagus in one of them, open and empty, with its edges and corners chipped by centuries of souvenir seekers. This artifact is the legendary place of Juliet's final rest, although there is no such pink remnant mentioned in the play. Nor should there be. Even in Verona, there is disagreement about the age of that marble artifact, whose it was, and how it got there.

Whatever the case, the sarcophagus was really not my concern. If a real Juliet was ever laid inside it, it would have been after all had been said, and a stonecutter had been engaged to make the stone coffin, if that is what it is. To be honest, I was vaguely uncomfortable with the Tomb of Juliet; quite empty, with added tourist entry and exit stairs, and its quasi-Gothic stone window frames which make no sense. My quest began, and ended, with the playwright's final lines, with lovely Juliet lying lifeless on her bier.

The cloister at *Friar Laurence's Monastery. In the corner, beyond the arch, are the steps down to the Capulet crypt where Juliet would have been interred. (Author's photo)*

I had reduced my adventure with *Romeo and Juliet* to one final step, a step that required a fresh examination of a city map of Verona, a visit to the office of the diocese, a bit of reading, and a brief visit to what had become my favorite police station. Here was one final puzzle to solve, and like that unique reference to the sycamores, here was another reference that can be found only in the playwright's version of *Romeo and Juliet*; it is not to be found in any other literature. As with the sycamore trees, no one has noticed it; after all, wouldn't it be yet one more of the author's inventions? Never mind that its name is repeated in the play — indeed *three times* — with the actors probably shouting. It is "Saint Peter's Church," and named in the play at a place editors later labeled "Scene 5" for "Act III."

In that editorially designated scene we first hear about this church. I had to find it; I had to believe it was not a fiction conjured at a London writing table — certainly not after discovering the accuracy of the play's sycamores, its old Freetown, and the uncanny ambience of the Verona neighborhood which is reflected in the play. An "uncanny ambience" is hardly proof of anything, however, and I wanted one more solid landmark that the playwright alone gave us — one that was unique to him, was exact, and was also in the right place in Verona. The test would be not

Capulet family crypt. *These are the steps leading down to the crypt from the St. Francis Monastery cloister. (Author's photo)*

only to find a Saint Peter's Church in the city, but a Saint Peter's Church that exactly fit the lines in the play.

I was beginning to suspect that this playwright had a peculiar practice in writing his Italian Plays, and as I discovered throughout my adventures in Italy, my suspicions were confirmed. It was his method, his "trick" of pointedly naming or describing some obscure or unique place that might look like an invention or mistake but which turns out to be actual. It would be one that is not necessarily a place for a scene, but somewhere that today we might say is "off-camera," and with an identity that has little (or nothing) to do with the plot: a one-of-a-kind place which reveals an unusual, intimate, knowledge of Italy. I promised myself that as I continued my explorations the length of Italy with the Italian Plays in hand, I would exercise special alertness to verify that my suspicions were correct. Meanwhile, here in Verona, I would search for the playwright's Saint Peter's Church.

It all happens in that "Act III Scene 5." Juliet's father is furious with her. He has arranged her marriage to Count Paris, and she is holding back. *Not once, but three times in succession*, Saint Peter's Church is invoked as the place where the marriage to Paris is to take place. It seemed to me that said three times is the playwright's demand for our attention; it is his call.

Juliet's mother is first to say that it

Tomb of Juliet (alleged). (Author's photo)

will happen at "Saint Peter's Church." Then Juliet repeats the name. And third, Capulet names it, threatening Juliet to be dragged there if she won't go willingly. No one but the playwright, not even the Veronese, has ever mentioned this Saint Peter's Church to embellish their story.

Because no wedding will really happen there, nor will any scene of the play, this threefold repetition of the name of the church is passed over or regarded as a fabrication. What characteristics would such a church need to have to be consistent with the complexities of *Romeo and Juliet*? What elements would give it the ring of reality, be beyond the pale of untraveled contrivance?

It would need to be a Franciscan church. Religious orders were — still are — proprietary, jealous of their jurisdictions and prerogatives; and Friar Laurence, who would officiate at the marriage, was a Franciscan. Young women of any social level, especially with protective parents, would customarily marry in their own parish church, not so much out of sentiment but because that is where necessary family records were maintained, where a favoring priest would preside, and where the local community would gather to look on, all these factors forming a body of verification of a lawful and binding marriage in a lasting form. The party most needing such verification for her protection was the bride; and it would be the bride's parish church, not the groom's.

Is or was there a church called Saint Peter's in medieval Verona? Now I had a problem. There are four: *San Pietro in Castello*; *San Pietro in Archivolto*; *San Pietro Martire*; and *San Pietro Incarnario*. And every one of them was there during the fourteenth century; three of them there before that. Each had to be seen, its records found, its function learned. And so I began, and this is what I found:

San Pietro in Castello is inside the Castelvecchio, the vast city fortress of the Scaligers. It was never a parish church. It was a military church for soldiers who needed convenient confession and the healing mystery of the mass. It did not exist when Bartolomeo della Scala, Prince Escalus, was the ruler of Verona. The construction of Castelvecchio began fifty years after Bartolomeo's death, about 1354. And it looked to be too far to the west of Juliet's house, away from the pattern of the traditional scenes of the story which I had adduced.

San Pietro in Archivolto was built in the thirteenth century, well before the time of *Romeo and Juliet*. It is a small and charming sanctuary with a seated figure of Saint Peter, "Keeper of the Keys," above its door. This medieval building served, and still serves though infrequently, as a subsidiary of Santa Maria Matricolare, the magnificent cathedral of Verona, and stands just across a narrow street from the south door of the cathedral. It was never a parish church; and it is even farther to the west of Juliet's neighborhood.

San Pietro Martire is a medieval church of a different kind. It is adjacent to the great Dominican basilica built about 1290 and dedicated to Saint Anastasia. This lesser church, or chapel, stands on the left side of Piazza Sant'Anastasia as an adjunct to their monastery, and was originally called San Giorgio dei Dominicani. The man called "San Pietro Martire," sometimes called "Peter of Verona," was a Dominican friar, not a Franciscan; and Piazza Sant'Anastasia is also to the west, not the east, of Juliet's house.

San Pietro Incarnario, the last of the four, seemed impossible to find, nor would I have found it without the pencil sketch that a kind *carabiniere* made for me at the police station in the Piazza dei Signori. It wasn't a great sketch, but was good enough, although he warned me that I might not recognize the building for the medieval church it once had been.

With sketch in hand, I left the police station, went through Piazza Erbe, entered Via Cappello, walked past Juliet's house toward the river, turned right on Stradone San Fermo and continued walking. This seemed like déjà vu: this was the first part of Juliet's route to Friar Laurence's Monastery, where both Juliet and her Romeo had paid their visits and where they had been secretly married by the Friar in the Monastery's church.

But the sketch I was given didn't go that far. In only a few blocks I had arrived at my destination, and it was as the *carabiniere* had said: before me stood a small church building, now with a white plaster exterior.

"Saint Peter's Church," San Pietro Incarnario. The church was founded in 955 A.D. and has been renovated over the centuries. (Author's photos)

It was located at the corner of Stradone Scipione Maffei (a renamed segment of Stradone San Fermo) and, to my great surprise, a street named "Via San Pietro Incarnario." I was stunned. This was the very corner where I had turned toward the river on my earlier search to find the Monastery! In my haste at the time, I had not noticed the church, whose street still bears its name. Unmistakably, however, here was the Capulet parish — and the play's — thrice-named Saint Peter's Church.

In 1302, this Saint Peter's was not a white-plastered building. Over the centuries, its original appearance has been altered significantly, resulting in the mixture of architectural styles seen today. The church hardly merits a second glance by a weary traveler, especially one focused on a quest — neither is it especially attractive, nor does it appear old. But by craning my neck, I could make out its early medieval origins: the original bell tower still exists.

For a long time, this Saint Peter's has not actually served as a church, and it is the only one of the four San Pietros to have undergone extensive modifications. These were done in the second half of

the nineteenth, and again in the twentieth, centuries. In 1882, the church suffered heavy flood damage and during World War II was partially destroyed. It has suffered mightily over the centuries, but there it is: shortened by flood, altered by violence, no longer needed for any parish — now used only as a simple meeting hall.

But both in the sixteenth century, and in the days of the story of Romeo and Juliet, the diocesan records reveal that this was, indeed, a parish church. Founded in 955, in the thirteenth century it came under Franciscan jurisdiction and remained so for the next six hundred years. I had, indeed, located Saint Peter's Church. It fit every ingredient given for it in the play, and was yet one more of the playwright's very own, almost secret touches to his *Romeo and Juliet*.

True to the pattern of the story's places in the city, this Saint Peter's Church not only was in Juliet's parish, but directly on the path between lovely Juliet's house and the monastic cell of her confessor.

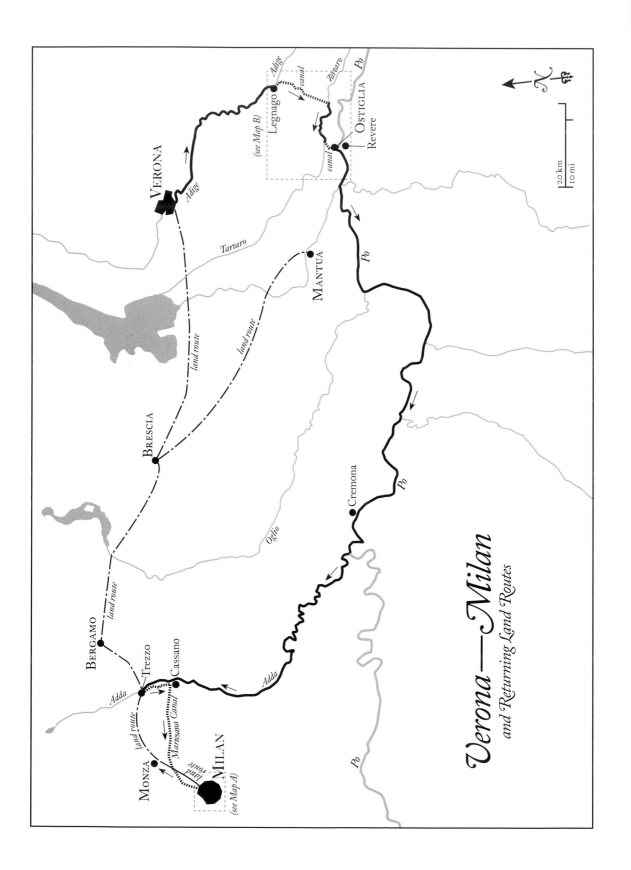

Verona–Milan
and Returning Land Routes

2

The Two Gentlemen of Verona – Part 1
"Sailing to Milan"

T he leading characters in *The Two Gentlemen of Verona* are two young fellows named Valentine and Proteus, each the son of a nobleman, and thus called "gentlemen." Their adventures can be viewed in a light hearted way and left at that, and so it has been through the centuries. Yet, there is far more to the play, virtually all of which has been ridiculed as the product of the playwright's fertile imagination.

This is the play with the most, and most highly varied, descriptions of and allusions to things Italian in the entire Shakespeare canon. Indeed, if critics were to choose one single Italian Play to criticize, this is that play. Critics say it has an absurd Italy, with seacoasts and harbors that never existed, and historical events that never happened. Not only is the playwright accused of inventing such things, but also of being so absent minded about Italy as to misname Padua for Milan in one of its dialogues, and to refer to an emperor in Milan when it only had a duke. They say that anyone who spent any time in the relevant places in Italy would never have made such blunders.

One thing was already clear to me by finding that the settings for *Romeo and Juliet* are actual, none invented. But what about the allusions to places, things, and events in *The Two Gentlemen of Verona*? They really do seem to be outlandish, but were they real nevertheless?

Verona is where this play begins, and where the allegedly ignorant blunders begin. Though I had concluded my searches about *Romeo and Juliet*, I was still in Verona, and was free to stay longer. I had brought along, "just in case," my marked-up paperback of *The Two Gentlemen*, and some research material.

When walking the streets of Verona, it had been easy to visualize Escalus, Juliet, Romeo, Nurse, and all the other characters in the dramatic story in one place or another. It wasn't as fulfilling this time around, when the characters and events are those in *The Two Gentlemen*.

As I walked about Verona with a copy of the play in hand as a guidebook, its usefulness began to pale. At first I thought it was because the preponderance of Verona's streets and buildings are marvelously medieval, overshadowing the elegant Renaissance achievements within its walls. Then, as I continued to scrutinize this play, the real reason became clear: there are no specific allusions to, or descriptions of, places, streets, or buildings in Verona such that they could be explored or photographed. In *Romeo and Juliet*, the playwright describes or alludes to enough specific sites that anyone disposed to study the terrain and its history, can be rewarded. This is not the case with *The Two Gentlemen*.

In *The Two Gentlemen*, the playwright turned instead to address Verona's position as one of the important hubs of Italian trade and transportation. That done, he turns then to tell of the people, places, and things in Milan, a very different Italian city. To do this, he sends his two fearless young men of Verona there to tell of that city as best as they can.

When this play begins, its two young gentlemen are on the stage. The one named Valentine, about to depart for Milan, is taking leave of his best friend, Proteus, who has been pleading with him to stay at home. In his speech, Valentine says in part:

Cease to persuade, my loving Proteus;
Home-keeping youth have ever homely wits.
…
I rather would entreat thy company
To see the wonders of the world abroad
Than (living dully sluggardiz'd at home)
Wear out thy youth with shapeless idleness …

This is an argument that a restless young gentleman of means in England might well have offered against the contemporary Puritan view held in high places there — such as those of Elizabeth's great minister, Lord Burghley — that travel in Italy was corrupting.

Valentine has more to say about this, then, near the end of their conversation — and anxious to depart — he says:

Once more adieu; my father at the *road*
Expects my coming, there to see me *shipp'd*.   (Emphasis mine)

Then, among his added final words he says: "At Milan let me hear from thee by letter …." And now we know: Valentine is sailing from inland Verona to inland Milan in a ship.

Valentine's father is not at a paved or dirt road for pedestrians and vehicles. Valentine is using a nautical term frequently misunderstood. *The Riverside Shakespeare* is not alone when it footnotes "road" as meaning a "seaport," which any mariner would know is exactly what a road is not. No sailor, Elizabethan or modern, would think it was.

Along select channels of the seas, and in the large and smooth rivers the world over, there are wide places for ships to anchor called "roads" (though some recent dictionaries call them "roadsteads"). Roads are the preferred places for ships to ride at anchor, either to be served by lighters, or else to come up, in turn, to a nearby quay, to load or unload passengers and cargo. A port, on the other hand, is a haven or harbor of calm water with surrounds of solid land, often enhanced with protecting jetties. Ports are a refuge from the stormy hazards of seas or great lakes, as well as being a suitable place to accommodate long-range commerce and transportation.

The playwright's precise knowledge of sailing, and the language of sailors, is famous. He made the germane distinctions, for example, in Act I Scene 1 of *The Merchant of Venice*, in which Solanio describes Antonio as "Piring [peering] in maps for ports and piers, and roads." These nouns are not synonyms, and nowhere in *The Two Gentlemen* did he write that there was a port or "seaport" at Verona, nor at Milan, either.

Since Roman times, Verona was a city of major importance as a center for shipping, serving traffic, trade, and travelers going through the Brenner Pass above it. By means of the Adige River, one could sail to and from it to many cities in Italy. One could also sail from Verona, through the mouth of the Adige, and reach the Adriatic arm of the Mediterranean Sea — and thence, to the rest of the world. In 1580, when the famous French essayist Michel de Montaigne saw Verona's road, he remarked in his *Diary* about Verona's "vast quay." The road and that adjacent quay were just downstream from the great stone bridge called "Ponte Navi" (Ship Bridge). The bridge can be seen as it was a century after de Montaigne's description in the painting by that Italian master Bernardo Bellotto (1720–1780).[1]

The venerable Ponte Navi has long since disappeared. It was heavily damaged from the storm waves of Alpine waters raging down the river in 1805; then in 1882, there was a catastrophic inundation of all of

View of Verona showing the "Ponte Navi" (Ship Bridge), by Bernardo Bellotto (1720–1780).

Verona. Slowly repaired after 1805, and yet again after 1882, the bridge was irreparably destroyed in World War II. Now, to cross the river where the old bridge stood, the visitor finds a streamlined steel span. But in a romantic mind's eye, the ships — long since replaced by trains and great diesel trucks — still come and go, with passengers and cargo.

*I*n addition to using the somewhat unfamiliar word "road," Valentine spoke of being "shipp'd." "Shipp'd" in those days meant going by vessel, not by land; it is only in our time this word embraces travel by truck and train — and aircraft, too. We also have learned that Valentine is going to Milan, yet anyone can see on a map of northern Italy — without ever going there — that Verona and Milan are inland cities, far from any sea on which to sail.

The nearest sea to Verona is the Adriatic. It is an arm of the Mediterranean Sea, and it is 100 kilometers *east* of Verona, in the *opposite* direction of Milan. Milan, 160 kilometers *west* of Verona, has its closest salt water in the Tyrrhenian Sea, the western arm of the Mediterranean, which is far to its south, up and over the Apennine Mountains, and down to the Gulf of Genoa. Not only does the playwright send Valentine to Milan by water, in Act II, he dispatches another person, Proteus, on the identical voyage, thus insisting on its feasibility.

The Ponte Navi:
20th-century
replacement.
(Author's photo)

Among the many fault-findings with the playwright's geography over the years, this one, asserted a hundred years ago, is representative:

> Shakespeare had a clearly conceived geography of the land, and accurately maintained his conception, though it was, for the most part, an ideal, not a real geography. For instance, Verona is a port upon the sea, with tides that ebb and flow, and boats that may sail from thence to Milan; Valentine's father at the road expects his coming, there to see him shipped; and Launce [servant to Proteus] "is like to lose the tide."
> — Horatio Brown, *Studies in Venetian History*

Examples of such conclusions are restated even today, some through essays, such as Mr. Brown's, and others appearing in footnotes, such as that found in *The Riverside Shakespeare*, that prominent work frequently used in college courses, which states:

> Shakespeare seems to have supposed that Verona was a seaport.

~

Even the critics of this play who have not misdefined "road" also believe the playwright put Verona on a false sea. They believe it because the idea of salt water is assumed by them from the repeated use of the word "tide" in Act II.

We hear it first from the mouth of Proteus in that short Scene 2 of Act II. Proteus has learned that he, too, on his father's orders, must go to Milan. He rushes to Julia, his love, to bid her farewell, and among his parting words he says:

> My father stays my coming. Answer not. The tide is now.
> Nay, not thy tide of tears! That tide will stay me longer than
> I should. Julia, farewell!

Today, "tide" is a word that makes us first think of the ebb and flow of the sea, but this was not always so. This Anglo-Saxon word originally meant "time," and its corollaries, such as "hour," or "moment." Since those ancient days, tide has come increasingly to mean the flow of the sea, as well as other things, both literal and figurative, such as "rush" and "flood." In *Shakespeare's Language*, Eugene F. Shewmaker[2] defines tide as "floodtide; the most opportune moment," citing *Troilus and Cressida* in its Act V Scene 1: "I have important business, / The tide whereof is now."[3]

Proteus' words to Julia, though heartfelt for him, create a bit of levity for the audience. They are puns on the word "tide," and the punning will continue with Launce, in the following Scene 3. In fact, in Scenes 2 and 3 of Act II, the playwright drenches us with punning "tides"—then drops his "tide" fun altogether.

Proteus' parting words to Julia employ three different meanings for "tide." An alert audience, onto the game, could realize that Proteus, had he used three *different* words, would have said something like:

> My father stays (awaits) my coming. Answer not.
> The *time* is now. Nay, not thy *rush* of tears!
> That *flood* will stay me longer than I should.
> Julia, farewell!

❧

Scene 3 opens with a solitary figure on stage; it is Launce, Proteus' dense young servant. This evocative name seems slyly chosen to muddle the listener again; causing him to mistakenly think of the sea, since a "sand launce" is a little fish that buries itself at ebb tide in sandy beaches. I do not see Launce standing on a street, as editors of the play have suggested in their notes. I see him dawdling at the water's edge, on Verona's quay, fussing about, as time ebbs away.

Ordered to accompany Proteus to Milan, Launce is terrified of leaving home; he's never done that before. More, he is grief-stricken over the fate of his beloved dog, "Crab," another tricky seaside sort of name, and a cipher or cryptogram, i.e., crab spelled backward yields "bark" for bow-wow; and "bark" is a synonym for "ship." Launce jabbers and dallies, and he dallies too long. Onto the stage comes Panthino, the major-domo of the noble house of Proteus' father, Antonio—which makes Panthino Launce's boss—and Panthino is irate. His fierce words cripple poor Launce's weak understanding, and in response, Launce confounds his speech, mixing the homophone, "tied" into his words—and continuing the punning word game begun by Proteus:

Panthino: Launce, away, away! Aboard. Thy master is shipp'd, and thou art to post after with oars. What's the matter? Why weep'st thou, man? Away, ass. You'll lose the tide if you tarry any longer.

Launce: It is no matter if the tied were lost, for it is the unkindest tied that ever any man tied.

Panthino: What's the unkindest tide?

Launce: Why, he that's tied here, Crab, my dog.

Launce cannot cope with ambiguities or homophones (later in the play, he misinterprets other words as well), and he's deaf with fear for himself, and with worry over Crab. Like the sand launce, this Launce is buried in fright — instead of sand.

But Panthino has had enough. He explodes, and tries a *different*, clearer, word:

> Tut man! I mean thou'lt lose the flood, and in losing the flood, lose thy voyage, and in losing thy voyage, lose thy master ...

Not: "lose the tide," but "lose the flood." Panthino is trying his best to use what he thinks is more understandable language. But for Launce, it still isn't clear. For him, "flood" is ambiguous, too. And even though "flood" can be a synonym for "tide," Panthino here seems to mean something other than the movement of the sea. Since his attempt to differentiate for Launce is clear to the audience, what does Panthino (the playwright) mean by the word "flood"? If it can be understood in a clear sense, it must have something to do with a rush, or a rising, of water. But if so, where?

Launce remains frozen. He wails:

> Lose the tide, and the voyage, and the master, and the service, and the tied! Why man, *if the river were dry*, I am able to fill it with my tears; if the wind were down, I could drive the boat with my sighs.   (Emphasis mine)

Here Launce has specifically indicated that the voyage he is about to take is on a river. And even though the guileless lad is always truthful, his very clearly spoken reference to a river has never been properly scrutinized as fact. Weary of this dunce, Panthino halts all attempts at explanation, and just flatly orders Launce to set out.

The word play ends, but the mystery lingers: Panthino has said that if Launce doesn't depart immediately, he will miss "the flood." When he said "tide," he could have been talking about "time," some opportune moment; we have seen that usage before, when Proteus says goodbye to Julia. But now, "tide" begins to sound like *both* a literal flood of water *and* a critical moment. The untraveled Launce seems to understand neither the significance of Panthino's "flood" nor his "tide." How could he? This is to be his first big trip away from home. In Launce's lack of understanding — which includes the Shakespearean world — he has never been alone.

And so, down by the Verona quay, with Panthino urging him on, with Crab wildly barking and wagging, we can envisage Launce tearfully taking up his oars and sniffling while rowing down the river, heading to the place of his newly bidden chores.

❧

The trouble with the idea of taking the Adige to Milan is that after a while the Adige turns to the *east* and flows into the Adriatic Sea. Milan is far to the *west*. Why not go directly westward by land from Verona to Milan? There were many towns on the way with lodging, however awful: Peschiera, Lonato, Brescia, Rovato, and Bergamo, for example. A trip to Milan by land appears to be, and therefore has been accepted as, the only one which makes any sense.

It isn't as though the playwright didn't know about this. He knew land travel was possible, but he also knew of its dangerous difficulties. He even said so in Act II Scene 7. There Julia resolves to follow Proteus, and find him in Milan. In conversation with her companion, Lucetta, Julia implores her:

> … tell me some good mean
> How, with my honour, I may undertake
> A journey to my loving Proteus.

Lucetta replies, "Alas, the way is wearisome and long." Later in this conversation Julia says:

Then let me go, and hinder not my course.
I'll be as patient as a gentle stream,
And make a pastime of each weary step,
Till the last step have brought me to my love;
And there I'll rest, as after much turmoil
A blessed soul doth in Elysium.

Julia is not going to sail to Milan; she will walk all the way, the kind of travel that was by far the cheapest and the most common.

~

In the word game between Panthino and Launce, where Launce was instructed to hasten down the river to intercept Proteus, it was clear to me that whatever the "flood" was, it wasn't to be found in the city. Panthino's flood was somewhere downstream.

In my rental car, I left Verona and searched, stop-and-go, along the edge of the Adige River, all the way to Legnago, just where the Adige swings irrevocably eastward. I found nothing. Since early in the twentieth century, the river's edges have been bordered by huge earthen dikes, obliterating what might have once existed at the river's edge. Legnago itself is no longer the ancient town that it was. It is almost entirely new, built up after the ruinous high waters of 1882 had subsided.

~

I decided that if there were a way to solve the puzzle of sailing from Verona to Milan and I couldn't find it in Verona or along its Adige River someplace near Legnago, then perhaps I could find answers at the other end of those criticized voyages; someplace in, or near, Milan.

I turned to Act II Scene 4, of the play, when Proteus arrives in Milan. He is greeted by Valentine, who is already there, and anxious to talk; but Proteus, at the end of the scene, excuses himself:

Go on before; I shall enquire you forth.
I must unto the road, to disembark
Some necessaries that I needs must use,
And then I'll presently attend you.   (Emphasis mine)

The playwright has added another "road." We now know that there was a road both at the beginning of the young gentlemen's voyages and at the end. This off-hand allusion revealed to me that the entire trip from Verona to Milan could be made by water using the Adige, then, by some connection to the Po, which involved a "flood," and then, somehow, by water directly into Milan. But a road in Milan? Milan does not have a navigable river, let alone a seacoast. How could it have a road?

It could, because Milan had something other than a great river, something of the greatest importance to that city, and had had it for centuries before the voyages of Valentine and Proteus. For this, a map or two of Italy can be very useful, but not in the same way the critics have used theirs.

Incidentally, it is the opening lines of the next scene, Scene 5 of Act II, that have prompted the greatest doubt about the playwright's knowledge of Italian geography. Speed, Valentine's man, meets Launce, Proteus' man, newly arrived in Milan, greeting him by exclaiming: "Launce, by mine honesty, welcome to Padua!" This remark is the basis for the opinion that the author does not know what city he is writing about. Critics have forgotten that Launce is a dolt and Speed, a teaser. Speed is pulling Launce's leg, but the unobservant editors of this play, such as *The Riverside*, the *Collins*, and the *Yale*, have invaded the text to change "Padua" to "Milan." They are certain of a playwright blunder, although Speed, by saying "by mine honesty," is giving the audience a tip-off that he's purposely deviating from the truth.

*I*mportant rivers come down from the Alpine regions of Italy, flowing southerly in somewhat parallel routes to join the waters of the mighty Po. Brimming with this snowy water, the Po then flows eastward to the Adriatic Sea. In Lombardy, where Milan is the principal city, the Ticino is one of its most prominent rivers and connecting with the Po near Pavia. The Ticino is navigable, but is thirty kilometers or so, as the crow flies, to the west of Milan. About twenty-five kilometers to Milan's east is the Adda River, which also flows into the Po, near Cremona. With two good navigable rivers nearby, but both still too far away, the citizens of Milan knew what they had to do.

Eight hundred years ago, the Milanese faced up to the fact that they would be perpetually short of irrigation water for their expanding farms in fertile Lombardy if they didn't do something about it. So they did. With nothing but their sweat, shovels, and ox-carts, they dug a canal, an amazing fifty-two kilometers long, matching the contours of the earth from the Ticino across farmlands and around hills, all the way to their city. In 1269, they widened and deepened this canal to make it navigable, so that boats could sail right up to a Milan city gate. They named the gate the "Porta Ticinese"; and the canal, steadily improved thereafter, and still to be seen today, was proudly baptized the "Naviglio Grande."

Ships, even fleets of ships, had been plying the Po, a virtual inland sea, for centuries before Valentine and Proteus took to its waters. Even before the Roman Pliny mentioned it in his writings, there were sails on its surface stretching from the Adriatic all the way westward to Turin, about 130 kilometers still farther west beyond Milan. Then, with the Naviglio Grande, ships and barges not only could turn up from the Po to the Ticino, reaching the gates of Milan; other vessels could travel the rest of the way up the Ticino to Lake Maggiore, and its quarries, to collect the stone used to build Milan's towering cathedral.

The Milanese connected their Naviglio Grande to the city's old protective moat, widening and deepening it too, to transform it into a circular canal embracing the city's core. They named that internal canal the "Naviglio Interno." Fed by both the waters of Naviglio Grande and those of the local streams, which had watered it from the time it was a moat, the Naviglio Interno had a clean, subsisting current. With quays at convenient intervals, and wide places to anchor or tie up, the Naviglio Interno was the equal of a continuous road for arriving ships. Even a ship from Trebizond, Palermo, or Barcelona — if it could run a Venetian customs blockade while in the Adriatic — was able to enter into the very heart of Milan with cargo, or passengers.

But this was not enough. A shorter, better route to Milan from the Po was wanted. So more than a century before the playwright arrived, the Milanese dug yet another canal, this time a total of twenty-nine kilometers eastward, to reach the Adda River. They baptized this canal the "Naviglio Martesana" or Martesana Canal. Using it, and then the Adda, the Milanese had a second, shorter way to and from

Canal system of Milan from a map dated 1623. Until the middle of the 20th century, Milan was classified as one of Italy's principal maritime ports.

the Po. But the Martesana, suitable for some craft, wasn't adequate to serve ships desiring to reach Milan; so finally, in 1573, the Martesana was deepened and widened. Canal gates called "mitre gates" — invented a century before by Leonardo da Vinci — were installed for the locks. A commodious passenger vessel, or cargo ship, could now travel from the Po, up the Adda, and then, on the improved Martesana Canal, enter the Naviglio Interno, and thus reach the heart of Milan. The year 1573, was a time of great celebration in the city, and soon there were visitors from far and wide coming to see this engineering marvel. In 1928, the Naviglio Interno was filled in for streets, a project which blocked the Martesana's entrance into Milan, but the canal is still there, outside the city's walls, and can be sailed on today, as I have done.

~

The playwright had chosen well for his young travelers. In the sixteenth century — as well as even before and after — freshwater travel was reasonably safe, while land travel was not. There were bandits in Italy's woods, especially in the woods between the Duchy of Milan and the Venetian Republic. Bridges often went unrepaired, uncertain fords could suddenly swamp beasts and men, and there was the toll-exacting greed of petty lords *en route*. Land routes were little more than wandering tracks in places. Only by post-horses, traveling lightly but expensively, was land a faster way to journey from place to place.

Travel by river and canal, on the other hand, was steady, provisioned, and comfortable. The traveler could bring all sorts of baggage and equipment, and bread and bottles and sausages, and avoid those vermin-infested inns and bandit-ridden woods. And one could have servants come along, too.

Until there were rails in the nineteenth century, both travelers and cargo moved on the rivers and canals of Continental Europe. To compare a water voyage to travel by land in the sixteenth century, a pack-horse plodding along a land route could carry an eighth of a ton — 250 pounds; and a wagon drawn by a single horse, five-eighths of a ton — 1,250 pounds. All done slowly. But a tow-horse could pull a barge along a river with a cargo of thirty tons — 60,000 pounds; and fifty tons — 100,000 pounds, along a canal. A single boatman manning a sweep on a canal or river could do almost as well as a tow-horse, and with far less expense and complication. Nobles traveled in boats and barges on canals, with all their clutter and paraphernalia, especially when going to visit another court. Freshwater sailing was ideal.

Arriving at a basin on the Naviglio Grande, c. 1905.
(From I Navigli Milanesi: Storia e prospettive, *Silvana Editoriale, 1982, p. 26)*

So important did Milan's canals continue to be over the centuries, that until 1958, the Italian government, having taken over all the canals in the mid-nineteenth century, continued to classify Milan as one of Italy's *Principali Porti Maritimi*. And more than four centuries before Italy's unification, Milan was thought of in that same way. Well into the twentieth century, in listings that also included Genoa, Naples, Venice, Trieste, Livorno, Messina, and Bari, Milan was ranked third in cargo tonnage out of all of Italy's maritime ports.

～

With what I had now found out, I had "sailed" a long way, but a critical link in the young gentlemen's voyages from Verona to Milan was still missing. In Milan, I realized that I could not stay there to enjoy it in the company of Valentine and Proteus until I had first retraced their voyages to solve a gnawing question. How could they get their ships across the twenty kilometers of dry land, between the Adige and the Po? In the play itself there is the clue, although it has been furnished in that oblique, roundabout way, so often used by the playwright in the Italian Plays. This one clue was Panthino's "flood."

The Naviglio Grande today.
(Author's photo)

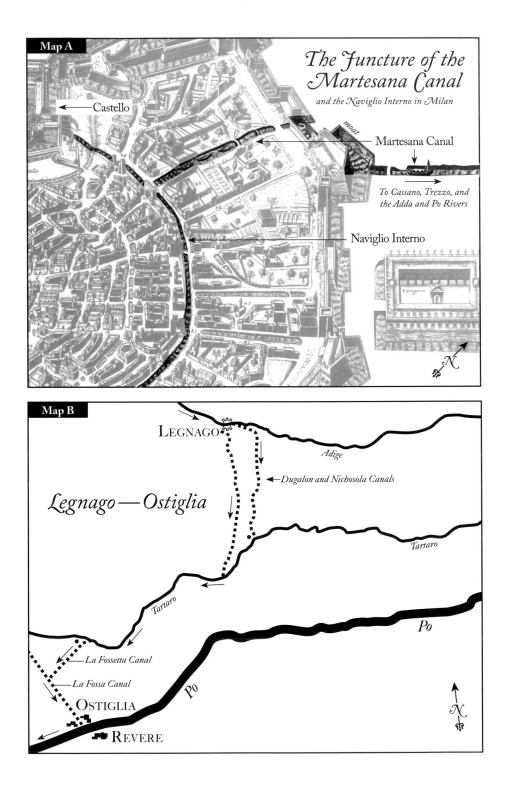

Map A

The Juncture of the Martesana Canal
and the Naviglio Interno in Milan

Castello

moat

Martesana Canal

*To Cassano, Trezzo, and
the Adda and Po Rivers*

Naviglio Interno

N

Map B

LEGNAGO

Adige

Dugalon and Nichosola Canals

Legnago — Ostiglia

Tartaro

Tartaro

Po

La Fossetta Canal

La Fossa Canal

OSTIGLIA

Po

REVERE

N

**The Martesana
Canal in Milan.**
(Print from Milan
C'era una volta il
naviglio, *Enzo Pifferi
Editore. First printed
1886)*

**Horse shipping
on the Martesana
Canal.** *(From*
I Navigli Milanesi:
Storia e prospettive,
*Silvana Editoriale,
1982, p. 27)*

The Porta Ticinese in Milan. *(Print from* Milano C'era una volta il naviglio, *Enzo Pifferi Editore. First printed 1886)*

He had said to Launce:

> … I mean thou'lt lose the flood, and in losing the flood, lose thy voyage, and in losing thy voyage, lose thy master, and in losing thy master …

∽

Some time before coming to Verona I had the good fortune of receiving from Ruth Miller, an independent scholar who was my long-time friend, copies of the writings of Sir Edward Sullivan that were concerned with Shakespeare and Italy. One of Sullivan's articles, published in 1908 and aptly entitled *Shakespeare and the Waterways of North Italy*, is a carefully researched defense of the Italian Plays that have allusions to such waterways. With regard to *The Two Gentlemen*, not only did Sullivan describe the origins and characteristics of the Naviglio Grande and the Martesana Canal in Milan, he does it by citing the knowledgeable works of *Italian* historians and travelers, something rarely done by anyone else engaged in Shakespearean studies. Of Milan, he wrote, in part:

… we find the city in 1497 in ship communication on one side
(by the Naviglio della Martesana) with the Adda, and on the
other (by the Naviglio Grande) with the Ticino, the Po, and
Lago Maggiore — a condition of things sufficient to justify Carlo
Pagnano's statement in 1520 that Milan, far as it was from the
sea, might easily be taken to be a seaport town.

Left: *The Naviglio
Interno at the via
Senato.* (*Print from*
Milano C'era una
volta il naviglio,
*Enzo Pifferi Editore.
First printed 1886*)

Right: *The Naviglio
Interno at the via
Senato,* c. 1920.
(*From* I Navigli
Milanesi: Storia e
prospettive, *Silvana
Editoriale, 1982,
p. 103*)

For myself, the notable inclusion in *The Two Gentlemen* of a
road at the beginning and a road at the end of the voyage,
with Panthino's "flood" in between, was equal to a bidding
that I stay in Italy until I found the answer. There is nothing in Sullivan's
article suggesting he himself had gone over the ground in Italy, but I was
now there, primed for a search. There simply had to be a canal connecting the Adige and Po Rivers, the two most important in Italy. It would
be an important canal, so important it might need to operate on a sched-
ule at *known times,* when the locks were successively raised (*flooded*),
and lowered with flood-gates and sluice-gates: a timed flooding that the

river mariners knew about and could rely on in planning for passage of their ships between the Adige and the Po. Something that would shine a light on Panthino's anxiety, "Tut man! ... Thou'lt lose the flood ..." when he sees Launce dawdling on the quay.

Before, when I had searched along the Adige's edges, it had been from Verona down to Legnago. This time, I would search farther to the south, on all the intervening land between the two rivers. On my map, putting the point of my compass pencil on Legnago and swinging an arc that reached the Po, I saw that on its banks, about twenty kilometers to the southwest, there was an ideal place for the other end of my theoretical canal: the ancient river port of Ostiglia.

In one footnote to Sir Edward Sullivan's article, he remarked:

> The fossa, or canal, which joined the river Tartaro with the Po at Ostiglia (ancient Ostia) ... undoubtedly existed from about the year 1000 A.D. ... and was in all probability the canal by which the Venetian ships in 1510 escaped into the Adige [from the Po], as described by Guicciardini. [Referring to Francesco Guicciardini's famous sixteenth-century *History of Italy*.]

Legnago, too, is a town of ancient origin, which means that like Ostiglia, it had an ancient reason for being where it is, in this case, either as the place for a westward portage between the rivers, or

A mitre gate on the Naviglio Grande in Milan.

the nearest place for a connection across to Ostiglia by means of my imagined canal. If the Milanese could dig a fifty-two kilometer canal in 1269, and a twenty-nine kilometer canal in 1470, it seemed to me that the Veronese or the Mantuans could have dug a "mere" twenty-kilometer canal in plenty of time for Valentine and Proteus to use it. But there was no such canal on the maps I had.

Out in the countryside between the rivers, however, I did see large canals running through the farmlands, but diked or leveed as they are, they looked to be modern irrigation canals. And between the Adige and the Po I also found that lesser river, the Tartaro that Guicciardini mentioned, passing through those farmlands and coursing eastward *between* the two great rivers. But it, too, is now disciplined with levees, making it look very like a man-made irrigation canal instead of a natural river.

Remembering Sullivan's allusion to Ostiglia, and a canal he called "fossa," I turned my car toward that town, it being the other end of my imagined canal. On arriving there, sadly, I found no vestige of any such canal. However, I did discover through interviews between my accompanying professional interpreter, and older folk in Ostiglia, that indeed, there once *had* been a canal which connected to the Po and they *did* call it "*La Fossa*." So far as anyone in Ostiglia

Monument in Milan to Leonardo da Vinci, *designer of the mitre gate. Leonardo's design allowed for wider canals that could accommodate larger vessels, significantly impacting the economy of 16th-century Italy. (Author's photos)*

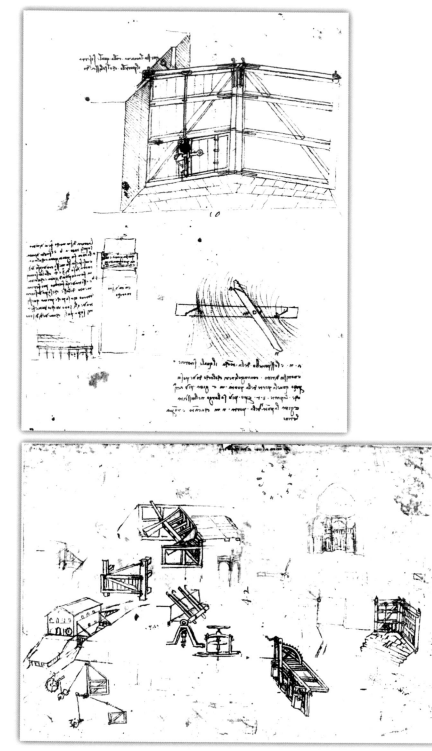

The mitre gate designed by Leonardo da Vinci, drawn in his own hand. The mitre gate is composed of two canal lock gates. The gates swing out from the side walls of the canal and meet at an angle pointing toward the upper level of the canal. The design doubles a canal's width and is easy to operate. Leonardo's revolutionary design is still in use today. (*From* Milano C'era una volti il naviglio, *Enzo Pifferi Editore. First printed 1886*)

knew, this La Fossa had reached only as far as the Tartaro River and by 1928, had become a disused mosquito nuisance, so was filled in.

During my interviews with people in Ostiglia, I learned that across the Po, in the venerable town of Revere, there was a learned man who had written books about the history of Ostiglia. I went across the great river — by a modern bridge, of course — to Revere's Gonzaga Palace, which had become the city hall. I was flattered to be greeted by the mayor of Revere himself, and he, with his delightful interpreter, took me to meet Professor Gino Magri. Professor Magri is a

16th-century burchiello ("barque" or "bark"), any small sailing vessel. (J.F. Costa, engraver, from Riviera del Brenta, *Paulo Tieto, Panda Editioni, p. i)*

Traveling by barge on Italy's canals. Time had another meaning to people of the past. Although traveling by barge was slow, it was more comfortable and spacious — not to mention far safer — than traveling by land. Note the single boatman at the rear manning a sweep. (Photo from the film "L'albero degli zoccoli," by Ermanno Olmi. This picture of a period reenactment taken from I Navigli Milanesi: Storia e prospettive, *Silvana Editoriale, 1982, p. 44)*

serious scholar of the Po, and he generously gave me documented details about La Fossa, as well as books he and others had written about it, the Po, and related places of interest. An important work was his *Ostiglia Napoleonica*, printed in 1982 at Ostiglia, which became the catalyst for our more detailed conversations.

In one place Magri refers, in an off-handed way, to "La Fossetta" being navigable from Legnago; and in another to the "usual way by water from Legnago," and so forth. I asked him to explain the historical background to those references. As a boy in 1928, he had watched as the old La Fossa and La Fossetta canals were filled in, and he told me where, in Ostiglia, I could buy old photographs of them made in 1895.

*I*n 1405, when the province of Verona became a part of the Venetian Republic — to be called "the Veneto Lombardo" — the Adige became a Venetian possession from the Alps to the Adriatic. Ancient Legnago thus became a strategic Venetian stronghold at the new "Veneto Lombardo" border.

In 1438–39, Gianfrancesco Gonzaga, Marchese of Mantua, was at war with Venice. Gianfrancesco attacked Legnago, there to destroy the Venetian warships that were riding on the Adige. To get his own

Barge docked at a "road." *Canal travel was critical to moving commercial cargo and travelers and their belongings throughout northern Italy. Landings, or "roads," were located inside cities and at regular intervals along the length of each canal, much like modern bus stations. (Photo from the film "L'albero degli zoccoli," by Ermanno Olmi. This picture of a period reenactment taken from* I Navigli Milanesi: Storia e prospettive, *Silvana Editoriale, 1982, p. 48)*

Ostiglia: Via XX Settembre in the town center showing La Fossa canal (photo dated 1895). (Postcard: Author's collection)

warships up from the Po, Gianfrancesco Gonzaga had improvements made to La Fossa, even digging a short-cut called La Fossetta, which went from part of La Fossa across to the Tartaro. (La Fossa itself joined the Tartaro at a bad angle for his warships.) Now I had an even stronger clue. If Gianfrancesco was shortening La Fossa with La Fossetta, and was going to attack Venetian ships on the Adige, then he must have used a canal that started someplace on the Tartaro near its La Fossetta

Ostiglia: Via Bertioli parallel to La Fossa canal (photo dated 1895). (Postcard: Author's collection)

junction, and went the rest of the way across to the Adige. But just where and how, in specific terms, Magri couldn't recall, though he remembered there were actually two such canals, both of which disappeared in the late nineteenth or early twentieth century.

I told Magri about the voyages to Milan in an old English play called *The Two Gentlemen*, and about the allusion to one of those Milan-Venice hostilities in another such play called *The Taming of the Shrew*. Magri then reminded me that Ostiglia, La Fossa, and La Fossetta, up to the Tartaro, were all in *Mantuan* territory, and anything on the other side of that boundary river would be under *Venetian* rule. He said that there were probably references to be found in the public library in Verona about any canal system from the Tartaro to Legnago, and maybe something useful in the Archivio di Stato di Verona as well.

As our conversation continued, I learned some interesting and significant — and rather complicated — facts. I learned that, yes, there had been a canal system connecting the Po, the Tartaro and the

Ostiglia: La Fossa canal at Via Aia Madama where the canal becomes wide and straight (photo dated 1895). (Postcard: Author's collection)

Ostiglia: La Fossa canal (photo dated 1895). (Postcard: Author's collection)

Adige, but no, there weren't any modern traces. I learned that a boat sailing on the Po with the Adige as its destination would exit the Po at Ostiglia, would sail through Ostiglia and enter the La Fossa canal, would turn right into the La Fossetta canal, and would thus connect to the Tartaro River. The boat would continue on the Tartaro to either the "Nichosola" canal or the parallel "Dugalon" canal, and sailing up one of these canals, would reach the Adige at Legnago. I tried making a sketch of this involved water route, by referring to a commercial map of the area that I had been using in my fruitless quest, and Magri nodded, saying it looked right, so far as he knew.

On returning to Verona, I went to its public library, accompanied by my professional translator. A librarian there searched the card catalogue, selected four books, and leafed through them. She found nothing really useful, although bits here and there seemed to confirm what Magri had said. Later in the week, my translator and I went to Verona's Archivio di Stato (State Archives) where, after a discouraging search, a map entitled *Confine delle Stato Veneto coll. Eclesco Lungo il Fiume Tartaro* was found in the collection. I held my breath as the map, worn with age, was carefully unfolded. When I saw the lines — with the Adige, the Tartaro, and the Po connected by a system of canals — my heart stopped. Here was my proof. At last, spread out before my eyes, was solid evidence that my long-held conviction had been correct.

The map, dated 1713, was embellished with color. Not only did it corroborate Magri's description, I saw with delight that it almost duplicated the drawing I'd made myself. I knew it would be critical that this map, here in Verona's archives, should be reproduced for my book. But looking closely at the negative I was given, I was concerned that it was not going to be clear enough for publication. I had no choice but to make my own sketch, set to scale and to that commercial map I had in hand. But that technicality aside, my instincts had been spot on: water travel between Verona and Milan — not just for our two young gentlemen in the play — had once been a reality.

NOTES

1. This superb painting, which also portrays portions of the quay, can still be seen in Edinburgh.
2. Facts on File, 1996.
3. *The Oxford English Dictionary* devotes seven columns to the various means of "tide."

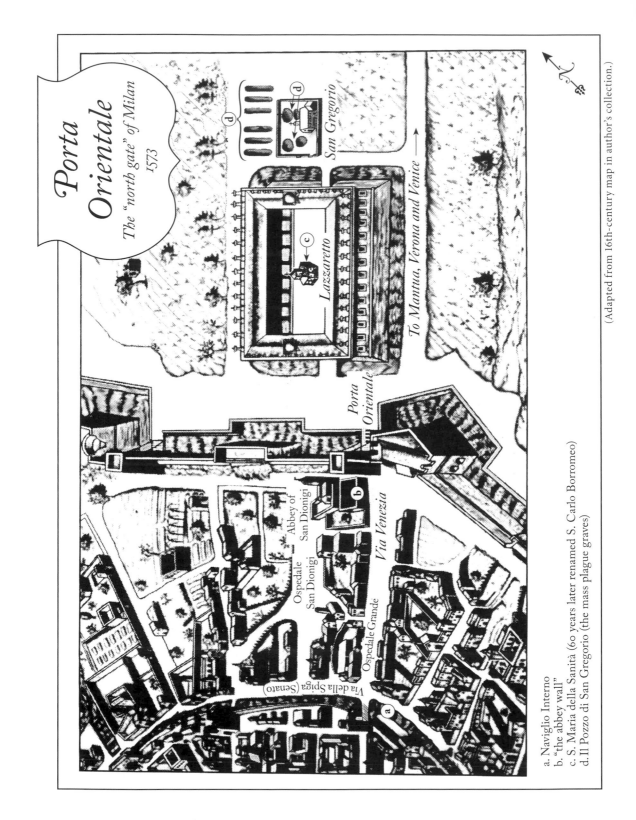

Porta Orientale

The "north gate" of Milan
1573

San Gregorio

d

Lazzaretto

c

To Mantua, Verona and Venice →

Porta Orientale

Naviglio Interno

Abbey of San Dionigi

Ospedale San Dionigi

Ospedale Grande

Via della Spiga (Senato)

Via Venezia

b

a

N

(Adapted from 16th-century map in author's collection.)

a. Naviglio Interno
b. "the abbey wall"
c. S. Maria della Sanità (60 years later renamed S. Carlo Borromeo)
d. Il Pozzo di San Gregorio (the mass plague graves)

3

The Two Gentlemen of Verona – Part 2
"Milan: Arrivals and Departures"

Proteus had not been told the whole story, when Valentine sailed away at the beginning of *The Two Gentlemen of Verona*. Perhaps Proteus already knew the real reason why Valentine is heading to Milan; but from their conversation in Act I Scene 1, it doesn't seem as though he does.

When the scene begins, Proteus has been trying to convince Valentine to stay at home in Verona. This is Valentine's reply:

> Cease to persuade, my loving Proteus;
> Home-keeping youth have ever homely wits.
> To the sweet glances of thy honour'd love,
> I rather would entreat thy company
> To see the wonders of the world abroad
> Than (living sluggardiz'd at home)
> Wear out thy youth with shapeless idleness.

Whether Proteus does, or does not, know what Valentine is up to, the audience certainly doesn't. Not yet. But when we get to Scene 3 of Act I, we find out — maybe before Proteus does — and it's a lot more important than merely going "to see the wonders of the world abroad." In fact, it's the chance of a lifetime.

When that Scene 3 begins, Proteus's noble father, Antonio, is on stage with Panthino, his major-domo. The men share an instructive conversation:

Antonio: Tell me, Panthino, what sad talk was that
             Wherewith my brother held you in the cloister?

Panthino: 'Twas of his nephew Proteus, your son.

Antonio: Why, what of him?

Panthino: He wonder'd that your lordship
             Would suffer him to spend his youth at home
             While other men, of slender reputation,
             Put forth their sons to seek preferment out:
             Some to the wars, to their fortune there;
             Some to discover islands far away;
             Some to the studious universities.
             For any or for all these exercises
             He said that Proteus your son was met;
             And did request me to importune you
             To let him spend his time no more at home,
             Which would be great impeachment to his age,
             In having known no travel in his youth.

Antonio: Nor need'st thou much importune me to that
             Whereon this month I have been hammering.
             I have consider'd well his loss of time,
             And how he cannot be a perfect man,
             Not being tried and tutor'd in the world.
             Experience is by industry achiev'd
             And perfected by the swift course of time.
             Then tell me, whither were I best to send him?

Panthino: I think your lordship is not ignorant
             How his companion, youthful Valentine,
             Attends the Emperor in his royal court.

Antonio: I know it well.

Panthino: 'Twere good, I think, your lordship sent
             Him thither.

There he shall practice tilts and tournaments,
Hear sweet discourse, converse with noblemen,
And be in the eye of every exercise
Worthy of his youth and nobleness of birth.

Antonio: I like thy counsel; well hast thou advised
And that thou mayst perceive how well I like it,
The execution of it shall make known.
I will dispatch him to the Emperor's court.

Panthino: To-morrow, may it please you, Don Alphonso,
With other gentlemen of good esteem,
Are journeying to salute the Emperor
And to commend their service to his will.

Antonio: Good company. With them shall Proteus go.

These young gentlemen of Verona are going to Milan for an event of the utmost importance for their futures: "To salute the Emperor, and commend their service to his will." Of course, if they happen to see some wonders on the way, so much the better; but each of them is leaving town for the particular business of getting ahead in the world, of winning a personal plum by making *una bella figura*, as the Italians say, before "the Emperor."

The Italians have always had a word for a personal goal, whether an appointment of office, or title, or honor, or be what it may: the *particulare*. And for exact instructions on how to attain it, an expert had written a handbook for them. His name was Baldassare Castiglione and his important book, *Il libro del cortegiano* (*The Book of the Courtier*), had already been published, in Venice in 1528.

What the young men are embarking upon — commending their service to the Emperor's will — might seem out of line because they are Veronese, and therefore the subjects of the autonomous Venetian Republic; yet they are about to offer homage to a ruler sitting in the capital of the Duchy of Milan. They are crossing frontiers, going from one to another of two separate states that were often hostile, and always at loggerheads. But not to worry, not where the *particulare* is involved. Such technicalities were never a serious problem in the sixteenth century.

Valentine and Proteus are simply doing what is expected of them. Their fathers have chosen well among laudable choices. Panthino placed their pursuits on an equal footing with other proper things for young noblemen to do: going to the wars;[1] discovering distant islands; studying at a university; "for any or for all these exercises." The playwright has not only listed them, he will treat some of them in his other plays: Count Bertram, though French, will go "to the wars" in Tuscany in *All's Well That Ends Well*; and Lucentio, the wealthy young man in *The Taming of the Shrew*, will attend Padua's famous university.

While it is true that in the rest of Europe, the privileged had begun to study *The Courtier* soon after 1528, there was a difference ever so natural in its employment in sunny Italy. This difference is said to endure. As Luigi Barzini wrote about Castiglione in his entertaining *The Italians*:

> Perhaps the author's teachings sank so deep into his countrymen's conscience that they are now a part of their very nature, or, more probably, he being Italian, merely codified what everybody more or less knew then and would still know centuries later.

In any case, the young gentlemen would embark for Milan with either those teachings in mind, or their native instinct for personal success. And there could not be a better time and place than at an emperor's court — not a duke's court nor even a king's court, but the greatest of courts — where there would be an array of opportunities beyond imagination. And this court was so accessible, just across the border in Milan, so easy to reach, sailing on safe and untroubled rivers and canals, all the way from their own city's river quay, right into the heart of downtown Milan.

There is a problem with this grand event. The playwright's critics have written and rewritten about it, asserting that his notion of there being an emperor's court in Milan is absurd, and making observations such as the following from the "Longer Notes," at page 190, in *The New Folger Library* edition (1990) of *The Two Gentlemen of Verona*:

> 1.3.28. Emperor: The ruler that Shakespeare presents as residing at the court in Milan is sometimes referred to in the play as an emperor and sometimes as a duke. Editors have noted that

at one time Charles V, emperor of the Holy Roman Empire, also ruled the Duchy of Milan. This fact may be pertinent, or the confusion may be simply another of the inconsistencies in this early play.

The critics have been totally confident of their conclusions, observing that never, not since the fall of Rome, has Milan been the capital of any empire. Milan was only a duchy, it's true; its ruler was merely a duke. The author, they say, has made yet another mistake. But had he? While he wrote that these travelers were to see one, no emperor ever appears in the play. The only person of authority that can be found in *The Two Gentlemen* is "the Duke of Milan." It is now customary in the fault-finding to ascribe this to the playwright's ignorance of Milan's history and status.

When this playwright drums at something specific, it is time to get suspicious. "Saint Peter's Church," said three times in *Romeo and Juliet*, is a prime example. And here, in *The Two Gentlemen*, he not only alludes to "the Emperor" three times, he refers three times to his "court," either as "the Emperor's" or as "the Imperial's." It seems he has gone to a lot of trouble to make another Italian "mistake." What emperor could this have been? And why is he not in Milan where he is expected to be?

For most of the fifteenth century, Italy had prospered: its Renaissance had burgeoned to fascinate the world. Though skirmishing among themselves, its local rulers in its north had been strong enough to withstand most foreign interference; but this would change in 1494. It was then that the invasion of Charles VIII of France took place. He had been invited by the Duke of Milan — Lodovico Sforza, called "Il Moro" — to come to Italy with an army to help him put down his troublesome neighbors. The French invasion marked the beginning of more than thirty years of hell for much of Italy. One French king after another would invade, loot, and destroy, met only by disorganized resistance and misalliances among those Italian neighbors. Next, another and very different Charles from beyond the Alps and the Pyrenees would send his troops from Spain, Germany, and the Swiss federation to Italy in what was advertised as a relief expedition.

Portrait of
Charles V in 1548
(Titian). The
Emperor, seated, is
wearing the black
Spanish attire he
favored.

This different Charles, who called himself "Carlos," was the most powerful monarch that Europe had seen since Charlemagne. He was Charles V, King of Spain (1516) and Holy Roman Emperor (1519). Besides Spain and central Europe, his dominions covered all the Spanish New World possessions, the Low Countries and the Kingdoms of Naples, Sicily, and Sardinia. He had conquered or inherited control over strategic Mediterranean islands and parts of North Africa. And, too, some of the dukes of Italy were under oaths of fealty to him as their feudal overlord.

It was this Emperor Charles who confronted the French and their allies on Italian soil, among the latter, the de' Medici Pope Clement VII in Rome. He defeated the French king, Francis I, at Pavia in 1525, and his unruly mercenaries attacked and plundered Rome itself in what has gone down in history as the "Sack of Rome," a tragedy that left the city in ruins and impoverished, for many years to come. The event was so beyond all comprehension that historians have given up trying to describe the whole of it. Within twenty-four months, using replaced and disciplined troops, the Emperor made peace with Pope Clement VII and laid siege to a rebellious republican Florence, to restore the overthrown rule of the de' Medici.

Finally, on 5 August 1529, by the celebrated Treaty of Cambrai, peace was restored to Italy. Milan, and most of Italy, became a dependency of the Spanish crown. Later, the Emperor arrived on Italian soil, to make a triumphant progress, and in 1530 at Bologna, he achieved his greatest prestige, his crowning as Emperor, by the same Clement VII who, meanwhile, had taken sides with the Emperor. In fact, Charles V hardly needed such a papal enthronement. As John Julius Norwich observed in his *History of Venice*:

> [This] was not an indispensable ceremony; several of his predecessors, including his grandfather Maximilian, had done without it altogether, and Charles himself had already been ten years

on the throne without this final confirmation of his authority. The fact remained, nonetheless, that until the Pope had laid the crown on his head he could not technically call himself Emperor, and, to one possessing so strong a sense of divine mission, both the title and the sacrament were important.

The Emperor wished to consolidate his sway over the Dukedom of Milan. Its Duke Francesco was not formally his feudal subject, even though the Emperor had engineered the marriage of his own twelve-year-old niece, Christina of Denmark, to that aged and ill, yet kindly, Duke. With the presence in northern Italy of the imperial army, by 1533, the Duke gave in to various pressures and inducements. He invited the Emperor to Milan, to receive his oath of fealty, and the submission of his duchy, to the imperial power. And the Emperor graciously accepted Francesco's invitation.

When it was heard that the Emperor was due to arrive in Milan for the appropriate formalities, the excitement in the city, in the whole duchy, and far beyond, was incomparable; and so were the preparations. Not only did Italy's nobles and common folk begin to gather, but artists and artisans arrived from far and wide to help embellish the city. Federico Gonzaga, Duke of Mantua — already long beholden to this emperor — sent his famous court artist, Giulio (Julio) Romano — the only artist the playwright ever named[2] — to put up a fantasy "imperial arch of triumph." The Milanese made the great tournament field and tiltyard ready; and grand entertainments of a great variety were arranged. The imperial coat-of-arms was placed on all of the city gates, on the great door of the Cathedral, and inside and out of the Castello Sforzesco, the gigantic stone pile that still looms at the city's Renaissance edge, and in which the Spanish troops of Charles had already been garrisoned to give the Duke a further sense of commitment.

The ducal residence, which was inside the Castello, was rearranged. This *Cortile della Rocchetta* ("courtyard of the small fortress") — aptly named, being a fortress inside of the fortress — was prepared for the Emperor, while the Duke and his household took temporary rooms in the Renaissance convent of Santa Maria delle Grazie, already a place of wide note, since Leonardo had painted his *Cenacolo,* or *Last Supper,* there less than forty years before.

The palace of the Duke of Milan, *the Cortile della Rocchetta, located inside the Castello Sforzesco. (Author's photo)*

The world-famous Milan Cathedral received its festive decorations; and, in addition to those, and the fastening of the imperial arms, this inscription was placed on its central door:

> Post profligatos Turcos, republicae christiane reducta pace, Italia novo foedere iuncta, tam diu expectate Caesar Optime, Urbem hanc tot cladibus guassatam et afflictam fove et adiuva (After having defeated the Turks, pacified the Christian Republic, united Italy in a new pact, O, highest Caesar so long expected, console and help this city, weakened by innumerable destructions).

Charles V arrived in Milan late in the evening of 10 March 1533, by way of the Porta Romana, the traditional entry gate of the emperors of Rome. With trumpets blaring the imperial toccata, banners flapping, and nobles attending in the black Spanish-style clothes that Charles V himself wore, the Emperor proceeded to the Cathedral for imperial ceremonies, entering it by that same central door. That done, he was escorted to the waiting Cortile della Rocchetta where, in addition to the finest provisions made for him and his entourage, a throne and other appropriate court furnishings were in place. On the following day he received the Duke's oath of fealty, and during the next two days he rested and presided over some official affairs and various conversations.

On the next day, 14 March, in the morning, the Emperor went outside the city with his imperial party to go hunting. He was expected to be gone two or three days. He did not return. Instead, it was discovered that he and his party had quietly crossed the Ticino and the Po Rivers, had gone over the Appennino Ligure mountains and down to the coast, and at Genoa, he had boarded a ship for Spain.

This is the journal record; and like all proper journals, no commentaries by its recorder were included. In his *The History of Italy*, however, Francesco Guicciardini (1483–1540) did make the remark that the Emperor "was very eager to go to Spain for various reasons, but mainly because of his desire to procreate sons, his wife having remained there."

Milan never saw Charles V again. He vanished from the city, indeed too soon to appear in the play, but soon enough for Valentine and Proteus to get involved in a different sort of activity. The Duke moved back to Castello Sforzesco, and the city's decorations, save for the imperial arms, were taken down. And, too, the eloquent plea for a handout was removed from the Milan Cathedral door. But dates of the imperial presence are precise: 10 March 1533, in the evening; to 14 March 1533, in the morning.

The playwright had included something more than a piece of embarrassing Milanese history in his play: a reminder not only about the Emperor himself but perforce about his obedient son Philip, who, when this play was written, had inherited lands where the sun never set and nursed a triple grudge against England that included (1) the offense bequeathed by Charles V for the outrage deemed done in England upon Katherine of Aragon, his aunt and Philip's great-aunt, whom Henry VIII had put aside and virtually imprisoned to marry the woman who would become Queen Elizabeth's mother; (2) the rudeness done Philip by Englishmen upon his marriage to Katherine's daughter, Mary Tudor — the Mary they called "Bloody" — being a marriage at which he had the presumption to have himself declared "King of England"; and (3) the refusal of his marriage proposal to Elizabeth after Mary's death. Charles V had left it to Philip to manage a complete encirclement of France, having fallen short of a needed conquest of England, and Philip had failed thus far in his filial duty.

With the Emperor gone and springtide approaching, our promising lads are left high and dry, along with everyone else in town.

Left: ***Il Lazzaretto*** *in Milan. The rooms represented by the first five arches are today occupied by the Russian Orthodox Church.*

Right: ***Interior*** ***view*** *of the surviving remnant of il Lazzaretto. (Author's photos)*

Valentine has arrived and Proteus is arriving, but there is nothing imperial for them to enjoy. Their fathers will be disappointed, but the boys don't seem to care. Being from out of town, it's a good time to get into trouble, and Valentine has had a head start. He is already in love with Silvia, daughter of the "Duke of Milan" and the beauty of the famous song—in Act IV Scene 2 Line 38—that queries, "Who is Silvia?" This Duke of the play is not, of course, the real duke of history; that duke had no daughter. We thus have returned to the world of imagination.

~

A century or so ago, critics of *The Two Gentlemen of Verona* decided that the playwright knew at least one thing about Milan that appeared to be accurate: he had referred, in this play, though indirectly, to a church outside the walls of Milan, by using its actual name: "Saint Gregory's." Specifically, however, what he alluded to—in Scene 2 of Act IV— is not the church *per se*: his allusion is to "Saint Gregory's *Well*." A number of critics have written about the well, saying it existed and expressing surprise that the author knew about it, but variously representing, as fact, either that it was a small water fountain, or an actual well.

In support of the thesis that the author had never been outside England, such assertions are "explained" as discoveries he could have seen on a sixteenth-century map of Milan: the "Braun and Hogenberg" map of Milan, being one of the maps of cities of the world in the atlas entitled *Civitates Orbis Terrarum*, and issued in Germany, between 1572 and 1598. This atlas was sold in many places, including England. That map shows an erroneously located St. Gregory's *Church* but no well. It also shows a huge, four-sided building just outside the northern city wall, and next to a city gate labeled "Porta Orientale." Rarely did sixteenth-century cartographers depict anything outside a city's walls, unless they considered it particularly important.

This huge building was Milan's *lazzaretto* (disease quarantine compound), which the Milanese simply called by that name: *Il Lazzaretto*. Within its great central courtyard, there is a sketch of a very small church, with the word "Gregorio." My excellent guidebook of Milan[3] says the little church was called *Santa Maria della Sanità* at that time, not *San Gregorio*.

Many cities in Italy had a lazzaretto, named for biblical Lazarus, who rose from the dead. Meant to confine lepers, and to detain travelers who looked diseased in the terrifying times of plague, it was the mandated place for frightened and frightening victims. It was a place outside the city walls to minister to them, to offer prayers, and to attempt medication, but a place where nearly all would die. Inside the city walls of Milan, but nearby its lazzaretto, was the abbey, residence of the saintly friars who cared for the dying.

The dimensions of Milan's Lazzaretto were exceptional. With four sides of about 500 yards each, the Lazzaretto enclosed an area of approximately one and one-half million square feet, or about 140,000 square meters, or fourteen hectares. The perimeter lines of its walls and moat—almost completely gone by 1880—are delineated today by four streets: Via San Gregorio; Via Lazzaretto; Viale Vittorio Veneto; and Corso Buenos Aires. Absolutely enormous. It could hold many thousands of the sick; and twice, at least, it did. In 1575, a plague descended on many parts of Italy, and by early 1576, it had reached Milan. It sent the multitudes of its sick and dying out into its Lazzaretto, where, at the peak of the plague there were as many as 16,000 victims.

Today the street maps of modern Milan show a church named for San Gregorio, directly *across the street* from the now nearly vanished

Lazzaretto. It is a very big church, built around 1900, in a location that was outside the sixteenth-century city wall. There I found a priest in the sacristy, preparing for a mass, but having just enough time for me and two of my burning questions.

First, I wanted to know if this San Gregorio had always been where it is, or if it had once been in the middle of the Lazzaretto. Second, I wanted to know if the church — in either place — once had a well, or other kind of source for water. I told him that it had been reported there was such a well at a church named for San Gregorio, which was inside the old Lazzaretto. When he asked me, "Who would report such a thing?" I told him some English and American writers had, saying it was called *il Pozzo di San Gregorio*: "Saint Gregory's Well." I deliberately avoided mentioning the playwright.

I asked the priest what he knew, though by the expression on his face I already knew one thing that he was sure about: there was an uninvited lunatic from America standing in his sacristy. The priest was kind, and might have been patient if he hadn't been required at that moment in the chancel. Even while I was asking, he was shaking his head:

> No, no; our San Gregorio was never inside the Lazzaretto. You all have been looking at that old German map. It is wrong. San Gregorio was always outside. Our first building was some meters down the street, this street, this same side. Now our church rests on the bones. The Lazzaretto was over there, across the street.

What about the water, the well?

> No. No water, no spring, no fountain, no well, no source. Big, no; little, no. *Niente*. Not for this church; not for the old church; not for the little one in the Lazzaretto. *Inventato*.

That last word amused me for a second: it means "figment of the imagination." I asked what had happened to the little church that was in the Lazzaretto.

> It is still over there! It began as an open altar where mass was said for the sick. Now it is a small church; and is named *San Carlo Borromeo al Lazzaretto* for our heroic saint of the plague[4] *il Peste di San Carlo*. It is just over there on Via Lecco. Go see it.

He had his vestments adjusted now, and was leaving. Then, in an afterthought, he rushed to a file cabinet and withdrew a single sheet. "Here," he said, "this picture is true. You can have it. Part of our old monastery is at the bottom." Almost at the door he added, "Read Manzoni," and he was gone.

I quietly left; a choir had begun singing. Then, out on the steps, I stopped. The priest had also said, "Now our church rests on the bones." What did *that* mean? I had lost the chance to say, "Bones? What bones?" I wandered away to the little church that was in the Lazzaretto, but my search there was fruitless.

❧

I was sure, when the priest said, "Read Manzoni," he was talking about *I Promessi Sposi — The Betrothed —* the landmark Italian novel by Alessandro Manzoni (1785–1873), renowned Milanese author, historian, and statesman. I had read it years ago, and I remembered it had something in it about a terrible plague in Milan, so I made a mental note to look for an English edition; but at the moment, I had more pressing business at hand. If there really was a San Gregorio *Well,* it might still be down the street, where he said the church had been before. There, I searched about for a well, but found nothing.

Fortunately, I had earlier been introduced to Doctor Eleanor Saita of Milan, a specialist in the history of her city. It was she to whom I had turned for research about the vanishing Emperor. In describing this second "Milanese problem," I told her of the strange remark I had heard when visiting in Venice. There, when telling a Venetian friend about my upcoming plans for Milan, I had said I intended to hunt for a mysterious well called *Il Pozzo di San Gregorio.* The friend had gasped, and then elaborated:

> Whatever it means, it is something horrible. My grandmother was from Milan; and when I was a little girl I remember her saying that name as though it was some kind of synonym for Hell, but that is all I ever knew about it.

Dr. Saita agreed to search for answers.

Santa Maria della Sanità. Located in the center of the Lazzaretto, the arcades were originally open so that plague victims, lying on pallets, could witness the elevation of the host. Following a second ghastly plague, the church was renamed "San Carlo al Lazzaretto" (circa 1630) in honor of the nobleman, Carlo Borromeo, who had selflessly ministered to plague victims. (Author's photo)

*T*his is how the subject of "Saint Gregory's Well" comes up in the play: The moment Proteus set eyes on Valentine's beautiful Silvia, he, too, falls in love with her, head over heels. The gullible Valentine doesn't notice this. He is distracted by a fellow named Thurio, also rich and naïve, who is in town — also from Verona — and he, too, is trying to win Silvia's hand. Worse luck, Thurio has been given the nod by her father, the Duke. Proteus decides to get rid of him.

Proteus is frank with us. He says, "Already I have been false to Valentine, and now I must be as unjust to Thurio." He already has Thurio eating out of his hand. Thurio is even more dense than Valentine: he believes the perfidious Proteus will make a plea on his behalf to Silvia. Deciding that a private planning session with Proteus would be a good idea, he asks Proteus where the two of them should meet. And now we have it: Proteus says, "At Saint Gregory's Well." Proteus — which is to say the playwright — has picked a terrifying place according to my Venetian friend's grandmother. He has directed his rival to go there in the dark of night, and with no means to return through the small gate called a "postern" into the safety of the city.

There is an easily retraced route described in the lines of *The Two Gentlemen*. It begins at Castello Sforzesco, home of Silvia and her father, and ends in a forest outside of Milan — the final scene of the play, and with, I was sure, a Saint Gregory's Well somewhere between the beginning and the end. I trusted the playwright's knowledge of this route, the one that first Valentine and Speed will take, then Silvia will take, and finally, nearly everyone else in the play will take. When I zeroed-in on its specifics, putting aside all of the unrelated events and dialogues, such as the matter of Silvia's serenade, the shameful treatment of Julia by Proteus, and so on, I plotted a route that is exactly the same, in its sixteenth-century facts, as the descriptions the playwright has provided for it.

There are three events of departure from the great Castello Sforzesco, which stands inside the western wall of the city. The first trip begins when Valentine has been caught by the Duke and sent packing (Act III Scene 1); the second departure is by Silvia (Act V Scenes 2 and 3); and the third, by the Duke, Proteus, and Julia, and joined by Thurio (Act V Scene 2).

*Il **Lazzaretto** and the **Church of S. Gregorio** in 1629.*

At Valentine's departure, the double-dealing Proteus offers to convey him across the city and through "the city gate." Valentine then instructs Launce, "if thou seest my boy [Speed], bid him make haste, and meet me at the North-gate." Launce will do as instructed, later saying to Speed, "thy master stays for thee at the North-gate." The north gate in question is, in fact, called "Porta Orientale." It is in the north city wall, correctly named on that same Braun and Hogenberg map, and on almost every other map of Milan, both antique and modern, though now often called "Porta Venezia." "Orientale," of course, means "eastern" and "Venezia" is as far *east* as one would go by using it. It is not named for where it is, but for *the direction* in which the road through it will soon *lead*.

Some have opined that a traveler to the east wouldn't be using a north gate, that he should go out of an east gate, and straight east across the intervening flat lands to get to Mantua. These ideas stem from an unfamiliarity with the terrain and the long-established route to Mantua or Venice, which first went northward for a time, before swinging eastward. A major crop grown in those flat lands between Milan and Mantua was rice, with vast flooded paddies. There were irrigation canals in every direction, and the streams and rivers flowing down from the Alps branched and widened out on those plains, making fording often impossible and bridging unfeasible. Travelers went where the land was dry, the streams were narrower and easier to cross, where bridges and ferries were reliable, and where there were towns, inns, and relays along the way. Thus, we find the Duke correctly saying to the others when they depart to find Silvia (Act V Scene 2):

> ... mount you presently and meet with me
> Upon the rising of the mountain foot
> [*the up-slope edge at the rising of*
>   *the Alpine foothills*]
> That leads toward Mantua ...

The writer knew exactly how that road went.

*I*n Act IV Scene 1, Valentine and Speed have left the city through that north gate, and once they are past the Lazzaretto they are soon involved with some comical outlaws. It was well known to travelers in Italy in the sixteenth century that once outside a city's encircling walls, law and order ended. It was further known that outside Milan, especially to its north, the landscape was full of outlaws. So serious was their presence in this area — the same area in which the common boundary between the Duchy of Milan and the Republic of Venice was located — that in 1572, the two governments, ordinarily uncooperative, signed a pact — renewed of necessity in 1580 — by which officers of either government were permitted to pursue criminals up to six miles beyond their own frontier.

Where, exactly, are the two exiles when they meet the outlaws? In the popular *The Riverside Shakespeare*, the place noted for this Act IV Scene 1, is "Location: A forest between Milan and Mantua." The *Cambridge Edition* uses the same words. *The Yale Shakespeare* varies: "A forest between Milan and Verona." There is nothing in the dialogue that would justify such a surrounding — nothing at all. The author has explicitly stated the correct description and it is *not* a forest. The untraveled Englishmen who inserted this headnote got it wrong. This is what the Second Outlaw asks Valentine:

> Are you content to be our general,
> To make a virtue of necessity
> And live as we do in *this wilderness*?   (Emphasis mine)

The *Oxford English Dictionary* defines "wilderness" as "wild or uncultivated land," and "a wild or uncultivated region or tract of land, uninhabited, or inhabited only by animals." In examining the playwright's use of "wilderness," both here and in his other works, nowhere has he used that word as a synonym for "forest" or "woods," yet editors have done just that. Is this important? It most assuredly is, if the issue of the author's exact knowledge of Italy matters.

This much is clear: Valentine and Speed are in a wild or uncultivated region that is uninhabited, and they are far enough outside the city's walls to be where outlaws are also a part of the landscape.

Leaving Valentine and Speed in the Castello-to-wilderness segment of the route, let us turn to the less direct way taken by Silvia and the knight, Sir Eglamour. In Act IV Scene 3, Silvia asks Eglamour to accompany her in her flight to join Valentine, "To Mantua, where I hear he makes abode." Sir Eglamour asks, "Where shall I meet you?" Silvia replies: "At Friar Patrick's cell, where I intend holy confession."[5] No place name, no monastery name, but a friar's given name: an Irish name.

Not too many years before this play was written there was an Irish Franciscan friar named Patrick O'Hely, who went to Spain to study at the University of Alcalá. At some point, O'Hely became involved in a plot to overthrow the English domination of Ireland and put Don John of Austria, the illegitimate son of Emperor Charles V, on an Irish throne.

After gaining a reputation for his studies in Spain, O'Hely was summoned to Rome, where, on 4 July 1576, Pope Gregory XIII named him Bishop of Mayo, an area of Ireland. After his sojourn in Rome he traveled overland to reach his Irish diocese, stopping — it has been said — at Milan. We can guess, in line with the known facts, that he would have waited for Milan's plague of 1575–76 to end before coming through that city. Milan was the accustomed resting place for northbound travelers to gather strength and provisions, before the task of crossing the perilous Alps. When he landed in Ireland at County Kerry, O'Hely was immediately arrested by the English, and on 22 August 1578, he was hanged.[6] King Philip II, Don John's half-brother, said he had never approved any such Irish plot, but the English never believed him. (It is only my conjecture to suggest that Friar Patrick O'Hely was the Friar Patrick referred to in the play.)

The first part of the road to Mantua was, and still is, the same as the road to Verona, and on to Venice, until it splits in two at Brescia, a distance away to their east. The route from Milan to both cities departs from Milan by means of that north gate.

Sir Eglamour is at that appointed place, the abbey near Friar Patrick's cell. Silvia arrives sounding hurried, and says:

> Go on, good Eglamour,
> Out at the *postern* by the abbey wall.
> I fear I am attended by some spies.   (Emphasis mine)

In medieval and Renaissance times, the great city gates were closed at night. On either side of a gate there was a much smaller guarded passageway called a "postern." A properly identified person, or perhaps one offering a satisfactory bribe (as Lorenzo did in Chapter XXXIV of *The Betrothed*), could gain ingress to or egress from the city after public hours. I realized Silvia does *not* want to go through the great open Porta Orientale. She says, "I fear I am attended by some spies," probably her father's henchmen. She wants to give them the slip, to use the small postern gate "by the abbey wall," once the great gate is closed for the night. Moreover, it will soon be dark, as Eglamour notes at the beginning of this scene, as the time when "The sun begins to gild the western sky"; by then they could have a cover of dusk or darkness.

I scrutinized the exterior of the north city wall on foot, from where the original Porta Orientale (now gone) had stood, to the site of the next gate to the west, the Porta Nuova. The huge area next to that wall, and just inside the city, formerly occupied by that abbey and its humanitarian facilities, is now occupied by the Senate Palace, the headquarters of the Italian Touring Club, the Museum of Natural History, and the Planetarium, all of them surrounded by Milan's great *Giardini Pubblici*, the Public Gardens. If once there was a postern, I did not find it, though I thought I saw traces of one about twenty meters west of the site of the old Porta Orientale, and just opposite the former Lazzaretto location, just outside the city wall. Could this faint relic have once been "the postern by the abbey wall?"

This would be the shortest distance, and the most unobtrusive way, for the overworked friars to travel to and from their abbey, which they needed to do again and again, night and day, to attend the sufferers in a time of plague.

Of course, Silvia and Eglamour, on leaving the city by such an arrangement, would go past the corner of the Lazzaretto building and enter the road to Mantua. All this has seemed probable to me, but I cannot offer proof of such a postern.

I went to the remarkable *Bertarelli Collection* of prints and maps in the Castello Sforzesco, to study more maps of Milan. There I learned the abbey had been Franciscan, just as the priest whom I met is, *and* as Patrick O'Hely was. It, and its enormous hospital and other facilities, can be identified on many maps such as the one made by Antonio Lapreri in 1573. I examined others, in a chronological sequence reaching to 1699, depicting those same abbey buildings and the walls. The abbey was named for Saint Dionigio, Saint Dionysius, who was a Franciscan. Manzoni described it in *The Betrothed*.

When I explained to some of the personnel at the Bertarelli what I was looking for, they said no postern should be expected on maps made for public sale; it would be irresponsible to show an available postern in the city wall. I remarked that my possible postern could have been the best way for the friars to go to the Lazzaretto, and they asked, "Who would need to know about it besides friars, who already would?"

In Act V Scene 1, when Silvia gives Eglamour instructions to leave by the postern, Eglamour replies:

> Fear not, the *forest* is not three leagues off;
> If we *recover* that, we are sure enough.   (Emphasis mine)

Eglamour is not referring to the wilderness just outside the city; he is referring to the forest three leagues farther on. *The Oxford English Dictionary* says a "league" is an "itinerary measure of distance, varying in different countries, but usually estimated roughly at about three miles." Thus, according to Eglamour, safety will be reached, once they are in the forest. We thus know the forest itself is something less than nine miles from the north wall of Milan. The accuracy of the playwright continues. In fact, the intervening distance in the sixteenth century from the city wall to the forest was about seven or eight meandering miles. As Manzoni remarked in *The Betrothed*, the only straight part of the road was the brief segment alongside the Lazzaretto.

In Act V Scene 3, the bandits have now captured Silvia. Sir Eglamour has run away. They are *not* in the forest, as the many editors of this play have claimed; they are in that wilderness outside Milan. It is there that the Third Outlaw instructs the First Outlaw: "Go thou with her to the west end of the wood." In the sixteenth century, the wood — the forest — was to the north and northeast of the wilderness, nine miles beyond the city gate, and the road went through part of it on the way to Monza. It was beyond Monza where the road began rising, and turning eastward toward Verona and Mantua.

Meanwhile, in Act V Scene 2, back at the Castello, the Duke has information that Silvia did not go to confession, as she said she would. Instead she has been seen in the forest. The Duke is now in haste; he instructs Thurio, Proteus, and "Sebastian" (who is actually Julia, as we have earlier learned): "But mount you presently and meet with me upon the rising of the mountain foot that leads toward Mantua, whither they are fled." The Duke is unaware that Silvia is still in the west end of the wood some distance off the road, taken there by the bandits.

With this, out of the north gate, or its postern by the abbey wall, across the wilderness and into the forest, the route of the lovers ends, and so does the play, with Act V Scene 4.

Our playwright has herded nearly his entire cast into the woods, the forest, near Monza. There they are assembled to speak their final lines. From the distinctions between "wilderness," and "wood" or "forest," and the distance of three leagues between them, I am satisfied that the playwright was personally familiar with the lay of the land beyond the walls of Milan.

~

It was time for me to leave Milan and its duchy, and return to California. After a time, I received a very large envelope from Dr. Eleanor Saita, containing all that I had hoped to learn and which proved, once again, that the playwright knew whereof he wrote.

In the devastating plague of 1575–76, thousands of the afflicted were brought to the Lazzaretto. It had two gates: one, nearest the Porta Orientale, was the usual place to enter; the other gate, on the opposite side of the Lazzaretto, faced the church of San Gregorio across the road. Beyond San Gregorio was the great "wilderness," through which a road first made its way northward to a forest near Monza, and then angled to the east.

Inside the huge quarantine compound of the Lazzaretto, many thousands would die. For the dead, who required a Christian burial in whatever way it could be arranged in such desperate times, an interment in consecrated ground needed to be close at hand. Bodies were piled in carts and taken to Saint Gregory's ever-expanding churchyard. At Saint Gregory's, there had first been trenches, but soon great pits were dug, and the carts would simply back up and dump out their grim contents, over and over, day after day, month after month. Saint Gregory's became a veritable Hell on Earth. It was not a fountain or a water source, but only a churchyard and mass graves, the whole of which would come to be called *il Pozzo di San Gregorio*: Saint Gregory's Well.[7]

The playwright chose the most ominous of all places in Milan for Proteus to frighten Thurio into going home to Verona. It was there, to Saint Gregory's Well, outside the protective wall of the city, around and behind the huge and desolate Lazzaretto, away from the traveled road, and at the beginning of a wilderness infested with desperados, that Thurio was sent. "Proteus," in the person of the playwright, had made a thoughtful survey of Milan's environs before sending off Thurio — who might even get kidnaped by bandits as he fled.

And now I knew what the priest meant when he said "Where the bones are." The nineteenth-century Church of Saint Gregory now stands on top of that tragic and horrible "Saint Gregory's Well."

❧

The playwright's juxtaposing of actual historical events of different times, e.g., the departure of Emperor Charles V on 14 March 1533, with the end of the plague in 1577, or thereabouts, has not bothered his audiences. Elizabethans' sense of time was not as nervous as our own.

NOTES

1. Oliver Logan wrote in his *Culture and Society in Venice 1470–1790*: "Those numerous provincial nobles who followed a career of arms usually did so in the armies of other European powers, particularly Imperial ones, and provincial aristocracies often looked sympathetically towards the Habsburgs, in whose adjacent dominions they were, they believed, better treated."

2. *The Winter's Tale,* Act V Scene 2.

3. *Guide de Agostini — Milan*, Instituto Geographico de Agostini, 1990.

4. Not the one of 1576–77, but the later one of 1630.

5. Both Juliet and Silvia use going to a monastery as an excuse to get away from home to meet a lover, evidently an effective ruse for young women in Italy though one unavailable in a Protestant England.

6. *Dictionary of National Biography.* Anthony Munday also commented on O'Hely in *The English Romayne Life*, 1582.

7. There were two different names used by the Milanese for those huge burial pits in the San Gregorio churchyard. In addition to *Pozzo di San Gregorio*, they were also called *Foppone del Lazzaretto*, a name also of the old Milanese dialect, in which *foppone* means "big pit."

These frightening matters are detailed in the histories of Milan, including the following:

- Fra Paolo Bellantani da Salo, *Dialogo della Peste*, cura di Federico Oderici, Milan, 1957: the recollections of the friar who was responsible for the organization and direction of the Lazzaretto during the plague of 1630, being virtually identical to the plague of 1575–76, as all historians, including Manzoni, agree;
- V. Cavengo, *Il Lazzaretto: Storia di un quartiere di Milano*. Milan, NED, 1986;
- P. Biscide, *Relatione verissima del progresso della pesti di Milano*, Bolognia, 1630, for the illustrations; and
- S. Lattuada, *Discrizione di Milano*, Volume I, *Milan*, 1737, from which drawings of the pits were adapted.

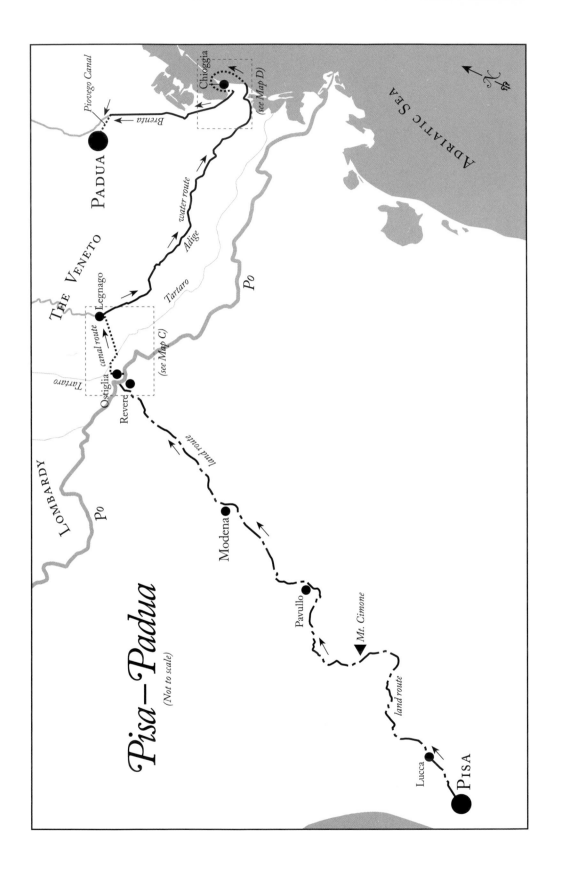

Pisa–Padua
(Not to scale)

LOMBARDY

THE VENETO

PADUA

Piovego Canal

Brenta

Chioggia

(see Map D)

water route

Adige

Tartaro

Legnago

canal route

(see Map C)

Ostiglia

Tartaro

Revere

Po

Po

Po

ADRIATIC SEA

land route

Modena

Pavullo

Mt. Cimone

land route

Lucca

PISA

4

The Taming of the Shrew
"Pisa to Padua"

Nearly all the scenes of *The Taming of the Shrew*, the famous play about the courtship of Baptista Minola's daughters, Katherina, called "Kate," and the younger Bianca, take place inside the sixteenth-century walls of Padua, the celebrated university city in northeastern Italy. Its events are preceded by a little two-scene preface: a playlet not set in Padua, but in England, which is about a practical joke on a drunkard named Christopher Sly. This playlet had no title until 1725, when the poet Alexander Pope, doing some editorial work on it, entitled it *Induction*, a name that has stuck. Because the subject of this investigation is Italy, not England, the *Induction* will not be addressed.

~

The Taming of the Shrew opens in Padua, with two young men on stage. The first to speak is Lucentio; and the other, doing the listening, is Tranio, his companion. Lucentio inundates us with information, saying who he is, where he came from, where he first began his journey, why he came, where he got his earlier education, who his father is, etc.; but through this chatter, we learn more of the playwright's specific knowledge about Italy. This is when Lucentio makes a peculiar reference to the wide territory in northern Italy called Lombardy.

I used to think Lucentio was making an off-hand remark, a few words slipped into his speech to provide some Italian "color"; but I have steadily learned that no remark in the Shakespeare canon is ever offhanded. There is always a reason, yet a reason that can very easily escape us. Here is "Lombardy" as it appears in the first four lines of Lucentio's speech:

> Tranio, since for the great desire I had
> To see fair Padua, nursery of arts,
> I am arriv'd for fruitful Lombardy,
> The pleasant garden of great Italy.

A slipup in the prepositions was made by someone where Lucentio says: "I am arriv'd *for* fruitful Lombardy." "For" makes no sense, even though it has consistently appeared since its first known printing in the First Folio. *The Yale Shakespeare* edition instructs in a footnote that "for" should be read as "in," making the line read "I am arriv'd *in* fruitful Lombardy"; *The New Folger Library* substantially agrees. This editorial alteration produces a geographical mistake. Padua is not *in* Lombardy; it's in the territory to its east called the "Veneto."

On a different tack, *The Riverside Shakespeare* translates Lucentio's "am arriv'd for" to mean "am on my way to." The trouble with this idea is that Lucentio is clearly *not* on his way to Lombardy, but to the Veneto, where Padua is located. Padua is not some awkward stop-over. It is Lucentio's declared, and now achieved, destination; one only need read his full speech to know this. Lucentio has come to Padua to stay, and to acquire some higher learning at its university — that is, until he gets a good look at Bianca, Kate's sister, which gives him a distinctly different reason to remain in that city.

Could this odd use of a tiny preposition be important? It could indeed, and I had to make some rational sense of it. Running through the entire list of prepositions, the only one that made any sense was "from." Could the playwright have actually written that Lucentio had come *from* Lombardy?

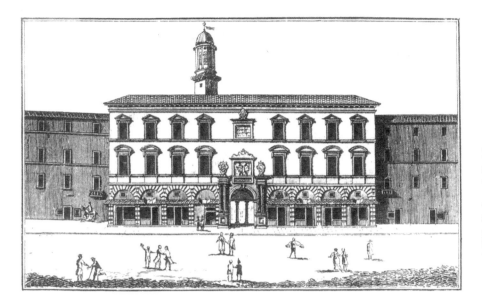

The University of Padua, called "il Bò," where Lucentio came to study. (From Guida per la Città di Padova, *Venezia, 1817)*

Numerous wording errors have been identified in the early printings of all the plays in the First Folio. They are so common as to demonstrate that the author was not involved in the proofreading of either the Quarto edition or the First Folio edition. As to *The Taming of the Shrew*, scholars have so minutely studied its word usages that by the end of the twentieth century, more than 350 insertions, substitutions, or emendations to it have been proposed, debated, and largely accepted in the various modern editions of this play. These include changing "yours" to "ours"; "seek" to "feet"; "bony" to "bonny"; "sconce" to "askance"; "me" to "in"; another "me" to "none"; and so on. While each of the thirty-six plays in the First Folio has undergone such editorial emendations, *The Taming* holds the numerical record.

～

Soon Lucentio will also say: "I have Pisa left / And am to Padua come." If my conclusion about his coming *from* Lombardy is correct, did he come from Lombardy or from Pisa? Or from *both*? Could he have come to Padua from both places on the very same trip? Since Pisa is much farther away, why mention Lombardy, even if he did come by way of it *en route*? He would have come by way of other places, too. There had to be a reason, maybe something the writer thought important and knew was accurate.

The ancient Roman roads, still gladly used in the sixteenth century, and even now—with modern paving—could easily have taken Lucentio through Lombardy on the way to Padua. Archeological maps that detail those roads are readily available in Italy. When I traveled the ancient routes that Lucentio might have followed from Pisa to Padua, I applied a reliable precept that has been used for a long time: when a modern Italian road substantially conforms to the route of a Roman road, it demonstrates that the Roman road has continued to be the best of all practical possibilities, massive modern earth-moving machines notwithstanding. Where those Roman roads coincide with routes of Italy's modern roads, a tourist traveling by car today can experience the temporary thrill of journeying through the ancient Empire on a Roman road, its timeworn stones merely having been topped by cushioning tarmac.

I had gone to Pisa, where Lucentio's trip began, from there to drive back and forth, on different possible routes across the Apennine Mountains, to Padua. I wanted to learn what the Renaissance options were in crossing the intriguing high barrier which separates Tuscany (where Florence and Pisa are) from the northern territories of Lombardy, and of the Venetian Veneto (where Padua is).

I found three practical routes that were available for Lucentio, each of which arrives at someplace on the mighty Po River, which forms the southern edge of Lombardy. Then, *from Lombardy*, a traveler could proceed onward to Padua by fresh water.

The shortest route departs from Pisa, on the former Roman road (now paved and called Highway S12). The road continues to Lucca, then crosses the Apennines to go down onto the southern plain of the Po. From there, in a nearly straight line, one reaches the banks of the river at the important town of Revere. Revere is directly across the Po from Ostiglia, the very same town to which Valentine and Proteus of *The Two Gentlemen of Verona* come, but in the *opposite direction*, on their water journey from Verona to Milan (see Chapter 2). The two gentlemen (separately) had sailed down the Adige from Verona to Legnago, entered the (now disappeared) canals that connected Legnago to Ostiglia, and thus reached the Po River at Ostiglia, on which they sailed right into Milan—all on their comfortable boats.

In this play, Lucentio and his companions will take this same route *backward*—using those same (now disappeared) canals—and comfortably sail from Ostiglia to Padua. When Lucentio, traveling by land on the Roman road from Pisa, reached Ostiglia, a switch to water travel would have been for reasons other than simply comfort and practicality. By Lucentio's day, the Roman roads, and any other hoped-for roads that might have been used to travel to Padua, had begun to disappear in the mud of overflowing rivers.

What is of major importance about Lucentio's itinerary is to know what Lucentio knows, does, and says; and what the playwright knows, has him do, and has him say. Both Revere and Ostiglia are in the Duchy of Mantua, an important part of *Lombardy*, while Legnago was a *Venetian* stronghold. Lucentio would be speaking the truth, saying to Tranio: "I am arrived *from* fruitful Lombardy" (my recommended change). He had journeyed from Ostiglia to Padua *in a boat*—a significant change from the first part of their travels, which involved a trek *on land* from Pisa to Revere. This was an important-enough difference in Italy for Lucentio to have named Lombardy as the pivotal point in his journey.

After Lucentio completes his opening lines, and Tranio responds, Lucentio turns in an off-stage direction, raises his voice, and says to someone we haven't yet seen:

> If, Biondello, thou wert come ashore,
> We could at once put us in readiness,
> And take a lodging fit to entertain
> Such friends as time in Padua shall beget.

This business of coming "ashore" in Padua has led to such nonsense as the observation in *The Riverside Shakespeare* that "like a number of other inland cities, Padua is endowed by Shakespeare with a harbor." The rivers and canals in Lucentio's trip from Revere, and across to Ostiglia, and on to Padua are still there, save for that now-vanished canal link between Ostiglia on the Po, and Legnago on the Adige. Lucentio is, yet again, using words that are true.

The Po River, which Valentine and Proteus had used going up-river on their westward journey to Milan from Ostiglia, actually flows eastward, down-river, to join the Adriatic Sea. It does this more slowly, and by a longer, more wavering course, than does the swifter Adige, flowing parallel to it on its north. Equally important for an unbroken water journey, the mouth of the Adige is much closer to the Brenta River (not to be confused with the Brenta Canal) than is that of the Po.

Before ever leaving Pisa, Lucentio would have known about both the land and the water routes to Padua. As he says himself, his father is a "merchant of great traffic through the world," who, being one, could have instructed his son on the most practical route to take from Pisa to Padua. Moreover, as an exuberant young man of privilege might do, wanting to have "a lodging fit to entertain" new friends in Padua as well as to live in his accustomed style, he would have brought along a number of better-class chattels, such as baggage and boots, bedding and books, clothing and candlesticks. After the wearying trek across the Apennine Mountains, foot-sore or saddle-sore, Lucentio would be happy to liberate himself from his freight, by turning it into cargo; indeed, it would have been irresistible. And, too, Lucentio and his traveling companions could have shading canvas overhead, food and wine, cushions and ease, and no more infested inns. So now we know: Lucentio hired or bought a boat, either at Revere or at Ostiglia, and using the earlier described canal and Tartaro connections, sailed or swept the rest of the way to Padua.

Once Lucentio had left the Adige's mouth and proceeded north along the Adriatic coastline, he would have turned directly into the Brenta River and then continued toward Padua. If the river's mouth was clotted with silt, as sometimes happened, Lucentio could use the Brenta River by first sailing into the Lagoon at the nearby city of Chioggia, then taking the canal called the Lombardo, which had been dug across to the Brenta River a long time before. The Lombardo canal cuts through a short piece of marshy land between the Lagoon and the Brenta River, at a place upstream from its troublesome mouth. Lucentio could then continue sailing up the Brenta River, about twenty miles (thirty kilometers), to enter the attached Piovego Canal, which runs straight as an arrow from the Brenta to the moat which embraces the sixteenth-century walls of Padua.

From there, the standing rule for vessels arriving on the moat was to steer to the right, and then continue around to the left, to reach the large landing place in front of a great city gate named "Porta

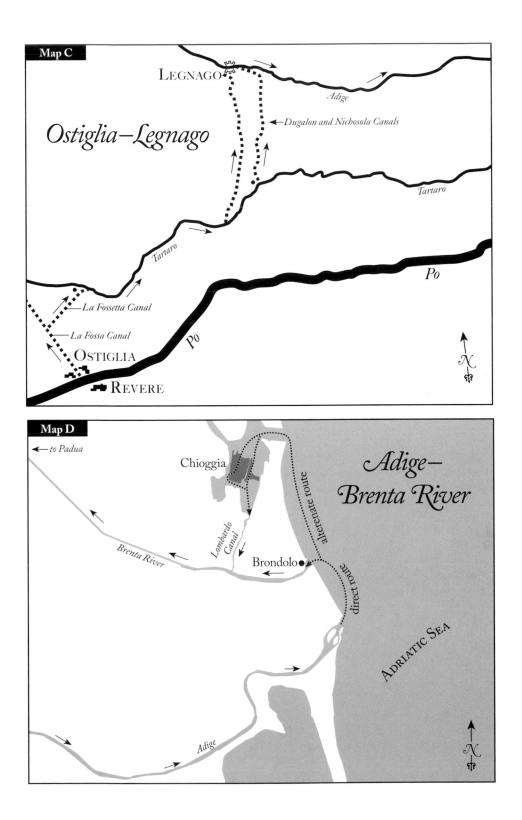

Map C

LEGNAGO

Adige

←*Dugalon and Nichosola Canals*

Ostiglia–Legnago

Tartaro

Tartaro

Po

—*La Fossetta Canal*

—*La Fossa Canal*

OSTIGLIA

Po

REVERE

N

Map D

←*to Padua*

Chioggia

Adige–Brenta River

Lombardo Canal

Brenta River

alternate route

Brondolo

direct route

ADRIATIC SEA

Adige

N

Portello." There, boats would unload, pay duty, and travelers could walk on into town.

Lucentio's boat didn't do that. At the moat, it turned to the left. Although it's no longer there, in Lucentio's day there was a small canal not far beyond this left turn. The little canal passed right through the city wall, next to a gate called "Porta Saracina," which in those days was by the still-existing edifice called "La Specola." This small canal served to connect that big sixteenth-century moat straightaway with the city's earlier medieval moat. By the time of Lucentio's trip to Padua, the medieval moat had become a circulating waterway, a canal, inside the larger city, just as the medieval Naviglio Interno in Milan had become such a canal inside a larger, sixteenth-century city. The natives of Padua called their canals (and still call interior ones) "rivers" — *fiume* — because in Roman times, they were actually branches of rivers; in Padua's case, the small and meandering Bacchiglione River. A street alongside a fiume is usually still commonly called a "riviera."

At which quay alongside a Paduan *fiume* did Lucentio's boat tie up? The playwright will tell us exactly which one, but we must carefully read again Lucentio's earlier-quoted lines, as he calls off-stage to someone named Biondello:

> If, Biondello, thou wert come ashore,
> We could *at once* put us in readiness
> And *take a lodging fit to entertain*
> Such friends as time in Padua shall beget.   (Emphasis mine)

This first scene in the play thus needs to be by a wharf, or dock, or quay, or a "road," where Lucentio's boat can be tied within easy earshot of Biondello and unloaded without fuss, and where the fellows can quickly "take a lodging." When Lucentio says "at once," he is telling us the lodging is but a few steps from where they are standing. It is close enough that he and Tranio have been able to inspect it, which includes meeting the landlord, striking a bargain for occupation, and going back outside to call over to Biondello to disembark.

No sooner has Lucentio given Biondello his instructions than five people arrive, all chattering away. At first, Tranio thinks they have come to extend greetings, saying to Lucentio, "Master, some show to welcome us to the town," but the group pays no attention to the young men; they have business to attend to.

These five are Baptista Minola, his two daughters, Katherina ("Kate") and Bianca; and two men, one a fellow named Hortensio, and the other an old "pantaloon," named Gremio. Both men, as it turns out, are suitors for Bianca's hand. No one has time for the young strangers; they have important matters to settle: their marriage prospects. But what is this? People discussing personal subjects out in public? The simple answer is that they are sixteenth-century Italians, and they don't think of themselves as being out in public, but rather as being in Baptista's "outdoor living room," the area of the street or square that is at his front door. Such a concept—and activity—is still seen in Italian towns and villages today, where neighbors often put out their chairs, and even tables, as soon as the sunshine turns to shade.

The playwright dispels any doubt about the closeness of Baptista's door. When the conversation turns to specifics about any marriage to Bianca, Baptista decides she shouldn't listen; he says, "Bianca, get you in." Not "go home," or "go away." They are in front of the Minola residence, with Bianca being told to step inside. When she doesn't obey, their location gets emphasized. Arriving at the point in the marriage negotiations where Baptista is about to discuss Bianca's

*Left: **The Piovego Canal,** which runs straight as an arrow from the Brenta River to Padua.*

*Right: **The Piovego Canal** as it reaches the 16th-century wall at Padua. (Author's photos)*

need for more education, he stops, mid-sentence, to repeat his order, saying, "Go in, Bianca." Not only is the front door right there, so are Lucentio and Tranio.

Now we have a list of stage requirements for this opening scene: a canal; a wharf or quay; a respectable hostelry; some kind of open space, maybe a street, maybe a plaza; and at least one, if not several, personal residences standing about. Houses within Italian towns, like other such houses in sixteenth-century Europe, were, and still are, rarely solitary; they stand cheek-by-jowl.

Could I take this listing I've made to be literally true? To really exist on the ground in Padua? As unique as this combination of features may seem, one could expect an alert host to open an inn, or hostelry, next to a place where travelers might tie up their boats. Yet I felt sure the playwright had written about one exact place. I hoped that there would yet be disclosed, in an early reading of his play, some singular, one-of-a-kind reference. Though I needed to be patient and pay close attention, the author did not disappoint me.

The landing place or "road" in Padua (bottom right of photo) where Lucentio's boat docked. (Author's photo taken from the bridge over the canal)

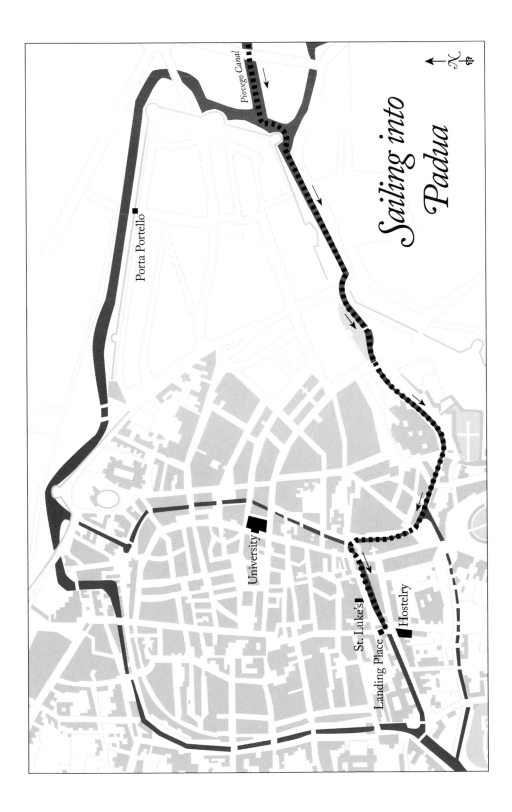

Sailing into
Padua

Piovego Canal

Porta Portello

University

St. Luke's

Landing Place

Hostelry

A respectable hostelry. Lucentio's lodging place, with an open space or plaza in front, located a few steps from the landing place. (Author's photos)

The story continues. Kate's brash suitor, Petruchio, arrives from the adjacent Venetian province of Verona to win her hand, and soon, to universal relief, since custom required that the elder daughter be the first to marry,[1] Petruchio makes the accepted dowry agreement with her father. It was common in those days in Italy for a marriage to take place as soon as — frequently on the same day — that agreement was reached. In Act III Scene 2, we are given a description of Kate's prompt wedding by Gremio, one of the witnesses. Consistent with sensible Italian custom, we can assume the marriage took place in Kate's own parish church. It can't be a very large, or important, church because, when Gremio describes the ceremony, he refers to the priest as the "vicar." Vicar is an ecclesiastical title that appears only four times in the Shakespeare canon, while "priest" or "priests" appear seventy-four times.

A vicar is a special kind of priest, and I would discover in Padua that the playwright knew precisely whereof he wrote. When a congregation is so small that a priest from someplace else is deputized to come to it to provide ceremonies, instruction, confession, etc., he is called a "vicar," having come to perform his duties vicariously, so to speak. Gremio, however, doesn't tell us the name of this little church, and the author isn't in any hurry to tell us, either, though he does accurately name the Italian churches in his plays. We have already encountered Saint Gregory's in Milan and Saint Peter's in Verona.

It is only at the end of Act IV Scene 4 where we finally learn the name of the parish church in Padua. In that scene, Biondello reports to Lucentio that the way has been cleared for him to marry Bianca, the prerequisite of Kate marrying first having been fulfilled. Biondello then says to Lucentio: "The old priest at Saint Luke's Church is at your command at all hours." And there it is: Saint Luke's Church.

Though not mentioned in connection with Kate's marriage, there were specific requirements for any marriage ceremony, which Biondello tries to describe to Lucentio after naming Saint Luke's when he says:

> … Take you assurance of her *cum pivilegio ad imprimendum solum* [irrelevant nonsense which is actually about publishing books]: to th' church take the priest, clerk, and some sufficient honest witnesses …

This was a specific mandate in the sixteenth century — aside from the "holy" Latin, which illiterate Biondello had overheard someplace — which goes nearly unnoticed today, since a requirement long since taken for granted now was not always followed in the sixteenth century in lands other than Italy. Nothing in the Italian Plays is really said offhandedly, but rather to some then-timely purpose. This remark of Biondello's is pointed directly at the authorities in England, and the disgraceful fraudulent marriages that were common there, to dupe innocent women. Such marriages were easily denied since they were deliberately performed with no witnesses, or church records, to prove they had taken place. Secret marriages, informal marriages, and marriages without suitable witnesses had reached epidemic proportions, especially in England. Courts could make brides destitute, and children into bastards, without reliable witnesses and proper church records as proof that a union had taken place.

While it is often said that the Roman Catholic Council of Trent took far too long to rectify ecclesiastical abuses and clarify other matters, on 11 November 1563 it declared to the Catholic faithful that all marriages not thereafter celebrated in the presence of a priest, and two or three witnesses, would be null and void. From that day forward, by canon law, Petruchio, Lucentio, and the old vicar at Saint Luke's would have had to comply. Such, however, was not to be the case in quasi-Protestant England. Neither the English Parliament, nor the Anglican Church, took a comparable stand, until the middle of the eighteenth century. Henry VIII had earlier attempted to correct this scandal by a statute, but it was repealed during the reign of his young son, Edward VI.

At the end of this Scene 4 of Act IV, the church is named again, when Biondello comically announces:

> … My master hath appointed me to go to Saint Luke's, to bid the priest be ready to come against you come with your appendix.

Now we have it: the playwright's method of repeating the name, insisting on it, his personal technique of urging the reader or audience to "Pay attention." The author is telling us that Baptista Minola and his daughters live in the parish of Saint Luke.

*D*ue, no doubt, to the conviction that the places and things in the Italian Plays are fictitious, no one has ever tried to find a *Chiesa di San Luca* (Saint Luke's Church) in Padua. But in five minutes time, at the diocesan office, its address was in my hand: 22 Via Venti Settembre, formerly called Via San Luca, between Vicolo Conti and Via Rialto. Later, from help at the city's Archives, and then in a book I bought at a nearby store, I learned Saint Luke's origins are medieval, built where it stands, well before 1350.

The writings of a certain Secondo Giovanni di Nono report that in the first half of the fourteenth century, the medieval walls of Padua (all now well inside the sixteenth-century walls) had nineteen gates, all of which he named. Most of the gates were named for the adjacent, or closest, church or churches, and there on his list is *Porta San Luca o Santa Maria in Vanzo*. San Luca is, in fact, just across a side street from Santa Maria in Vanzo, although it no longer has a medieval appearance. On the testimony of Secondo Giovanni, these two churches had been there for more than two centuries when *The Taming of the Shrew* was composed.

A parish church called Saint Luke's near the port and hostelry. (Author's photo)

*I*n 1815 (during the Austrian suzerainty over northern Italy), as stated in Latin on a plaque over the central door, San Luca underwent extensive renovations. The façade of the tiny church was "freshened up," resulting in its exterior neoclassical appearance of today. The little church has continued to receive loving attention over the years, the changing color of its outside walls attests to that: the yellow I witnessed two decades ago is now a cheerful pink. The interior of Saint Luke's, though welcoming, contains no distinguished art. It does have a nice altar, though, done by a local artist, Pietro Dameni, depicting Saint Luke writing his Gospel, and Saint Mary with four of the city's nineteenth-century patrons.

∾

The little Saint Luke's Church lies just inside Padua's medieval wall, close to an arched opening now called *Porta S.G. Barbarigo* (Portal of San Giovanni Barbarigo). Making my way through that arch, I found myself staring at the setting of Act I Scene 1 of *The Taming of the Shrew*. I was sure of this as I looked around me. To this

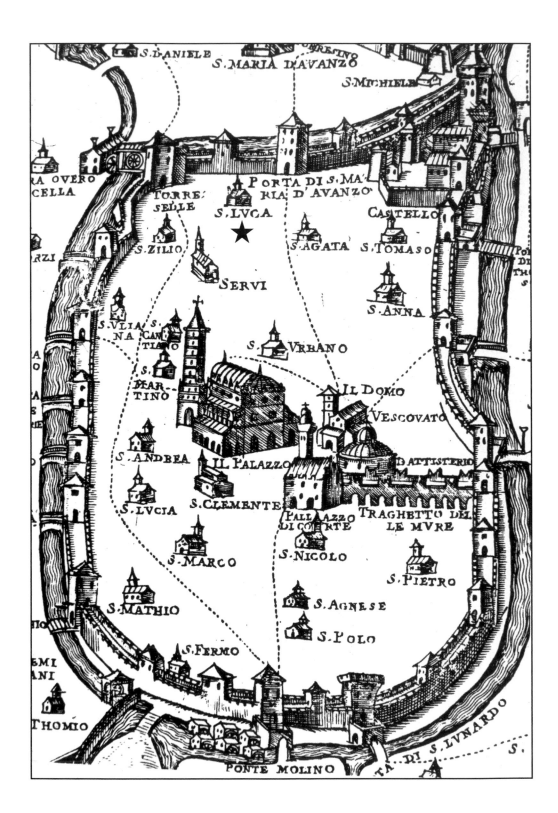

very day, the entire layout before my eyes possesses all the elements that exactly fit the describing dialogues in that opening scene:

- a waterway (now narrowed by centuries of cast rubble);
- a landing place, quay, or road where a boat could tie up (now reduced to a narrow ledge);
- a bridge across that waterway, connecting both to
- a street with a Saint Luke's church nearby; and
- a wide space with a cluster of buildings (part street, part plaza).

One, among that cluster of buildings, the one on a corner of that wide space facing toward the bridge — the only one that's a bit taller than the others — has a ground-floor arcade. This one building was about to be singled out.

~

Standing on the bridge, thinking about Lucentio and Biondello and Baptista and his daughters, I opened my portfolio of notes, maps and sketches and selected the photocopy I had obtained from the Museo Civico di Padova. The photocopy was part of an eignteenth-century drawing by a "surveyor," named Lorenzo Mazzi. Dated 17 December 1718, it was not a very good drawing — Mazzi was hardly a professional. His drawing is awkward, distorted, and without any consistent scale, but nevertheless, most helpful to my theory about this spot in Padua. One can only barely make out the name of Saint Luke's, and many of the buildings Mazzi sketched are no longer there. The waterway is boldly captioned *Fiume*, instead of *Canale* or *Naviglio*; and by the bridge, there is indeed a spot clearly labeled *Porto*, meaning "port" or "landing" — perfect for Lucentio to tie up his boat.

Mazzi's drawing also had something in tiny letters which I could barely decipher, but which, when I finally made them out, so startled me that I laughed out loud. Lettering at the foot of his depiction of that building, the one just over the bridge with the ground floor arcade, when examined closely, reads "Osteria," the Italian word for "hostelry" or "inn," or *lodging place*. This was a labeled sketch of Lucentio's home-away-from-home. The building is in excellent condition; it seems ageless. No wonder Lucentio, while standing in front of the Osteria above, chatting with Tranio, was able — in the same breath — to call to Biondello, patiently waiting for instructions, by their boat tied up at the porto below.

Opposite page:
Map of Padua *in the very early 13th century showing the little parish church of Saint Luke (S. Luca, indicated above the star) before its "face lift." (Reproduction of a medieval map from A. Barzon, Il Beato Crescenzio da Camposampiero, Padova, 1941)*

Opposite page:
Padua by Lorenzo Mazzi. *This drawing, dated 1718, depicts all elements in Act I Scene 1 of* The Taming of the Shrew: *the port (porto =* **1***) where Lucentio tied up his vessel; the hostelry (osteria =* **2***) where he lodged; and the parish church of Saint Luke (San Luca =* **3***) where Bianca and Katherine were married. (From A. Barzon,* Il Beato Crescenzio da Composampiero, *Padova, 1941. Also see* Storia e arte in S. Tomaso, *Padova 1966. The original map is in the Museo Civico di Padova, F. 6330)*

Still on that bridge, turning slowly, taking in the full circle sweep of the utter reality of all that the playwright described, I knew in a rush that I was standing exactly where the author of *The Taming of the Shrew* had stood four centuries before me, absorbing all he saw around him.

~

Late in Act II Scene 1, when vying for Bianca's hand, Gremio describes to Baptista some of the details of his wealth:

> First, as you know, my house within the city
> Is richly furnished with plate and gold,
> Basins and ewers to lave her dainty hands;
> My hangings all of Tyrian tapestry.
> In ivory coffers I have stuff'd my crowns,
> In cypress chests my arras counterpoints,
> Costly apparel, tents, and canopies,
> Fine linen, Turkey cushions boss'd with pearl,
> Valance of Venice gold in needlework,
> Pewter and brass, and all things that belongs
> To house or housekeeping …

Travelers in Italy familiar with *The Taming*, who have visited the interior of a Venetian villa in the Veneto which has retained its venerable furnishings, have remarked how strikingly like Gremio's description those Italian interiors are — and how unlike his description is to a wealthy Tudor house.

~

Some lines later in this Scene 1 of Act II, in Gremio's bidding for Bianca, he adds another alleged detail of his wealth. He says if Bianca becomes his wife, "she shall have, besides, an Argosy that now is lying in Marcellus' road." (Gremio's "Marcellus" is Marseilles, in the Kingdom of France.) There is something wrong with this: an "Argosy" was originally a merchant ship from Ragusa, the city-state across the Adriatic from Italy. This doesn't mean Gremio couldn't have owned one, but it does imply that Gremio was cunning enough to keep it in a foreign country, since it was illegal for a citizen of the Republic to own a foreign vessel (see Chapter 5). Earlier in Gremio's boasting, it

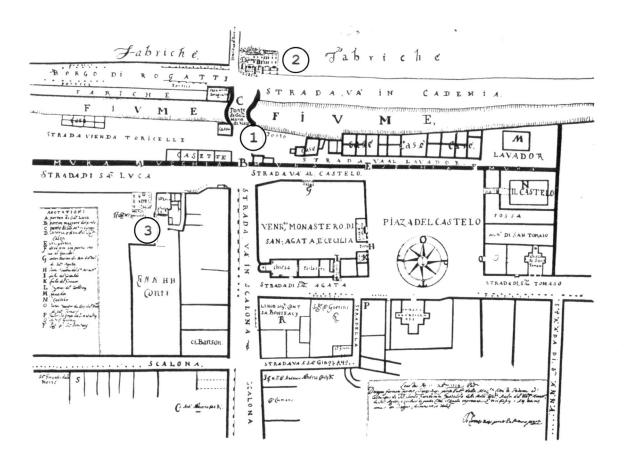

is obvious that he is a dairy farmer—at his farm, he proudly informs Baptista, he has 100 milch cows and sixty oxen. And now he has an Argosy, too, though he doesn't literally say that it is his property, only that Bianca will get it.

Gremio seems full of hot air; after all, he is a "pantaloon," a *pantalone* in Italian *Commedia dell'Arte*. The plots and characters of this form of Italian theatre so permeate the English playwright's Italian Plays that some in England would already know that a pantaloon was always a silly old man—and a sometime liar. This might explain the sudden appearance of this Argosy in Gremio's investment portfolio, which could provoke English laughter.

Tranio, astute though ignorant, pretending to be Lucentio, attempts to outbid Gremio for Bianca's hand. He layers on another lie about Lucentio's alleged father, claiming "... 'tis known my father hath no less than three great Argosies besides two galliases /

And twelve tight [*sic*] galleys." This is hardly likely, since Argosies were then owned by Ragusans.

In every edition of this play ever printed, there is the adjective "tight" for the galleys. This is a typographical error. The adjective should be corrected to "light," so as accurately to name a kind of Mediterranean galley of the sixteenth century constructed with a single mast. They are "light galleys," and the author would surely have known of them from his Italian travels, and may even have sailed in one. There was no such vessel in English waters.

*T*ranio realizes that to convince Baptista of his eligibility to win Bianca, he needs to recruit someone to pose as Lucentio's father; someone newly arrived in town who would be willing to fib, in affirmation of Tranio's falsehoods. We learn in Act IV Scene 2 that Biondello is sent to a city gate to find, and enlist, such a presentable person.

We learn this when Biondello enters this scene, and exclaims to Tranio:

> O master, master, I have watch'd so long that I am dog-weary! But at last I spied an ancient angel coming down the hill will serve the turn.

... "and twelve light galleys" ... This is a study, attributed to Raphael, of a single-masted Mediterranean light galley. (From the Galleria dell'Accademia in Venice)

Scholars have opined that Biondello calls his find an "angel," because of an old English coin with the figure of Archangel Michael. This idea can only be considered irrelevant. More likely, Biondello calls the man an angel because he regards his recruit as heaven-sent; after all, how easy is it to find a respectable-looking person both willing to impersonate someone's father, *and* assist in marriage negotiations?

Tranio asks Biondello "What is he, Biondello?" And Biondello answers:

> Master, a marcantant, or a pedant,
> I know not what, but formal in apparel,
> in gait and countenance surely like a father.

Biondello isn't at all sure what the man he has managed to recruit does for a living, but his appearance is respectable, something that would apply equally to both professions. A "pedant" was a school teacher, or tutor. As for a "marcantant," the Italian word for it is *mercantante*, which, when anglicized, loses its final "e." Thus, the proper spelling, in English, would be "mercantant."

It is my guess that the first "a" in the word, found in the First Folio and repeated ever since, is a typographical error for "e." Not only was "mercantant" an unfamiliar word in England, aside from this play, it has never been used in English literature. The *Oxford English Dictionary*, influenced by the appearance of the word in the First Folio, has given it the same misspelling; and the definition given there is "merchant," which, for a sixteenth-century mercantant, is sort of right, and sort of wrong. *Black's Law Dictionary* comes a bit closer, defining a mercantant as "a foreign trader," but even this definition requires clarification; because although a mercantant is a traveling commercial agent, he is one of a particular kind.

The man enlisted by Biondello is no pedant; he is, indeed a mercantant, as we learn from the details of his profession he discloses in his conversation with Tranio toward the end of this Act:

Mercantant/
Pedant: God save you, sir!

Tranio as
Lucentio: And you, sir! You are welcome. Travel you far
             on, or are you at the farthest?

Mercantant: Sir, at the farthest for a week or two,
             But then up farther, and as far as Rome;
             And so to Tripoli, if God lend me life.

Tranio:	What countryman I pray?
Mercantant:	Of Mantua.
Tranio:	Of Mantua, sir? Marry, God forbid! And come to Padua, careless of your life?
Mercantant:	My life, sir? How, I pray? For that goes hard.
Tranio:	'Tis death for anyone in Mantua To come to Padua. Know you not the cause? Your ships are stayed at Venice, and the Duke, For private quarrel 'Twixt your duke and him, Hath published and proclaimed it openly. 'Tis marvel, but that you are but newly come, You might have heard it else proclaimed about.
Mercantant:	Alas, sir, it is worse for me than so! For I have bills for money by exchange From Florence, and must here deliver them.

These lines reveal the specific knowledge the playwright had about one of Italy's important banking practices.

It is even more specific, and remarkable, when this Mercantant says he is from Mantua, of all places. First, we are informed that this man is a professional traveler, because of his scheduled and surprisingly wide itinerary: arriving in Padua from Florence; next going "up farther," by which he probably means Venice; then turning around to go back south "as far as Rome." After that, interestingly, he says he will go to Tripoli, across the Mediterranean in North Africa, on its Barbary Coast, where gold dust routinely arrived from the mines of Sudan, making it an important financial center.

Second, at the end of their dialogue, the Mercantant makes the purpose of his traveling profession even more specific, when he says he has *bills for money by exchange*. These financial instruments had been widely employed in Europe, the Near East, and North Africa since medieval times. These "bills for money by exchange" had what seemed a nearly magical use, which was the discount buying of a written order (bill) on a bank — usually one located elsewhere — to pay a stated sum of money on, or after, a specific later date. Thus, less than the stated amount of money was actually paid out for the paper at its place of origin on some earlier date, later to be exchanged at a particular bank in another city for the full stated amount. This difference in the amounts was the bill buyer's profit.[2]

～

This business of issuing, discounting, and then redeeming bills of exchange was done in many Italian cities, including Mantua, Padua, Venice, Florence, and Rome. Elsewhere in Europe, it was done in such places as Antwerp, Lyon, Frankfurt, and London, for example. In going to London, the bill carrier went by sea, and usually arrived on the Thames, hard by The City of London, where the banks were located. He was thus never encountered out on the road by English laymen — not enough, that is, to have acquired an English name instead of the Italian one.

Of particular importance to the play's Mercantant, there were bill discounters, and responsive banks, in Tripoli, a striking fact which the playwright obviously knew. From all that the Mercantant has now said, his profession is now fully defined; he is the collection agent for a bill discounter, or an issuer of bills, who lives in Mantua.

～

For years I have been bothered by the slavish practice of editors of *The Taming of the Shrew*, in marking the lines of the man imitating Lucentio's father, "Pedant." In his *Love's Labours Lost*, the playwright thoroughly ridiculed a *pedanto*, yet has done no such thing to this masquerader in *The Taming*. The failure, or conscious refusal, to insert the correct name — "Mercantant," instead of "Pedant" — might well be due to an earlier English scrivener's mistake. It would be an error resulting from someone who was unfamiliar with a mercantant, but who knew about pedants. Can this repeated error be attributed today to the same ignorance? While some editors did not hesitate to alter (erroneously) Speed's line in Act II Scene 5 of *The Two Gentlemen of Verona* (from "Welcome to Padua!" to "Welcome to Milan!"), all editors fail to correct "Pedant" by replacing it with the accurate "Mercantant."

*I*n the above-quoted dialogue between Tranio and the Mercantant, where the Mercantant reveals he is from Mantua, the playwright has sent another of his cryptic signals: Mantua is named *three times* in quick succession. Not only in this, but in the fib about a quarrel between the Duke of Venice (the state that included Padua) and the Duke of Mantua, the playwright has specifically referred to the Mantuan duke, who would have been a Gonzaga. The Gonzaga had been the ruling family of Mantua for centuries.

In Fernand Braudel's masterwork, *The Mediterranean and the Mediterranean Sea in the Age of Philip II*, Volume I, page 468, he wrote:

> The agents of the Gonzaga, who bought thoroughbred horses, were as at home in Tunis and Oran as in Genoa or Venice, coming and going with bills of exchange on Barbary (on the credit of Christian merchants settled there) ...

This would, perforce, include Berber-populated Tripoli, where payments could be received in gold, a metal in short supply in Italy, and far more desirable than silver, which kept losing its value due to the Spanish glut.

The playwright had learned something quite particular about the Gonzagas of Mantua, to which he has alluded in his typically oblique way. Through his character Tranio, we are told that the "Duke of Mantua" had seagoing ships, and this too has been a source of ridicule. The fact is, at Governolo, adjacent to the Po River, Mantua maintained a substantial fleet of both merchant ships, and ships of war, fully capable of plying the Po, the Adige, the Adriatic, and far beyond.

~

Far-away Pisa is named fourteen times in *The Taming of the Shrew;* not just because it's Lucentio's hometown, but because the playwright enjoys using Pisa for one of his wordplays. It seems the author especially likes this Pisa pun; he worked it into his dialogues twice in this play. Notwithstanding, his unusual punning on Pisa has escaped the notice of commentators. I, too, might not have noticed it, had I never been to Pisa, nor been aware of a parallel, and more obvious, pun in *Romeo and Juliet*. In its Scene 1 of Act III, Mercutio, run through by the outrageous Tybalt, lies dying in Romeo's arms:

Romeo: Courage, man. The hurt cannot be much.

Mercutio: No, 'tis not so deep as a well,
           nor so wide as a church door;
           but 'tis enough, 'twill serve.
           Ask for me to-morrow, and you
           will find me a grave man …

In Act I Scene 1, of *The Taming*, in telling where he was born, Lucentio says: "Pisa, renowned for grave citizens." Again, in Act IV Scene 2, when the "Pedant" (Mercantant) is asked if he has ever been in Pisa, he responds:

> Ay, sir, in Pisa I have often been;
> Pisa, renowned for grave citizens.

Like Mercutio, who is about to become "a grave man," and the "Pedant's" and Lucentio's "grave citizens" — meaning a "citizen" of the grave — the grave citizens of Pisa are not its living residents, however solemn Pisans may be thought to be. The Pisan "grave citizens" of which the playwright speaks, are its decedents, or at least the most honored or honorable of them. They are Pisans who were interred in the city's cemetery of distinction, the "Campo Santo," also known as the "Camposanto Monumentale." The Italian word for "cemetery" is *camposanto*, literally, "sacred ground" or "holy field," and the one in Pisa is unlike any other.

During the Crusades, Pisa became rich transporting pilgrims and soldiers to the Holy Land by sea. An archbishop of Pisa, Lanfranchi (1108–1178), noticed that the returning ships, emptied of the outbound faithful, employed stone, and exotic goods — often cheap ones — as ballast for the homeward voyage. Lanfranchi arranged that the holds of fifty-three galleys, on their return trips to Pisa, be filled with earth taken from Mount Calvary in Jerusalem, the place where Jesus was crucified. This earth was said to contain drops of Christ's blood. This holiest of soils was spread in a wide rectangle on a field near Pisa's cathedral (duomo) and baptistry, creating a burial place where the fortunate of the city could be interred in uniquely sacred relic soil.

About 100 years afterward, the burial ground was enclosed by an elegant marble structure of colossal proportions, whose interior walls were covered by vast frescoes painted by some of Italy's finest artists. The resulting Campo Santo, of enormous local pride and renowned throughout Italy across the centuries, remains, along with the nearby "leaning tower," as one of Pisa's most popular tourist destinations. The Campo Santo contains hundreds of tombs and important funeral monuments, and although burials ceased there when space ran out, the Campo Santo continued to receive the notable deceased even well beyond the sixteenth century, when this play was written.

~

Before making our way to the enchanting city of Venice in Chapter 5, attention should be drawn to the reference in Act V Scene 1, to a "sail-maker" in Bergamo.

The reference is made when Vincentio, Lucentio's real father, arrives in Padua to check on his son. Tranio appears and behaves insultingly. Vincentio recognizes him immediately and is shocked. To put an end to Tranio's masquerade and his lies about his rich father, Vincentio says: "Thy father? O villain! He is a sail-maker in Bergamo." Vincentio is stating what could be a fact, notwithstanding that Bergamo is a sub-alpine city as far as possible from the two seas which border Italy. Vincentio's statement is claimed as proof of the author's ignorance of Italy's geography.

~

In Alessandro Manzoni's novel, *The Betrothed*, or *I Promessi Sposi*, its humble protagonist is a weaver who finally, in 1630, found safety and employment in Bergamo. Bergamo is a city, from medieval times until now, devoted to the manufacture of textiles, which, depending on the era, has included velvet, silk, wool, broadcloth, and jersey; and always sailcloth, that ever-needed fabric made from hemp.

When this play was written, it is true that the very finest hemp in the Venetian Republic came from Piedmont, adjacent to Lombardy.

However, the next best hemp was produced in Lombardy itself, where Bergamo is located. The cloth woven from this hemp has the Italian name *canovaccio*. It is a word derived from the Greek, "kannibis," meaning hemp, and when englished, becomes "canvas."

All cloth, including sailcloth, was then woven on handlooms, hence, it was not very wide. For sails, the canvas had to be seamed together, trimmed to size, hemmed, and then the loop-holes made. Sailmakers worked where the canvas was produced, and readily available — not down at some crowded, bustling harbor. Sailmakers could work alone. They simply followed the instructions given in written notations for the shapes and dimensions required. In English, these instructions were called the "casting"; in Italian, *la valutazione*. Once made, the bulky sails could be rolled up and delivered anywhere in the Mediterranean World, by means of canals, rivers, and then seas, as they routinely were. All a sailmaker needed were the castings, a seven-foot bench, a pack of needles, a ready supply of good canvas, and initiative.

The playwright knew that Bergamo was the principal source of sails for the Mediterranean world, and knew that Tranio's father could, indeed, have been a sailmaker there.

NOTES

1. The rule that daughters were only to be married in the order of their birth is an ancient requirement is that many modern minds think to be unreasonable. It has existed at least since Biblical times wherein Laban, in *Genesis*, Chapter 29, required this. There, when Jacob sought to marry his daughter Rachel instead of the elder Leah, Laban said to Jacob, "It is not so done in our country to give the younger before the first-born."

2. A bill of exchange, unlike a promissory note, did not involve making a loan or levying a charge of interest. Lending at interest was both a punishable felony, and a punishable sin, and this was neither, although the end financial result was exactly the same: pure magic.

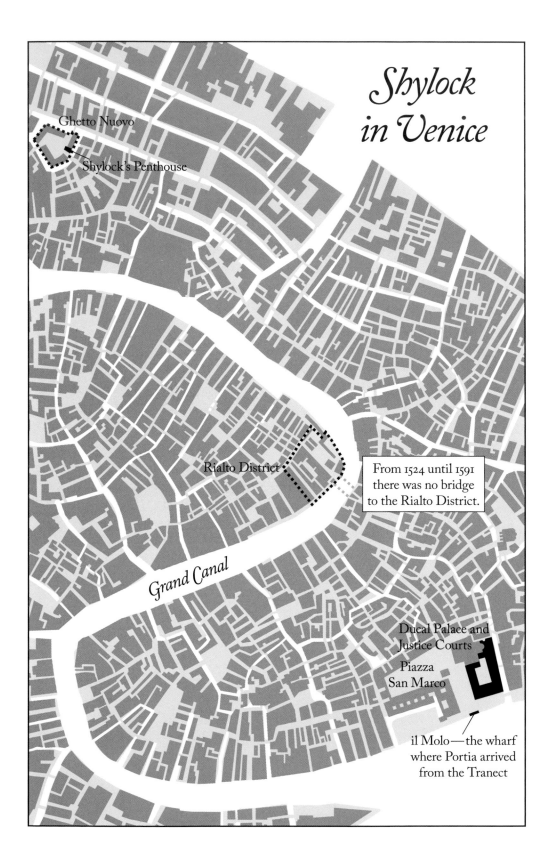

Shylock in Venice

Ghetto Nuovo

Shylock's Penthouse

Rialto District

From 1524 until 1591 there was no bridge to the Rialto District.

Grand Canal

Ducal Palace and Justice Courts

Piazza San Marco

il Molo—the wharf where Portia arrived from the Tranect

5

CHAPTER

The Merchant of Venice – Part 1
"Venice: the City and the Empire"

For centuries, the sweep of overseas possessions held by the Venetian Republic constituted an empire. And for a significant part of that time, that empire also included all the important cities and ports along the eastern coast of the Adriatic Sea. Moreover, this "Most Serene Republic of Venice," *La Serenissima*, had trading concessions in other Mediterranean ports further to the east. Importantly for both *Othello* and *The Merchant of Venice*, between 13 November 1473 and its final surrender to the Turks on 5 August 1571, the Venetians also counted the large and important island of Cyprus as one of their colonies.

In the latter part of the sixteenth century, the gifted English playwright arrived in the beating heart of this Venetian empire: the legendary city of Venice. He moved about noting its structured society, its centuries-old government of laws, its traditions, its culture, and its disciplines. He carefully considered and investigated its engines of banking and commerce. He explored its harbors and canals, and its streets and squares. He saw the flash of its pageants, its parties and celebrations; and he looked deeply into the Venetian soul. Then, with a skill that has never been equalled, he wrote a story that has a happy ending for all its characters save one, about whom a grief endures and always will: a deathless tragedy.

When *The Merchant of Venice* begins, there are three men on the stage: Antonio, the "Merchant" himself; Salerio, his lackey; and Solanio, his merchant friend. Antonio says:

> For sooth I know not why I am so sad.
> It wearies me, you say it wearies you;
> But how I caught it, found it, came by it,
> What stuff 'tis made of, whereof it is born,
> I am to learn;
> And such a want-wit sadness makes of me
> That I have much ado to know myself.

Salerio replies:

> Your mind is tossing on the ocean,
> There where *your Argosies with portly sail*
> Like signors and rich burghers on the flood,
> Or as it were pageants of the sea,
> Do overpeer the petty traffickers,
> That curtsy to them, do them reverence,
> As they fly by them with their woven wings.   (Emphasis mine)

MERCANTI.

Argosies were a specific class of vessels that were manufactured, owned, and operated by the merchants of the Illyrian city once known as Ragusa, modernly known as "Dubrovnik." These ships were easily identified by their banner of St. Blaise (Serbian, St. Vlah), the Patron Saint of Ragusa.[1]

An Elizabethan would know what an Argosy was, and from the lines of the play, would understand that this Venetian merchant, Antonio, had somehow deviated from an age-old Venetian rule. Antonio's merchandise was aboard a foreign ship, and though he denies it, he's not so much worried about the fate of that hired Ragusan ship as he is about what's inside its fat Ragusan hold. As Salerio says a little later, "I know Antonio is sad to think upon his merchandise."

In commiserating with Antonio, Salerio reveals more:

My wind cooling my broth
Would blow me to an ague when I thought
What harm a wind too great might do at sea.
I should not see the sandy hour-glass run
But I should think of shallows and of flats
And see *my wealthy Andrew* docked in sand,

...

... Should I go to church
And see the holy edifice of stone
And not bethink me straight of dangerous rocks,
Which touching but my gentle vessel's side
Would scatter all her spices on the stream,
Enrobe the roaring waters with my silks,
And in a word, but even now worth this,
And now worth nothing? ...

...

But tell not me; I know Antonio
Is sad to think upon his merchandise.   (Emphasis mine)

Through the words Salerio is given to speak, the playwright is telling us several things. One is very important information for English mariners intending to enter the Venetian Lagoon. The playwright warns them of the perils of running aground there.

In *The World of Venice*,[2] James Morris, citing Salerio, wrote:

> The Venetians have always been terrified of going aground.
> Storms, demons, pirates, monsters — all figure in the folklore
> of Venetian seamanship: but low water more dreadfully than
> any of them. The Saint Christophers of Venice, as often as
> not, are depicted conveying the infant Christ across the shal-
> low hazards of the lagoon, and many a sacred legend secretes a
> mud-bank among its pieties ...
>
> Very early in their history, urged by these apprehensions, the
> Venetians surveyed and charted their lagoon, marking its safe
> passages with wooden poles ...

Another thing he has told us is that not only is Antonio using Argosies for his business, some of his merchandise — "spices" and
"silks" — are carried in a second type of ship, what Salerio has called
"my wealthy Andrew." As Antonio himself has admitted during this
collegial chat, "My ventures are not in one bottom trusted ..."

Opposite:
16th-century
Venetian merchant*.
This is the
type of clothing
Antonio, the
"Merchant," would
have worn.*

*"The figure of the
merchant has always
been fundamental in
the history of Venice
where profit has
always accompanied
the philosophy of
experience, and the
search for pleasure
and beauty." Source
caption: Cesare
Vecellio. The
Merchant. (Degli
habiti antichi e
moderni di diverse
parti del mondo.
Venice, 1590). (From
Venetian Villas by
M. Muraro and
P. Marton, Magnus
Edizioni SpA, Udine,
Italy, 1986, p. 25)*

What kind of vessel is this?

An Andrew was a type of ship owned by the formidable Genovan *condottiere* Andrea Doria (1468–1560); and later, by his great-nephew and heir, Giovanni Andrea Doria. Andrea Doria was one of Genoa's greatest Renaissance admirals and statesmen. He was given the title of *Liberator et Pater Patriae* by Emperor Charles V, for his inestimable service to the crown. He was also the head of a Genovan family of enormous wealth, garnered from banking, finance, and merchant shipping. It was Andrea Doria's practice, continued under Giovanni, to use "Andrea" as part of the name for many of his ships, resulting in such names for his vessels as *Andrea la Spume* (Andrew the Sea Foam), *Andrea l'Onde* (Andrew the Wave), *Andrea il Gabbiano* (Andrew the Sea Gull), and *Andrea il Delfino* (Andrew the Dolphin).[3] Thus, Andrea — Andrew in the English tongue — became the nickname for any vessel that flew the Andrea Doria flag. Antonio was not using Venetian ships at all; his merchandise was carried in the holds of Argosies and Andrews.

The playwright's specific information about a Venetian using foreign ships — and in the very opening lines of this play — is significant. Here was something new and startling. It was common knowledge, in England as well as in the rest of Europe, that the Venetian custom — the law — was, and had been for several centuries, that Venetian merchants were neither to own nor hire foreign vessels. Through the words of his characters, the playwright has inserted information he wants his audience to know: there was a new development in Venice.

This information was the author's alone, woven with his usual artistry into his own story, because the tales which had inspired his *Merchant* say nothing of such things.

~

There were two: one was *Il Pecorone*, The Blockhead, sometimes called "The Pound of Flesh Story." This old tale was written around 1378 by Ser Giovanni Fiorentino. It was not printed until 1558 and was translated into English only some forty years later, in 1596.

The other story, "The Casket Story," is a tale about winning the hand of a fair maiden by correctly selecting the right casket, or decorative box. Set at various sites on the Continent, "The Casket Story" was part of a collection of stories in Latin entitled *Gesta Romanorum*, dated 1472. The collection was not translated into English until 1595.

Although there are some ships carrying merchandise in "The Pound of Flesh Story," they are ships that evidently originated in Venice. There are no ships in "The Casket Story." Reference to Argosies and Andrews is the playwright's own idea.

Was there an explanation for this departure from a long-standing Venetian rule? And why does the playwright emphasize those different nationalities? I returned to my favorite historian, Fernand Braudel, and next, to John Julius Norwich, in his *A History of Venice*, and then to other, more specialized works. And once again, I discovered that the ingenious dramatist was never haphazard in his Italian details.

Some time around 1550 English ships had virtually disappeared from the Mediterranean. The reasons are many and complex, but they do include the increased hostilities of the Holy Roman Empire and the Papacy. The English dealt with this by getting their Italian grapes and wines, oil, and other Mediterranean desirables, from Venetian — and, yes, Ragusan and Genovan — vessels. But in 1573, Venetian ships ceased arriving in England. The young men of Venice had rebelled against the tradition of going to sea because of the radically increasing danger from piracy. To compound the problem, Venetian shipyards were having difficulty getting ship timber. It had become much cheaper to use the merchant vessels of other states, especially those of Ragusa and Genoa.

In that significant year 1573, the English began to respond to all this, and to probe the Mediterranean with vessels of their own. When they did, they discovered that the Spanish were not as formidable as they'd been led to believe: Philip II had turned his attention, and his warships, almost entirely away from the Mediterranean, focusing his energy on the New World. At the same time, to their happy surprise, ships from England discovered they were welcome, especially at Tuscan and Venetian ports. So the English increased their presence, and set out to gather more intelligence about Mediterranean opportunities. Along with this, English of a certain class began coming to

Italy to study the Italian language or history, and to enjoy its burgeoning theater arts.

There were great opportunities for English entrepreneurs in shipping. For transport of goods, English and Dutch ships were the cheapest, largely because they were the swiftest, and most reliable. Contrary to the age-old practice of all Mediterranean sailing since the beginning of time, English sailors from the North didn't weave their way along the meandering shores of the Mediterranean, keeping the coastline in sight. Instead, the English sailors sailed in straight lines, using the compass. Their crews were paid by the trip, not by the week, as Italian sailors were; and their ships were not the cumbersome and slow-moving galleons that are described by Salerio in his opening remarks:

> … as it were pageants of the sea,
>   Do overpeer the petty traffickers,
>   That curtsy to them, do them reverence,
>   As they fly by them with their woven wings.

This is charming poetry, but it is also a graphic description of the small and swift merchant ships from the North, such as the English ships, capable of sailing circles around those fat, awkward ships favored by Mediterraneans. This advantage would be demonstrated in the later English destruction of the Spanish Armada.

The growth of the English presence, and its financial success in the Mediterranean, became the most important of England's foreign enterprises, with its Queen, on 11 September 1579, formally issuing the royal patent for the Levant Company to trade in the Levantine area of the eastern Mediterranean.

~

The dramatist has provided additional proof of his knowledge of contemporary Venice. This time it is given indirectly, by listing the destinations of Antonio's Argosies. In Act I Scene 3, Shylock, the money lender, speaking of Antonio's creditworthiness says:

> … he hath an Argosy bound to Tripolis, another to the Indies,
>   I understand moreover upon the Rialto, he hath a third to

Mexico, a fourth for England, and other ventures he hath squandered abroad …

And later, in Act III Scene 2, Bassanio receives a letter from Antonio, and when reading it exclaims:

Hath all his ventures fail'd? What not one hit?
From Tripolis, from Mexico and England,
From Lisbon, Barbary and India,
And not one vessel scape the dreadful touch
Of merchant-marring rocks?

Shylock has named five specific destinations, and adds that there are others; and Bassanio names six, nearly all corresponding to those of Shylock. All of them are historically accurate.

❧

Venetian ships arriving in England with holds stuffed with exotic goods had been a common sight; but after 1573, they ceased to make the voyage there due to the Venetian concern with interference by a newly hostile Spain. The hostility arose when Venice, out of genuine need, made a trading treaty, "The Peace of Constantinople," with the Ottoman Sultan in Moslem Turkey. Philip II characterized this treaty as anti-Christian, and banned all Venetian vessels from the ports of his vast Spanish Empire. Since Mexico was part of that empire, it became entirely off-limits to ships from Venice.

This is the country, Mexico, which is singled out when critiques about the playwright's knowledge of Venice are made. Critics assert that since Venetian ships were not permitted to trade in Mexico, it was a serious mistake for the playwright to have used it as the destination for one of Antonio's ships. However, as we have seen before, and will again, the mistake is not the playwright's; it is the failure of knowing that an Argosy was not a Venetian vessel. Ragusan Argosies were always welcome in Mexico, and indeed, one of them could have—and probably would have, were money involved—carried Antonio's merchandise there in its hold. Shylock and Bassanio also name other ports where a Venetian ship wouldn't, or couldn't go—but where an Argosy could.

*A*s for the "Indies," there were two places with that same name in European and English vocabularies of the time. It was only later that this ambiguity was cleared up by separating the Indies into "West Indies" for the Caribbean world, and "East Indies" to mean India, Ceylon, the Spice Islands, etc. There is no record of Venetian voyages reaching the East Indies in that era, but there are some records, though sparse, of Ragusan ships having sailed there. The West Indies, of course, were a part of the Spanish Empire, being the Caribbean and its adjacencies.

Another destination mentioned by both Shylock and Bassanio for Antonio's merchandise, "Tripolis," could also ambiguously refer to two different places: either the city on the Levantine coast, or the one on the coast of North Africa. As in the case of the Pedant (Mercantant) in *The Taming of the Shrew* (Chapter 4), this Tripolis is more likely to have been the Tripolis just east of Tunisia, on the coast of North Africa, where gold could be obtained. Gold was much needed when doing business with the Turks, due to their disdain for

The Rialto was for centuries the principal center of business in Venice for merchants, bankers and shipowners. The opposing views were painted in the early-to-mid-18th century by Giovanni Antonio Canaletto (1697–1768).

Opposite page: View of the public square, Campo di San Giacomo di Rialto.

This page: The church of San Giacomo di Rialto.

western silver. Either Tripolis, however, could be a port of call for Venetians and Ragusans; and both were welcome at certain ports the length of the Barbary Coast of Africa, as well.

In sum, ships flying the flag of Ragusa were welcome in all the places listed by Shylock and Bassanio. But for Venice, especially after 1573, it was otherwise. The merchants in sixteenth-century Venice knew this and knew what to do — and the playwright knew as well.

〜

Of all the noteworthy places within the city of Venice, only one is cited in *The Merchant of Venice* by name. It is the Rialto, the financial district of the city. The center of the Rialto consisted of a relatively small public square, called *Campo di San Giacomo di Rialto*, which is adjacent to the Grand Canal of Venice, about midway along its S-shaped course. Though the Rialto is mentioned by name five different times in the play, none of its scenes is set there.

Over a thousand years before *The Merchant* was written, the Rialto was considered the center of Venice, both physically and financially. By tradition, this was the very spot of dry land where the first Venetians laid the foundation of their City of the Lagoon. The event took place on a date of which they are certain — Friday, 25 March 421 A.D. at high noon. It is a date which Venetians continue to celebrate. Part of that tradition maintains that the modest church on the square, San Giacomo di Rialto, was the first church built in Venice, although the present building dates from about 1097.

*T*he Rialto has often been confused with the great white stone bridge, lined with small shops, that spans the Grand Canal and is a favorite destination for tourists to Venice today. That bridge, called the Ponte di Rialto, connects the Rialto *district* to the other side of the city, and until 1854 — when another bridge was finally built — remained the only possibility in Venice for getting across the Grand Canal on foot. For some reason, it is usually — though incorrectly — assumed that Venice bankers did business on the Ponte di Rialto, instead of in, at, or on the Rialto itself.

The bridge is high and wide — some think handsome — and decked, stepped, and partially roofed to accommodate small shops and vendors' spaces. There seems to be enough room for bankers, too; but as Brooklyn is not the bridge by which it is reached, neither is the Rialto its bridge. In fact, for much of the sixteenth century, there was no Rialto Bridge at all.

Its predecessors were a succession of clumsy structures made of wood. A good likeness of the last one can be seen in the 1496 painting *The Miracle of the Cross at the Rialto*, by Vittore Carpaccio. This wooden bridge collapsed into the Grand Canal on the disastrous day of 14 August 1524. Decades were spent in debates over architectural proposals, and finally, on 9 June 1588, the first stone of the now-famous replacement was laid. The bridge was not fully completed until 1591, and in the meantime, the Grand Canal was crossed by standing upright, with Venetian aplomb, in small ferry-boats called *gondolone da prada*, similar to the large gondolas on the canals of Venice today. If ever a date is determined for the playwright's visits to Venice, only then will it be ascertained if he saw a bridge crossing the Grand Canal to the Rialto with his own eyes.

Of specific importance to the story of *The Merchant of Venice*, the Rialto was the place where the city's nobles, merchants, and financiers gathered each weekday. It was a beehive of activity. There, the merchants of Venice would transact business, gossip, report news — especially shipping news — and make trade agreements, form joint ventures, buy and sell cargo,

The Rialto Bridge *(detail) as seen here in the painting "The Miracle of the Holy Cross," by Vittorio Carpaccio (c. 1465– c. 1522). The original Rialto Bridge seen in Carpaccio's painting done in 1496 was constructed of wood. In 1524 it collapsed into the Grand Canal. Almost seventy years later (in 1591) the wooden bridge was replaced by the stone Rialto Bridge known today.*

and borrow and lend money. There, each weekday morning, the bankers' benches were set up in the arcades of the *Fabbriche Vecchie* building, and with ledgers opened, their day began. The Rialto may well have been the most important, and certainly the most famous, financial exchange in the western world. It was also the place to which mercantants would come — from Mantua, for example — on their errands with bills of exchange (see Chapter 4).

❧

For other places in Venice where a play scene is set, the playwright uses dialogue to describe what sort of place it is. With a stay in Venice, poking about with a copy of the play in hand, a sojourner attempting to reconstruct the footsteps of Antonio, or Shylock, or Portia, might well attach to some scene or other an actual Italian name, as is possible with the Ghetto.

The world-famous Jew of Venice is, of course, Shylock. But there are two other Jews in the play as well: Jessica, Shylock's eloping daughter; and a troubling man named Tubal. No Jew residing in Venice in the sixteenth century would have been regarded as a Venetian. He, or she, would be a foreigner, permitted residency in the city by acquiescence of the Venetian Senate. Jews, banished entirely from England already in the late thirteenth century, were harassed, then chased out of Spain and Portugal; were assaulted and bullied in Germany, and so on. If Jews in Europe were to live with a modicum of safety, it would be in Italy, especially in territories under the rule of the houses of the Gonzaga of Mantua and of the Estensi of Ferrara — and in Venice.

In Venice, from the late fifteenth century onward, Jews were welcomed, though grudgingly. Although most professions were closed to them, banking was not. There were almost no venues where they could put their capital to work; lending at interest became a means of livelihood.

It is no surprise, therefore, to meet Shylock in the process of making a large loan, at a negotiated interest rate, to a Gentile merchant. The Gentile — Christian — merchants gladly accepted these loans in order to leverage their businesses, but then came the twist: they would complain, calling the collection of interest a sin, while ignoring the reality of their direct participation in that same alleged sin. The cycle created distrust and great animosity.

Shylock first appears in Act I Scene 3. He is engaged in a conversation with Bassanio, and the subject of the conversation is three thousand ducats — a very great sum of money. Bassanio, a young, dead-broke noble, wants to pay off his many past-due debts and use the rest of the money to make him look classy enough to win, and wed, the very wealthy Portia, heiress and mistress of a grand villa located somewhere in the Venetian Veneto.

In Venice, lending at interest was ordinarily forbidden both by law, and by the Church, but a loophole, which made it lawful in some cases, existed since the days of Moses. It is in the *Bible*, in *The Third Book of Moses* commonly called *Deuteronomy*. In Chapter 23, Verses 19 and 20, as they appear today, in the *Revised Standard* edition, Moses commanded:

> You shall not lend upon interest to your brother, interest on money, interest on victuals, interest on anything that is lent for interest.

> To a foreigner you may lend upon interest, but to your brother
> you shall not lend upon interest; that the Lord your God may
> bless you in all that you undertake in the land which you are
> entering to take possession of it.

Today, on the mere mention of Shylock, there is the widely indulged temptation to expound on his depicted character and situation;
whether meant to be inflammatory against Jews, or simply intended
as a representation of matters as in fact they were in Venice, a frequent conclusion has been that this play is thoroughly anti-Semitic.
Many, especially in recent years, have boycotted performances of *The
Merchant.* Remarkably few have been aggrieved by the fact, however,
that this sixteenth-century play is also one in which Antonio and his
ilk are bullies, liars, and thieves, without an ounce of Christianity;
and one in which Shylock, but one member of a defenseless minority,
is their selected victim, driven to the edge of madness by their numerous insults and evils over the years.[4]

As Scene 3 of Act I begins, the conversation between Shylock and
Bassanio is much like that between any professional lender (including
a banking loan officer today) and prospective borrower — especially
a possible deadbeat — without the loan arrangements being discussed
with his proffered surety. Shylock asks: "may I speak with Antonio?"
And Bassanio makes it conditional, saying, "If it please you to dine
with us."

This is a snide invitation; no observant Jew would dine at a table
that was not kosher. Shylock is sure that Bassanio knows this. Aside
from all that he has already been through with these men, this remark alone is reason enough for Shylock to take offense. The playwright understands some of these striking cultural differences, even
though, at this moment in history, there were no known observant
Jews in England. In his response, Shylock puts Bassanio straight, and
thereby the English audience is given some fundamental information
about Jewish observances as they were in sixteenth-century mercantile Venice. Shylock tells Bassanio:

> I will buy with you, sell with you, talk with you, walk with
> you, and so following: but I will not eat with you, drink with
> you, nor pray with you.

With this, Antonio arrives on the scene, but instead of greeting him, Shylock speaks an aside to the audience of his hatred for Antonio. When Bassanio calls for his attention, Shylock says:

> I am debating my present store,
> And by the near guess of my memory
> I cannot instantly raise up the gross
> Of full three thousand ducats: what of that?
> Tubal (a wealthy Hebrew *of my tribe*)
> Will furnish me ...   (Emphasis mine)

For someone who was familiar with the Jews of Venice, a "Hebrew of my tribe" would not be a redundancy; it reveals the playwright's awareness of the differences among Jews according to their origins. Shylock is referring to the different "nations" of the Jews in Venice and thus to their dress, their everyday language (Hebrew was not an everyday language), and their particular trades or specializations.

For such a small segment of the total population of Venice as the Jews were, there was a surprising diversity among their nations. There were the Italian Jews, of course, who were a minority, although they were the first to arrive, and many years before the others. The largest nation at the time came from either Germany or Central Europe. These were the Ashkenazi (the Hebrew word for German). The next largest tribe were the Levantines, principally from Turkey, but also Syria, and other parts of the eastern Mediterranean known as the "Levant." The Levantines often maintained important business ties with their homeland, along with certain features of their distinctive oriental dress, such as yellowish caps made of voile. Wearing such garments was a statement of solidarity with their compatriots. Next, but growing, was the Spanish nation, refugees from Ferdinand and Isabella, Charles V, and then Philip II — the lively and cultured Sephardic Jews (Hebrew for Spanish). And there were other tribes as well, originating from smaller nations.

In giving Shylock the comment he makes about Tubal, the playwright has disclosed that he knew about the "nations" of the Ghetto: hardly everyday knowledge for an Englishman who'd never been beyond his native shores, or met a known Jew.

The author also knew about Jewish clothing in Venice. He referred to it in Act I Scene 3, when Shylock, recounting past insults, says:

> You call me misbeliever, cut-throat dog,
> And spet upon my Jewish gaberdine …

Jewish gaberdine. *Gabbano* was the Italian name for the garment; *gavartina* or *gaberdina* was the material. Worn since the Middle Ages, the gabbano was a large, loose cloak, more like an overgarment. It reached to the feet, and was often girt at the waist. It was an encompassing and

protective form of dress and of wide usage, especially for travel. While it was unsuited for manual labor, the gabbano would not be impractical for a Jew to wear, since he was forbidden by law to engage in such labor anyway. Being conservatively attached to this loose and flowing garment, the Jews — especially the Ashkenazim — continued to wear it after it had ceased being worn by Gentiles.

This would be enough reason for Shylock to call his gaberdine Jewish; but there is the added probability that he called it that specifically, because two centuries before, on 5 May 1409, and again on 26 March 1496, the Venetian Senate had made it obligatory for Jews residing in Venice to sew the *rotella*, the letter "O" made of yellow cloth, onto their clothes at the breast, as stated in the statute: *il signo de tela zala in mezo del pecto.*

The playwright knew about this form of Jewish dress, the Jewish gaberdine — the distinctive and unique cloak worn by the Jews of Venice.

Jewish gaberdine. Shylock would have dressed similarly to the figure depicted here. This is the banker, Norsa, wearing the Jewish gaberdine. The Jewish badge, the rotella, a yellow circle, is displayed prominently on the breast. It is a detail in the painting, "Dedication of Santa Maria della Vittoria." [From The Ghetto on the Lagoon: A Guide to the History and Art of the Venetian Ghetto (1516-1797) by Umberto Fortis. Roberto Matteoda, trans. Storti Edizioni (1988–1993), p. 14]

*T*he first time in *The Merchant* we encounter the cloistered Jewish district of Venice — the name "Ghetto" never having been used by the playwright — is in Act II Scene 2. After a comic soliloquy by Shylock's clownish servant, the irresponsible youth named Launcelot Gobbo, his nearly blind father appears on the scene. He asks his yet unrecognized son, "Master young man, you I pray you, which is the way to Master Jew's?"

The old man is simply called "Gobbo," which has always caused a digression in Shakespeare commentaries, with the statement that *gobbo* in Italian means "hunchback." It is then pointed out that there is a stone pedestal in the Campo di Rialto in the form of what is usually called a hunchback. It stands by a small flight of steps, supporting a platform from which official proclamations were once read aloud. As interesting as this stone *gobbo* can be, I find no connection between it and the old drayman called "Gobbo" in *The Merchant of Venice*.

In fact, a *gobbo* is not necessarily a hunchback: this word also means "bent," as in "bent with a heavy burden." Pedestals rendered as hunchbacked, or bent, figures are not uncommon in Italy; they are sometimes found in churches supporting basins of holy water. I doubt Gobbo in *The Merchant* would be a hunchback: he is a workman with a horse and dray, although he is partially blind. He does not immediately recognize his son, Launcelot. Gobbo is on his way to the Ghetto, to Shylock's house, to show a polite regard for Shylock, the employer of his almost unemployable son, by presenting him with "a dish of doves."

This is a dish that was not an uncommon gift in Italy, as C. A. Brown observed in his 1838 *Shakespeare's Autobiographical Poems*. It was a thoughtful and modest Italian compliment. Modernly, tourists exclaim over the great flocks of pigeons — one breed of "doves" — in the St. Mark's Square of Venice. While picturesque to most, many Venetians find them to be a dirty nuisance. In Gobbo's day the birds were kept in rooftop cotes and had a legitimate purpose as an easy and cheap source of protein in the crowded city. Now their descendants fly around freely, depositing their droppings on pavements, parapets, statues, and churches; and once in a while, on someone's head.

Gobbo wants to find the way to the Ghetto, to locate Shylock's house, and deliver his gift. But notice Gobbo's lines: the first time he calls Launcelot "Master young man," and the second time "Master young Gentleman." He then asks the same thing twice: "I pray you, which is the way to the Master Jew's?"

After discovering in other plays the significance of the playwright's successive, almost insistent repetition of certain names, surely by now one ought to take special note — play close attention — to the words which the playwright repeats.

Gobbo didn't ask for the way "to the Ghetto." Ghetto is not a word that appears anywhere in the Shakespeare canon. It would not be until 1611 that the word Ghetto first appeared in print in England. One first sees it in Thomas Coryat's *Crudities*, where he wrote, "The place where the whole fraternity of Jews dwelleth together, which is called the Ghetto …"

Launcelot's answer to his father's repeated question is a classic, but comical, bit of Venetiana:

> Turn upon your right hand at the next turning, but at the next turning of all, on your left; marry, at the very next turning, turn of no hand; but turn down indirectly to the Jew's house.

Gobbo replies, "By God's sonties, 'twill be a hard way to hit!" Those are the kind of directions a stranger — and a native, too — might still be given from a local Venetian.

Both father and son know, once the old man arrives "indirectly," by using its tangled and zig-zag streets, that someone in that small district will be able to point directly to Shylock's house. There were no address numbers on Venetian buildings then; and the ones there now make sense only to the postman.

❦

Near the end of this father-and-son exchange, Launcelot tries to mislead his father by turning himself around, so the old man will feel the shoulder-length hair on the back of his head, instead of the hair on his face. With this, Gobbo exclaims:

> Lord worshipp'd might He be. What a beard hast thou got! Thou hast got more hair on thy chin than Dobbin, my fill-horse has on his tail.

Criticisms have been made of Gobbo's choice of words. First, that Gobbo, a Venetian, calls his horse by an English name. This play was written for an English, not Venetian, audience, and is no exception in the choice of names. In fact, virtually all the names given to animals in the Italian Plays are English names, immediately recognizable to English audiences.

Another criticism stems from the assertion that in Venice, there were no horses. The facts are otherwise. In the sixteenth century, Venetian nobles maintained their horsemanship skills, vital to their military prowess, by practicing in the open area next to the Venice Church of San Francisco della Vigna, where stables were nearby. As for Gobbo's Dobbin, a fill-horse is a shaft-horse, the work-horse harnessed between the shafts of a dray or cart. In Venice today, one still comes across an old bridge here and there, with risers that are gentle enough to avoid stumbling a horse; and with two parallel tracks made of ramped stone to accommodate the two wheels of a standard cart or dray.

❧

Ghetto. Of the many guesses as to the ultimate etymology, perhaps the most plausible is that it is an abbreviation of *borghetto*, dim. of *borgo*. Borough. — *The Oxford English Dictionary*

That is the best explanation of the word I have ever encountered, but it isn't the one that is always given when reading about Shylock's place of residence.

Customarily we are told that this word is a variation of the Italian word *getto*, though that is a word in which the "g," followed by an "e," would be pronounced in Italian as an English "j." *Getto* means a foundry for casting molten metal. Probably by leafing through an Italian dictionary, someone somewhere found this word and proposed that at one time, a foundry "must have" existed in that area of Venice. The logic has led to a piece of repeated disinformation. I've always had trouble with this explanation; the difference between the hard "gh" and a soft "g" in Italian is a big one, so much so that I can't imagine an Italian substituting one such "g" sound for the other.

The overall appearance of the Ghetto, as seen today, is much the same as it was when Shylock lived there. The only differences are

Aerial view of the Ghetto Nuovo, Venice. [*Cover photograph of* The Ghetto on the Lagoon: A Guide to the History and Art of the Venetian Ghetto (1516–1797) *by Umberto Fortis, Roberto Matteoda, trans. Storti Edizioni (1988–93)*]

the higher stories of the buildings which once, and then again, were added on in the sixteenth century as crowding increased; and, that a few buildings at one side of the very large square, the *Campo Nuovo*, were razed in order to make way for the Jewish retirement home that is situated there today.

The Ghetto was founded by a decree of the Venetian Senate on 29 March 1516. This decree stated:

> The Jews must all live together in the houses that stand in the ghetto near San Girolamo. And so that they do not go about at night, let two gates be made, one on the side of the Old Ghetto where there is a small bridge, and one on the other side at the bridge — that is, one gate for each place. And let these gates be opened in the morning at the ringing of the Marangona [the main bell at St. Mark's] and locked at midnight by four Christian gatekeepers, appointed and paid by the Jews themselves at a rate that our Council decides fair …

At the time of this decree, there were about 700 Jews in Venice, all of Italian or German origin. It was a figure that would grow, both from persecutions elsewhere, and the attraction of Venice as a world center of business with a climate of greater freedom to Jews than anywhere else in Europe. Some Jews had lived in Venice for generations, arriving as refugees from Central and Southern Italy around 1373, and initially settling in scattered places throughout the city.

Until near the end of the fifteenth century, the Jews, though heavily taxed, and their scope of business and professional activities severely limited, were nevertheless tolerated. Rarely were they subjected to physical harm. This changed with an ugly incident in 1490, and their presence in the city became a matter of increasing concern — and objection — from that time forward. Anti-Semitism in Italy was on the rise, stirred up on the street and by monastic preachers in the pulpit. Numerous proposals were advanced to the Venetian Senate for the Jews' segregation or ouster, resulting in that 1516 decree — a compromise measure — that they must all live together in the Ghetto.

For some perspective about Venetian segregation, it must be noted that German visitors in Venice had been required to stay in a single, though very large, building across from the Rialto. Serbs, Greeks, and Armenians were also confined at night to designated districts, although none had gates or enclosures. And in another Venetian limitation, while Jews were free to conduct their religious worship in the Ghetto, the Lutherans, far more numerous than the Jews, were forbidden to hold any of their ceremonies anywhere in the city.

The Jewish Ghetto is literally an island within the city of Venice. It is surrounded by a complex of canals on all sides, and accessible by only one, or the other, of the two iron bridges leading to its gates.

By reason of the way the gatekeepers were selected and paid, and the fact that the gates were closed only during the darkest part of the night, it is sometimes observed that the Ghetto had a dual purpose: on the one hand, a xenophobic and religious separation from Gentiles; and on the other — and perhaps more importantly — a protection of Jews from nighttime molestations from outside thugs and bullies.

There were other special features in the Ghetto: banks making loans to Gentiles, money-changers for travelers needing different specie; a pawnshop mandated by the Senate for making low-interest loans to Gentile poor; and shops that catered to all Venetians, selling both used and new clothes, exotic fabrics, jewelry, prepared foods, and other desirable things. This was a particular convenience to Gentiles because of the different Sabbath in the Ghetto, such that stores were open on Sunday while closed in the rest of Venice. And too, there were attractive theatrical and musical performances in the Ghetto's various squares.

In the matter of Gobbo seeking Shylock's house in the Ghetto, once again we find efforts to confirm the playwright's Italian ignorance. In the footnote to old Gobbo's question to his son in the *Arden* edition of the play there is this outburst: "The question is ludicrous, for 5,000 Jews could live in the Ghetto at Venice." Perhaps they *could*, but when and if they ever *did* is a different matter. In considering any Jewish population in Italy's history, it is essential to know the date on which a census was made, or a count was estimated. There were substantial fluctuations in the Ghetto populations year by year, and most especially throughout the sixteenth century.

For example, during the long recession between 1559 and 1575, and particularly during the long war with Turkey, 1570–73, there were some severe persecutions of the Jews in Venice, causing many families to migrate to the Levant. Following this period there were the shocking reductions in population due to the plague of 1575–76, an outbreak so terrible that 50,000 people in the city died — between one-third and one-half of the entire Venetian population. It was an event from which, as Fernand Braudel has reported, Venice never fully recovered. As late as 1585, there were only 1,424 Jews in Venice.[5]

To find someone in any small and isolated, but stable, community, then or now — even one with an alleged 5,000 people in it — a stranger asking a few questions here and there could easily learn where that person lived. And in that cloistered Jewish community, the sought person's surname would usually indicate his nation as well, speeding up the finding. With only a modest handful of facts, an inquiry at the appropriate synagogue or neighborhood would produce the wanted location. Even in Brooklyn, it has been said, Gobbo wouldn't need to search very long.

As to the ostensibly naïve errand, it was prompted by the instruction Shylock gives to Tubal at the end of Act III Scene 1. It is the scene, in my opinion, that portrays the final turning point in Shylock's life. It deserves to be read again and again. It is a masterpiece: the depiction of a repeatedly insulted Shylock, first being argued with by Antonio's obnoxious friends, Salerio and Solanio; and then told — actually goaded and humiliated — by his own countryman about the alleged wild squandering in Genoa of his stolen money and jewels — by his own flesh and blood. He is then wrenched to the limit by Tubal's report that his treasured early courtship gift from his beloved wife, Leah, was traded for a monkey.

Tubal either repeats false gossip, or deliberately burdens Shylock with these painful lies. (We will only learn much later, near the beginning of Act V Scene 1, that while Jessica truly is a thief, she had not gone to Genoa, but only as far as Portia's villa.) Having delivered that painful stab, Tubal abruptly changes the subject. He says, "But Antonio is surely undone."

That harsh reality strikes home. If the debt due Shylock is not paid on time, then at most — if one can call it that — Shylock is to get a useless pound of human flesh, "to bait fish withal," as he said earlier in this scene.

Three months earlier, Shylock did not have enough available coin to lend out those three thousand ducats upon the bond of Antonio, so he had borrowed it. Now, Jessica has brought him down. And soon he must return to Tubal, his own lender, that same number of ducats. Shylock instantly reckons, and replies to Tubal:

> Go, Tubal, fee (hire) me an officer: bespeak him a fortnight before. I will have the heart of him if he forfeit, for were he out of Venice I can make what merchandise I will. *Go, Tubal, and meet me at our synagogue; go, good Tubal; at our synagogue, Tubal.*   (Emphasis mine)

Seeking moral guidance from his rabbi at this moment would seem to be far from Shylock's mind, and he wouldn't need Tubal's company for that. Recognizing that Shylock's immediate peril is financial, all that I have been able to infer is that there is to be some business arrangement for his relief or discharge in which a "good" Tubal's participation, perhaps along with others at their synagogue, is essential. In the Ghetto, the governing body of the community was a small council headed by a rabbi, and synagogues were places to meet, not just for religious celebrations. Perhaps here is a moment of communal solidarity — one of the great strengths of the Jews throughout history.

S hylock says "*our* synagogue," not "*the* synagogue," for a very good reason. There was a synagogue — *scola* — for every Jewish nationality or "nation" in the ghetto. The Italian Jews, the Italian nation in the Ghetto, worshiped in a small scola until 1575, when the Scola Italiana was built. The Ashkenazi, or German nation, had their first synagogue, the Grande Tedescha, built in 1529, and a second smaller one, Santa Communità Canton, built in 1532. The Scola Levantina, the most elegant of all, was built circa 1538; and later a second one, the Scola Luzzato, was built next door to it. The Scola Spagnola was built in 1584. All of these are still in the Ghetto of Venice, and two of them can be visited by anyone today. At one time there were also the Scola Mesillamin and the Scola Kohanim. Until I had visited the Ghetto with the aid of a local guide, I did not recognize that the author of *The Merchant* was aware of what he was doing when he used that specific adjective, *our*, for the synagogue — "our synagogue," which would either be the Grand Tedescha, or the Santa Communità Canton.

The fact that Shylock and Tubal were to meet there indicates the playwright not only knew about the nations' synagogues, he knew as well that they served more than one function. In addition to the prayer hall there was a complex of other rooms: a "study house"; a place for the administration of religious and community affairs; a place for the men to meet; and other rooms for the needs of the congregation. Jewish men did not conduct business in homes or sanctified places, thus these ancillary facilities were used for the taking of oaths, the witnessing and sealing of contracts, and both personal and business conversations, particularly those of a sensitive nature.

This acquaintance with the interior of a Venetian scola, by the way, would not be limited to Jews. This was the "age of the sermon," the period when the art of the sermon as a scholarly oration came into its full flower, and humanism was in vogue. Intellectuals of whatever persuasion audited these sermons and philosophical discourses given in Italian — particularly those of the learned Rabbi Samuel Judah Katzenellenbogen (1521–1597).

There is a curious detail about the Venetian Ghetto in *The Merchant of Venice*, and it concerns Shylock's very own house. Aware that it might be a fool's errand, I was nonetheless determined to undertake an investigation. What prompted my search was the hint of something wrongful afoot among Antonio's crowd. The remark comes near the end of Act II Scene 2, when Gratiano says to Bassanio: "You shall not gauge me / By what we do tonight." Does this sound like it might be something evil?

On the heels of this remark, in the next scene, Scene 3 of Act II, Jessica is at home talking to Launcelot the clown. Like many extra-short scenes in Shakespeare, this one is packed with meaning. Launcelot is leaving Shylock's employment, and Jessica gives him a letter to deliver to her Gentile lover, Lorenzo, saying "do it secretly." Launcelot does indeed deliver the letter, in Act II Scene 4, but not so secretly. From what little conversation there is in that same scene, we learn that Gratiano, Salerio, and Lorenzo are planning something that involves wearing disguises, and doing something that has to be perfectly timed and requires "good preparation." We have already suspected that whatever it is, it's not good.

The Red Bank.
Attached to Shylock's penthouse, immediately to the left of it in the picture, is the four-arch arcade of the Red Bank. (Photo courtesy of Miranda Holmes)

Then Lorenzo discloses the contents of Jessica's letter: instructions on how to rob her father, and carry her away. These thieves are taking advantage of the Venetian practice of frequently wearing festive masks in public — not just at Carnival time. Masked revelers in costumes would stream through the streets on the slightest prompting, causing a grouchy Shylock to call them "Christian fools with varnish'd faces." Those masks and costumes were fun, but also provided ideal cover for thieves.

Act II Scene 6: Two of the conspirators, Gratiano and Salerio, appear dressed as masquers. From their conversation we can guess where they are: in the Ghetto. Gratiano says:

> This is *the penthouse* under which Lorenzo
> Desired us make a stand.   (Emphasis mine)

The penthouse. There it is — that curious detail.

In all the works of Shakespeare, "penthouse" is only used twice, once here, and once in *Much Ado about Nothing* in its Act III Scene 3. The classic Eleventh Edition of *The Encyclopedia Britannica* observes, "The Mid. Eng. form of the word is *pentis* … a small structure attached to, or dependent on, another building, from *appendere*, to hang onto." And happily for my need to be sure of things, *The Oxford English Dictionary* cited a 1625 usage of the word *pentis* in a Manchester Court Leet Record about "Erecting certain posts and covering them with large pentises"; because that is precisely what I found at one and *only one* location in the Ghetto: a second floor projecting from a building supported by a few columns. It is the only structure in the Ghetto of its kind.

Shylock's penthouse. View standing in the Campo del Ghetto Nuovo. The penthouse of Shylock is directly ahead, supported on three columns. (Photo courtesy of Sylvia Holmes)

And, interestingly, it is immediately next door to a building that has, as its ground floor, the four-arch arcade that was the site of those loan banks mandated by the Senate; the "Red Bank," so named due to the color of its pawn tickets.

This is the same startling precision for an obscure place and thing in Italy that the author knew about, and subtly described and wove into his story, as he did for the lodging house for Lucentio in Padua, for Saint Gregory's Well in Milan, and for the sycamore grove in Verona. And in succeeding chapters more such unusual and exact knowledge of Italy will be disclosed.

NOTES

1. The name resulted from the difficulty of an English tongue trying to pronounce "Ragusa." English shipping ledgers of the sixteenth century variously record merchant ships calling from Ragusa as a "Ragusye," "Arguze," "Argose," "Argosea," and so on. [*The New English Dictionary*, 1888, Clarendon Press.] The readily accessible *Oxford English Dictionary* observes that an Argosy is "a Ragusan vessel or carack, the transposition … no doubt due to the fact that Ragusa itself appears in sixteenth-century English as aragouse, arragouese, arragosa."

2. *The World of Venice*, James Morris, 1960, 1974.

3. Julia Coolie Altrocchi, *Ships and Spears in Genoa, Shakespearian Authorship Review*, Spring, 1959.

4. With respect to Jews in Shakespeare, one must look entirely to *The Merchant* to find any purported portrayals. No other work of Shakespeare has the word "Jew" except for these five odd remarks: "A Jew would have wept at our parting," and "Thou art an Hebrew, a Jew, and not worth the name of Christian," in *The Two Gentlemen of Verona*; "My sweet ounce of a man's flesh! My incony [rare, fine or delicate] Jew!" in *Love's Labours Lost*; "Of colour like the red rose on triumphal brier / Most brisky juvenal and eke most lovely Jew," in *A Midsummer Night's Dream*; and "If I do not love her, I am a Jew," in *Much Ado About Nothing*. The word "Hebrew" is used but three times: once in the above quotation from *The Two Gentlemen of Verona* and twice in *Merchant* as a variation on "Jew," one being by Shylock himself when referring to Tubal.

5. Braudel, *The Mediterranean*, Vol. II, pp. 814–21.

6
CHAPTER

The Merchant of Venice – Part 2
"Venice: Trouble and Trial"

W e have learned of Portia, the heroine of *The Merchant of Venice*, before we meet her. As described in the preceding chapter, in Act I Scene 1, when Antonio, the Merchant, and his kinsman Bassanio are alone, discussing the three thousand ducat loan from Shylock,[1] Antonio says:

> Well, tell me now what lady is the same
> *To whom you swore a secret pilgrimage*[2] —
> That you to-day promis'd to tell me of?   (Emphasis mine)

And Bassanio replies:

> In Belmont is a lady richly left,
> And she is fair ...

~

"Belmont." For centuries, there has been an ongoing effort to identify its Italian location. In *Il Pecorone*, that Italian tale mentioned in the previous chapter, which partially inspired the playwright's *The Merchant*, there is an imaginary seaside medieval castle named Belmont. Because of this, it is said that the Belmont of the play is situated on a coastline of the Adriatic Sea. But the playwright's Belmont isn't on the sea; nor is it a castle. In *The Merchant*, Belmont is a country villa, and as is clear from the words of the playwright's characters, located somewhere not too far from the Venetian Lagoon.

When the curtain rises on Act I Scene 2, we find ourselves looking into an elegant room in that very country villa. Blonde Portia is talking to a slightly younger woman, whose hair is shining black. She is Portia's companion, and with that hair it is no wonder that she is called "Nerissa."[3] The young women are discussing the men who have already called on Portia. These are suitors, one of whom will win Portia's hand by solving the puzzle that her deceased father, Lord of Belmont, laid down as the controlling prerequisite to becoming her husband. Now that the period of Portia's cloistered mourning for her father has ended, the competition has begun. Certainly, contemporary audiences would expect such a period would have been strictly observed by a noblewoman like Portia.

At this moment in Scene 2, Portia has already received several candidates, none of whom has met the requirement of her father's mandate. She mocks them all, but is especially hard on Falconbridge, the young English baron. After describing the mixed geographic sources of his clothes, and disapproving his behavior (which is likely a reference to his lack of *savoir-faire*), she adds:

> You know I say nothing to him, for he understands not me, nor I him: he hath neither Latin, French, nor Italian, and you will come into court and swear that I have a poor pennyworth in the English: he is a proper man's picture, but alas! who can converse with a dumb-show?

In the palazzi and villas of Venice, a fluency in the preferred Florentine variety of Italian, plus an erudite Latin and a decent French, would be essential for a noble seeking to be welcomed. All three of those languages were spoken, easily read, and understood in the sophisticated circles of Venice. Thus Portia considers the three to be absolutely essential for any proper husband; so too, I suspect, did her English playwright. The everyday language in Venice was — and frequently still is — a dialect far different from a pure Italian. "Venetian" Italian is peppered with ancient Lombard words, and words adopted from the numerous foreign tongues spoken there, such that it was — and still is — virtually a different language. Even today, a dictionary for it can be bought in Venice, and in Verona. No native of Venice would expect a foreigner to speak in their own complex Venetian tongue.

～

An Elizabethan traveler would be enchanted to discover around and about, on the Venetian mainland, those classic villas of the farming wealthy, standing in full view, impressive and unfortified. As the sixteenth century progressed, their numbers steadily increased, as did the need for locally grown crops, and other necessities formerly imported.

The Venetian economy was evolving, impacted by many factors, one of which was that construction of Venetian vessels was becoming more difficult, and Venetian merchants, such as Antonio, were finding that using foreign ships involved lesser costs. Moreover, cheaper insurance against cargo losses was readily available. Mixed into this, the perils of sea trafficking were on the rise — due to widening Spanish hostility — and Turkish and Barbary piracy was a constant worry. But while the wide world about them was changing, for wealthy Venetians, their own world seemed undiminished.

Nothing anywhere else in Europe was like those Venetian villas. A tourist today thinks of them only as palaces of pleasure and ease, newfound sources of escape from the crowded city, venues for entertainment and lavish hospitality. All this was true enough, but there was more to them than this. Those long wings on either side of a classically columned center palazzo weren't just decorative: they were essential. The wings sheltered farm workers and slaves, ploughs and harnesses, rakes and scythes, harvested crops, animals, wagons and carts, a new coach or two, and all else required for a serious farming enterprise on the adjacent wide acreage. These villas — in their singularly Venetian way — combined sweeping beauty with hard-nosed practicality.

Wealthy Portia had inherited just such an estate from her father. He had come to realize, like other wealthy Venetians in the sixteenth century, that in their preoccupation with overseas shipping and trade, the huge and sparsely farmed mainland of the Republic — which extended into parts of Lombardy — had been genuinely neglected.

Added to this, beginning in 1573, when the other Italian states turned hostile to her, Venice lost important sources of foodstuff, such as wheat from Sicily. It was in that year, too, as noted in Chapter 5, that Venetian ships ceased their visits to England and made what was to Venice an indispensable trade treaty with threatening and non-Christian Turkey. The Venetian Republic, more and more isolated externally, turned in on itself.

They began farming enterprises of their own, and a good number of the more wealthy among them turned to that brilliant architect, Andrea Palladio of Vicenza, to replicate his magnificent neo-classical architecture on their properties. Palladio's was a style of architecture that would become so enviable and so famous that it spread the world over. In 1570, Andrea Palladio was appointed the official architect of Venice. Buildings in his distinctive design continue to be constructed, and almost half a millennium after his death, his style, "Palladian," lives on, honoring his name.

Such were the noble villas of the Venetian Veneto, which steadily rose on the disused farmlands surrounding the Venetian Lagoon. Many of the most splendid examples are scattered along the Brenta Canal, and specialized tourist boats today delight visitors interested in architecture with water tours.

～

The playwright resists giving us clues about the location of his own Belmont until the end of Act III Scene 4. Finally, we learn a few important things when Portia is making her secret plans. She intends to travel to Venice disguised as a young man; present herself at the Courts of Justice as a lawyer; and defend Antonio from Shylock's dreadful demand of a pound of Antonio's flesh.

In that scene, with only her companion Nerissa present, Portia instructs her reliable aide, Balthazar:

> Now Balthazar,
> As I have ever found thee honest-true,
> So let me find thee still: take this same letter
> And use thou all th'endeavour of a man
> In speed *to Padua*, see thou render this

Into my cousin's hand (Doctor Bellario),
And look what notes and garments he doth give thee, —
Bring them (I pray thee) with imagin'd speed
Unto the *Tranect, to the common ferry*
Which trades to Venice; waste no time in words
But get thee gone. — I shall be there before thee.
(Emphasis mine)

Then, after Balthazar has left, in the closing lines of that scene, Portia turns to Nerissa:

> ... I'll tell thee my whole device
> When I am in my coach, which stays for us
> At the park gate; and therefore haste away,
> For we must measure twenty miles to-day.

To do this, Portia says she is first going "Unto the Tranect, to the common [i.e., public] ferry / Which trades to Venice." They will wait nearby, prudently keeping to their coach, until Balthazar delivers the materials from Doctor Bellario. Portia and Nerissa will then leave the coach, embark at the Tranect, and go across the water to Venice.

Portia's landing place, called "il Molo," *situated in front of the Ducal Palace and near the Courts of Justice. (From* Le Prospettive di Venezia: Dipinte da Canaletto e Incise da Antonio Visentini, *Pars Secunda, no. 11, Edito dalla Vianello Libri, 1984).*

The Brenta Canal
as it appears today,
just as it would
have looked in
the 16th century.
(Author's photos)

Tranect? What is this? In the First Folio, "Tranect" is capitalized; it is considered a proper name, most likely because it is something unique. In modern editions of *The Merchant*, the word is written
"tranect." As we have seen before, and will see again, spelling for this
playwright is of critical importance. Word meanings are significantly
altered if a capital — as opposed to a lower case — letter is used in this
playwright's plays. Editors seem unaware that the author capitalized

certain nouns to indicate that he was referring to a *specific thing,* one thing among a general class. He did this for accuracy and emphasis, but also for those who might read, rather than see, his plays.

~

The assumption can be made from the lines in *The Merchant* — visualizing Portia's and Balthazar's trips and meetings — that since Balthazar will be coming from Padua to the Tranect, and Portia will be coming from Belmont on the Brenta Canal to the Tranect, this Tranect needs to be where one can transfer easily to the ferry to Venice.

From this, it would follow that the Tranect needs to be someplace both near or on, dry land — where a coach could stand; and near or by, water — where the Venice ferry could dock. Was there such a place?

Indeed there was. But its name is not "Tranect"; the Italians call it "Fusina." No such word as Tranect appears on any map of the area of Venice, modern or antique, although Fusina does.

If the playwright can be relied on (and by now we should trust him), this Tranect — where Portia and Balthazar are to rendezvous — would have to have been at Fusina. (I doubt, however, that Balthazar would use the Padua-Fusina ferry; being in such a hurry, he should gallop to Fusina on the then-existing causeway alongside the Brenta Canal, since called Highway S11.) Carefully examining the geography around the Lagoon, I saw no other possibility than Fusina; and Portia's total mileage calculations fit — as we will see. From Fusina, the distance across the Lagoon is exactly five miles to the landing place called "il Molo," which sits in front of the Ducal Palace and Courts of Justice; the spot where Portia intends to go (see map in Chapter 5).

Portia's phrasing also suggests that the vessel going between Fusina and Venice was not the same kind of vessel as the one that went between Padua and Fusina. Her suggestion is correct. There were different means of water communication in the Venice of this sixteenth-century story. While the large public vessels on the Lagoon were powered either by sails or helmsmen using sweeps, the public vessels on the canals were towed by horses or mules (and also, where appropriate, powered either by oarsmen or helmsmen using a sweep).

Of all the presumptions in analyses of the Italian Plays, the "explanation" given for the Tranect is one of the most uninformed. Stratfordians have held that the word "Tranect" is a corruption of the Italian word *traghetto*, which can mean either ferry boat or ferry landing, depending on the context. For example, the *Signet Classic* edition of the play has a lower case "tranect" (though it was *specifically capitalized* by the playwright), and it merely notes, "*tranect:* ferry." *The New Penguin Shakespeare* edition uses the other frequent substitution of "traject" for "tranect" in a peculiar attempt to anglicize *traghetto*:

> *traject.* Q [symbol for the First Quarto edition of the play] and F [symbol for the First Folio] read "tranect"; probably from Italian *traghetto*, a ferry, found in Florio's *World of Words* (1598); and [Thomas] Coryat notes the "Thirteen ferries or passages [in Venice] which they commonly call Traghetti." Twenty miles from Padua, on the Brenta, is a dam to control the waters short of the Venetian marshes; this may have constituted a ferry or bridge, *known to Shakespeare by travelers's hearsay.* (Emphasis mine)

The Arden Shakespeare edition of the play footnotes its substitute word "traject" as follows:

> Q's "Tranect" is probably a misreading of "traiect"; this would represent It. *traghetto*, a ferry, which is found in Florio's *World of Words* (1598). Steevens [George Steevens (1736–1800), Shakespeare scholar and editor] identified "Tranect" with It. *tranare*, to draw, pass over, swim, but the sense is strained and the "-ect" ending is not explained.

George Steevens was right...

These are some typical "explanations" that ignore the fact that by their own tardy dating for *The Merchant*, i.e., 1596–97 (with which I do not agree), the play was written *before* both Florio's and Coryat's materials were published. John Florio's book was published in 1598; Coryat's in 1611.

Discarding all conjectures as spurious, I renewed my own search for answers. I arrived at the work of Violet M. Jeffery, a scholar who published her findings on the subject in the January 1932 edition of *The Modern Language Review*. Ms. Jeffery's documentation is thorough, and irrefutable: the place where Portia and Nerissa wait in the coach was a real place, with a known name. It was the "Lizza Fusina," simplified over the years to just "Fusina." Fusina means "spindle," and Lizza, in this context, seems to refer to "the place of" or "entry." Lizza Fusina would translate into something like "the place of the spindle"; and later simply "the spindle."

Jeffery has this to say about Lizza Fusina:

> This remote and tiny village is recorded by travelers solely on account of the dam and *the ingenious contrivance for transferring boats from the canal to lagoon.* But so remarkable did they find it that hardly one omits to make mention of it in describing the approach to Venice. And since the natural route for travellers coming from France, England and Flanders was through Padua, of necessity many passed over on the *carro ...*
> (Emphasis mine)

Jeffery found important parallel accounts in Latin, too, noting:

> The anonymous author of the *Itinerarium Italae Totius*, published in 1602, speaks of Lizza Fusina and the remarkable contrivance: "Hic pulchro artificio navigator non mari, sed terra."

And elsewhere she writes:

> In *Hercules Prodicius* [*Hercules Prodicius, seu Principis Inventutis vita et Peregrinatio*, per Stephanum Vinandum Pighium Campensem, Antwerp, 1587] it is spoken of as a *Machina Traductrix*, and is alluded to in much the same terms by Andrea Scoto and Paul Hentzer in their *Itineraries*.

Jeffery also listed preceding ownerships dating from 1444, citing the numerous documentations that are in the State Archives of Venice.

Both Jeffery and I had taken note of the travels of the great French essayist Michel de Montaigne, who made a long trip through Italy beginning in September 1580. Jeffery quotes Montaigne's French (and I from an English translation). Montaigne came to Italy, primarily to visit some of its famous spas, but also to spend time in some of its magnificent cities, such as Rome, Florence, and Venice. On his trip in 1580, almost daily, Montaigne made a record of his experiences and observations. When he was indisposed, his secretary made the diary entries. The entire record, *Montaigne's Travel Journal,* has survived the years, and still makes very enjoyable reading today.

On 3 November 1580, Montaigne arrived in Padua, where he stayed until November fifth. His *Journal* entry reads:

> We left there Saturday morning early by a very fine causeway along the river [the Canal], having on either side very fertile plains of wheat, very well shaded with trees sown in orderly rows in the fields where they have their vines, and the road furnished with plenty of beautiful pleasure houses, and among others a house of the Contarini family, at the gate of which an inscription states that the king [Henri III of France] lodged there on his way back from Poland. We came to Fusina, twenty miles, where we dined. This is only a hostelry, from which one embarks for Venice. Here all the boats along this river [Brenta Canal] land by means of machines and pulleys turned by two horses in the manner of those that turn oil mills. They transport these boats, with wheels that they put underneath, over a wooden flooring, and launch them into the canal that goes into the sea [Lagoon] in which Venice is situated. We dined here [at Fusina], and having got into a gondola, we came to sup at Venice, five miles.

Another account is the *Itinerary* by Fynes Moryson (1566–1630), English traveler and writer, published in 1617:

> In the spring of the yeere 1594 ... I began my journey to see Italy, and taking boat at the East gate of Paduoa, the same was drawn by horses along the River Brenta [actually the Canal]; and having shot two or three small bridges [a reference to locks, with which he was unfamiliar], and passed twenty miles, we came to the Village Lissafusina, where there is a damme to stop the waters of Brenta, lest in processe of time, the passage being open, the Marshes on that side of Venice should be filled with sand or earth, and so a passage be made on firme ground to the City ... Heere while our boat was drawne by an Instrument, out of the River Brenta, into the Marshes of Venice, wee the passengers refreshed ourselves with meat and wine ...

Moreover, Thomas Coryat (c. 1577–1617), another English traveler, included in his 1611 *Coryat's Crudities*, a like description of the *carro* and its operation.

~

"Tranect" is a Latin word, and Latin was the *lingua franca* of Europe, and a language of great importance to any traveler. Just as *connect* means "join with," tra-nect means "join across." A variant would be "transect," which has two different definitions available in almost any English dictionary. Both meanings are applicable, but in different ways, to the place where Portia and Nerissa wait in their coach. As a *verb*, it means to cut across, to go athwart, to make a short-cut, i.e., to cross or to join across. As a *noun*, it is a narrow strip of land; a section or slice of land. The playwright has simultaneously described both the thing and the action that would be found at Fusina: a strip of dry land *and* machinery to pull boats across it.

The development of more advanced engineering techniques sealed the fate of the Lizza/Tranect. Sometime in the seventeenth century, the sliver of land — the "dam" — that separated the fresh water of the Brenta Canal from the salt water of the Lagoon was sliced through, and locks were installed. Thus a direct water connection for vessels going between the Lagoon and the Brenta Canal was opened, and the Lizza (spindle), Portia's "Tranect," her "common ferry," became obsolete. But all this happened long after our playwright set down his own troubled tale.

~

After Portia has instructed Balthazar (in Act III Scene 4) to go to Padua, get the garments and notes from her cousin, return, and meet her at what we now know was the Tranect at Fusina, she and Nerissa go there themselves in her carriage to wait for Balthazar's arrival. The two young women will then board the next ferry to cross the Lagoon to il Molo, the landing place adjacent to the Ducal Palace.

Portia has been clear about how long this trip will take. She told Nerissa, "we must measure twenty miles to-day." (An English mile is the same as an Italian *moglio*.) Now we have some information with which to locate Belmont.

It is five miles from the Tranect to il Molo in Venice. If it were also five miles from the Tranect to Belmont, the combined distance would result in ten miles. After her defense of Antonio, Portia promises to return to Belmont directly. This would mean the mileage of her trip would be doubled. If my calculation is accurate, Portia's round trip is going to add up to exactly those twenty miles of which she speaks.

Is there a stately villa that could be the Belmont we're looking for, five miles from the Tranect? There is, indeed, and it is one of the most magnificent villas on the Brenta Canal. It is the "Villa Foscari," sometimes called the "Villa Malcontenta," due to its proximity to the small town nearby of that name.

One of the most famous of all Palladian buildings, the Villa Foscari-Malcontenta, constructed around 1560 and reflected in the waters of the Brenta Canal, remains in the Foscari family hands. The interior rooms are richly decorated with frescoes reminiscent of the paintings of Giulio Romano, and the villa was known for its grand receptions such as that given in honor of Henri III of France (1574–1589) in 1574. Though now the central seat of the University of Venice, the Villa Foscari-Malcontenta can be visited today. It was an easy reach to Venice and a fitting "Belmont" for an heiress, such as Portia, whose hand was sought by princes far and wide.

Portia's "Belmont." This grand palace on the Brenta Canal, the Villa Foscari-Malcontenta, was designed by Andrea Palladio (1549–1563). (Engraving by J.F. Costa, 16th century. From Die Wunderschone Riviera del Brenta *by Paolo Tieto, Panda Editiori, 1987, p. 12)*

Veduta del Palazzo del N.H. Foscari alla Malcontenta.

In reading *The Merchant* again and again, my eye caught an odd remark Portia makes to Nerissa after Balthazar hurries off on his errand. Portia is describing to her companion how both of them will dress when they board the public ferry on their way to Venice, "both accoutred like young men," although she herself will "prove the prettier fellow of the two." She adds: "And wear my dagger with a braver grace …" Portia is not going to wear a sword, that dangerous weapon that many men all over Europe habitually wore in public; she intends to carry a dagger.

A sword was considered a weapon of aggression; while a dagger was more often thought of as defensive. Carrying a sword in the City of Venice was strictly against the law. Musing on this, I turned to *The Harvard Concordance to Shakespeare* and found something interesting. Of all the thirty-six plays in the First Folio, thirty-five have men with swords. *Only one Shakespeare play has no sword whatsoever: The Merchant of Venice.* Although Scene 2 of Act I of *Othello* is also set in Venice, and both Iago and Roderigo have swords, theirs is a permitted exception, since both are officers of the Venetian army while in uniform.

Portia's "Belmont," *the Villa Foscari, as it appears today. (Author's photo)*

When Scene 3 of Act III arrives, we know Antonio has default-ed in repaying Shylock's loan. The borrowed money has been spent by Bassanio to pay off his creditors, and he has used the rest to im-press Portia and her people. Bassanio had calculated using marriage money from Portia to pay Shylock on time, but his marriage to the heiress becomes a reality a little too late. Under the literal provisions of the bond, it is already in default by the time of the intended mar-riage. Antonio is now to yield a pound of flesh to Shylock: the bond provides no alternative. In this brief scene, we learn that Antonio is to be jailed, pending trial on the issue of whether such a dread pen-alty is legally enforceable.

The substantive — as distinguished from procedural — law that would be involved here, is a part of that international body of rules, customs and usages adopted by merchants, traders, and their bank-ers, called the "law merchant," or "mercantile law." Today it is often called the "commercial law," or the "commercial code." It was in dai-ly use in sixteenth-century England as well as in Venice, cities in the rest of Europe, and places along parts of the Mediterranean coast-lines. The playwright merely calls it "the law"; and his English audi-ence would know what law he meant. Many would also know the part of the law merchant that was concerned with the terms and enforce-ment of bonds.

Shylock, beside himself before leaving the scene, can only utter over and over:

> I'll have my bond; speak not against my bond,
> I have sworn an oath that I will have my bond ...

Solanio, alone with Antonio, remarks:

> I am sure the Duke
> Will never grant the forfeiture to hold.

Antonio responds in a surprisingly reasoned way:

> The Duke cannot deny the course of law;
> For the commodity that strangers have
> With us in Venice, if it be denied,
> Will much impeach the justice of the state,

> Since that the trade and profit of the city
> Consisteth of all nations. Therefore go,—
> These griefs and losses have so bated me
> That I shall hardly spare a pound of flesh
> To-morrow, to my bloody creditor.
> Well, gaoler, on,— pray God Bassanio come
> To see me pay his debt, and then I care not.

In *Il Pecorone*, there is a similar passage, which in English would read something like:

> The Jew replied that he did not want the money since it was not paid at the appointed time, but that he would take a pound of flesh; and this brought about a great controversy, and everyone blamed the Jew; but since Venice was a place where the law was enforced and the Jew had his right fully and publicly, no one dared to speak against him, they could only entreat.

When the forms and provisions for mercantile papers, such as bills, bonds, notes and checks, and mercantile procedures prescribed by the law merchant, were properly followed, vagaries of testimony, tracery of titles, other evidence, and oral contentions were not allowed into evidence. The paper, the bond agreement, was to speak for itself; it stood alone. Something as bizarre as a bond penalty of a pound of flesh, to be excised from the promissory's person, should create an unacceptable problem which, it's safe to say, was never contemplated by the dispassionate law merchant, even in those often brutal times.

In Act IV Scene 1, the Duke[4] of the Republic of Venice— whom Venetians in their dialect called the "Doge"— has been squarely presented with this unprecedented problem. In point of fact, the Duke would not have presided personally at any trial; here he is a symbol for the Republic as a whole. This strange trial is pure theater, having nothing to do with either Venice or the Kingdom of England. As for technical criticisms, the playwright had intended that his *The Merchant* be performed in front of an English, not a Venetian, audience.

The trial of Antonio, a dramatic *tour-de-force*, has been criticized by many. Some base their criticism on the reasoning that the playwright has not followed the proper practices and protocols of mercantile law, as they in fact were during the late sixteenth century; others criticize the trial for its abuses of admissibility, reason and result. Portia's plea for mercy for Antonio would never be permitted under mercantile law. It should be noted that although she is allowed to do her lawyering in the play, her eloquent words fall on deaf ears. The procedure — a farce of mercantile law — actually turns on a "strict interpretation" of the bond, being construed to allow for flesh *only*, and barring the loss (taking) of blood.

Whatever the playwright may have intended in writing the trial scene — on the one hand, so famous for Portia's speech about the mercy she claims for Antonio, and on the other, the fines and forfeitures she demands of Shylock — this singular episode in *The Merchant of Venice*, as one Shakespearean scholar has observed,[5] is the "most ingenious satire on justice and courts of law in the literature of the world."

NOTES

1.   Ironically, Shylock himself is short of cash and must borrow the ducats from Tubal in order to lend them.

2.   Readers or audiences remembering this when Bassanio arrives at Belmont in Act III Scene 2, might well guess that this "secret pilgrimage" — never mentioned again in the play — was made to Portia at Belmont, there to seal their future and to learn which of the three caskets he is to choose.

3.   In Italian, the word for "blackness" or "darkness" is *nerezza*.

4.   He is consistently referred to in the Italian Plays as "duke," since "doge" was the unique title of the rulers of Venice and Genoa. The playwright substituted it with "duke" in order to impart some English appreciation of his high rank as a ruler of a "republic" of sorts, even though these titles symbolized very different sets of power and authority.

5.   Sinsheimer, H., *Shylock*, p. 139.

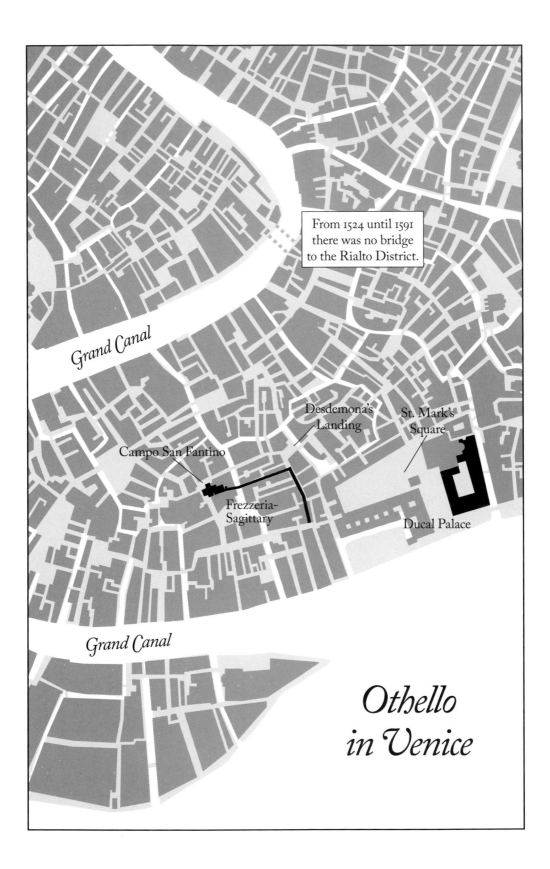

From 1524 until 1591 there was no bridge to the Rialto District.

Grand Canal

Desdemona's Landing

St. Mark's Square

Campo San Fantino

Frezzeria-Sagittary

Ducal Palace

Grand Canal

Othello in Venice

CHAPTER

Othello

"Strangers and Streets, Swords and Shoes"

*A*ll of the first act of *The Tragedy of Othello, the Moor of Venice*, is set in Venice. The rest of the play, Acts II through V, is set on the island of Cyprus. As the scope of this book is the knowledge and experience of the playwright concerning Italy, only a few lines from those later acts are mentioned in this chapter.

For the plot of *Othello* the playwright drew upon one of a collection of stories by the Italian scholar and writer, Giovanni Battista Geraldi, called "Cinthio" (1504–1573). The collection is entitled *Gli Hecatommithi*, and was published in Venice in 1565. Ostensibly, each story was told by one of a group of ten gentlemen and ladies on a sea voyage in 1527. Other than being identified as the seventh novella of the third decade, the story itself has no title. Typical of his Italian Plays, the playwright altered and deepened the source; and with his own superb dialogues as the vehicle, his version, his play, emerges as one of the world's great pieces of both literature and drama. No English translation of Cinthio's work, by the way, appeared before 1753, resulting in speculation over the years about how the playwright got hold of Cinthio's story. Here, with my emphases added, is an extract from Appendix 3 of the *Arden Shakespeare* Third Edition of *Othello*:

> A French translation by G. Chappuys appeared in 1583, and the first *extant* English translation not until 1753. Chappuys kept close to the Italian version except for a few details, and Shakespeare *could have* read one or the other, or *perhaps* a *lost* English translation ... Yet *a lost English version*, one that perhaps made use of *both* the Italian and the French texts, cannot be ruled out.　　(Emphasis mine)

This "lost English translation" proposition pervades nearly all analyses of the Italian Plays when the analyst cannot find an English version of the Italian, or Latin, source materials. It demonstrates the conviction that the playwright had "little Latin and less Greek," according to Ben Jonson's ambiguous remark in the First Folio. After advancing that "lost text" notion, the *Arden* continues:

> ... whether we consider Cinthio or Chappuys or a lost English version as Shakespeare's original, a surprising number of verbal parallels found their way into the play from Cinthio, with or without intermediaries ...

The Riverside Shakespeare in its commentary says:

> Such verbal evidence as can be found tends to show that he looked at Cinthio's Italian.

Looked? Heaven forbid it be suggested that the playwright could read Italian!

The Cinthio story begins with a brief recital about a Moor (unnamed) in Venice, who was personally valiant, had given proof in warfare of great prudence and skillful energy, and who was held in high esteem by the Venetian *Signoria* (the ruling body of the Venetian Republic). The recitation continues that a virtuous lady of wondrous beauty, called Disdemona [*sic*], impelled "not by female appetite but by the Moor's good qualities," fell in love with him and he with her. Despite the efforts of Disdemona's relatives to dissuade her, she married him. Then, the Cinthio story goes on, the Moor was sent to Cyprus as Commandant, and Disdemona went with him; and with this, the source story switches its action from Venice to Cyprus.

Published in 1565, the source does not involve the Turkish invasion of Cyprus in 1570 as its background, as does *Othello*. All of the details about Venice, its people and places, which are addressed in this chapter are those reported or alluded to in *Othello*. Nothing specific about Venice is contained in the Cinthio story.

~

As *Othello* opens on Act I Scene 1, it is night. There are two men on stage: Iago, the famous twisted sociopath, and Roderigo, the foolish romantic and Iago's constant dupe. Roderigo doesn't seem to be a Venetian; and Iago isn't. Except for those two, along with Othello and Cassio, who appear later, all the other figures in the play are Venetian.

It could have been that Iago, as a sixteenth-century Spaniard conditioned by his country's history, would automatically nurture a hatred for any Moor. Iago is a Spanish name, a version of "James" in English, "Jacques" in French, and "Giacomo" in Italian. The name has been familiar over the centuries to religious pilgrims coming to Spain, to Compostela, the town near its northwestern corner, where the huge pilgrimage basilica is dedicated to *Sant'Iago*, commonly written as *Santiago*.

By his own description of himself at the beginning of the play, Iago is a professional soldier and has served under Othello in other places before he came to Venice. There is a brief allusion to his country of origin in Act II Scene 3, at about its halfway point. There, when a bell happens to ring, Iago exclaims: "Who's that which rings the bell? Diablo, ho!" *Diablo*, "devil," is Spanish; the Italian equivalent is *diavolo*.

Roderigo is also in the military service of Venice, although his capacity isn't described. As in both medieval and Renaissance times, and long afterward, many armies were largely made up of mercenaries from all over Europe. It is clear, however, that Roderigo has been in Venice for a while, at least long enough that he is known to Desdemona's father, who tells him early in Act I Scene 1:

> I have charged thee not to haunt about my doors:
> In honest plainness thou hast heard me say
> My daughter is not for thee …

When this same scene opens, the conversation going on between Iago and Roderigo mainly consists of Iago complaining about Othello, who has been designated to command the Venetian military forces going to Cyprus. Iago claims he deeply hates Othello because Othello has declined to appoint him as his lieutenant at Cyprus. A "lieutenant" in a sixteenth-century army would be the second in command: literally, a "place-holder." Instead, Iago has been named as Othello's "ancient," a lesser military title meaning a standard-bearer in the field, although during the sixteenth century, the position involved some administrative duties as well.

Iago and Roderigo are standing on a street in front of the house of a Venetian Senator named Brabantio, who, in order to hold that prestigious office, is a nobleman. Most important, Brabantio is Desdemona's father, and as yet unknown to him, his daughter has eloped with Othello. Bent on creating as much trouble for Othello as he can, but intending whenever possible to stay unidentified, Iago instructs Roderigo to shout the bad news at one of Brabantio's upstairs windows.

When Brabantio opens the window shutters above, he is probably standing there in his night clothes, because Iago brazenly hollers at him: "Zounds, sir, you're robbed, for shame put on your gown!" This insubordinate rascal, out on a public street, has shouted out this impudence so that anyone in the area can hear it, making it a double insult to Brabantio's dignity.

Portrait of a Venetian Senator wearing his senatorial black gown. 16th century.

With regard to this "gown" of Brabantio's, Iago is referring not to a dressing gown or a bathrobe, but to Brabantio's Senatorial gown, the specific garb that all Senators in Venice were required to wear in public. The Senatorial gown, a distinctive long black robe — lined with linen in summer and ermine in winter — was worn by Senators on the streets of Venice, causing people to be pointedly and routinely aware of their government's presence, day in and day out, as each of the numerous Senators went about his affairs in the city, donned in his gown of office. This practice was entirely foreign to England and the rest of Europe. It is interesting to ponder how the author could compose such a precise line in his play about a Venetian Senator's gown unless he'd personally seen, and noted, its particularity.

Iago next proceeds to shout vulgar remarks about Desdemona equally demeaning to her father, saying such things as "You'll have your daughter covered with a Barbary horse." And "Your daughter and the Moor are now making the beast with two backs." To these broadcasts, Roderigo joins in with an embellishment of his own, saying Desdemona has not only gone, but that she was:

> At this odd-even and dull watch of the night,
> Transported with no worse nor better guard
> But with a knave of common hire, a gondolier ...

Confident that Brabantio will insist on finding Desdemona immediately, Iago slips away, but as he does, he instructs Roderigo to "Lead to the Sagittary the raised search ..." By this brief instruction, he has effectively told Roderigo exactly where Othello and Desdemona are to be found. Brabantio then arrives downstairs with servants and torches, ready, as expected, to begin the hunt for his daughter.

~

When Brabantio joins Roderigo down on the street, their anxious conversation includes the following:

Brabantio: Do you know
             Where we may apprehend her with the Moor?

Roderigo: I think I can discover him, if you please
             To get good guard, and go along with me.

Brabantio: Pray you lead on. At every house I'll call,
             I may command at most: get weapons, ho!
             And raise some *special officers of night.*[1]
             On, good Roderigo, I'll deserve your pains.   (Emphasis mine)

Being admonished that he must "get good guard," Brabantio turns to his servants and orders them to "get weapons." Those weapons would have to be miscellaneous household items, since the bearing of arms in Venice was restricted to authorized officials in uniform. He also instructs them to "raise some special officers of night."

That simple direction Iago gave to Roderigo to "Lead to the Sagittary the raised search" is something Roderigo will be able to carry out promptly; he knows the city well. But for the rest of the world, the Sagittary is a place which is still being sought. Where is this Sagittary? What, exactly, is it?

The lines of the play haven't been read attentively. Instead of precisely following them for their literal accuracy — as all lines by this playwright should be — different interpretations have been proposed, such as the following:

In the current *Arden* edition of the play, the footnote to "the Sagittary" says it is:

> An inn or house with the sign of *Sagittarius* (= the Centaur: a mythological figure, with head, trunk, arms of a man and lower body and legs of a horse. Alluding to Othello's "divided nature"?) ...   (Emphasis mine)

The *Riverside* edition says it is:

> an inn (so called because its sign bore the conventional figure of Sagittarius, the Archer — a Centaur shooting an arrow).

The Shakespeare Name Dictionary, after a similar explanation, adds this:

> Some critics asserted that the Sagittary was the residence, at the arsenal, of the commanding officers of the navy and army. It had supposedly an archer over the gates, a statue, but not of a centaur. Most critics dismiss this claim. Lists of inns of Othello's time do not mention a Sagittary, either, though that may mean Sh. [*sic*] borrowed it from something more contemporary, as he often does.

"Borrowed it from something" isn't information; it's an admission of not knowing.

The playwright's lines have deserved better attention than this. In Brabantio's anxious conversation with Roderigo — the one wherein the "officers of night" are called up, and Roderigo says of Othello, "I think I can discover him" — Brabantio says: *"At every house I'll call."* (Emphasis mine) The subject matter has to do with *houses*, not with inns.

The next episode in Act I takes place in Scene 2 on a street at the Sagittary. Iago is warning Othello that Brabantio is coming in anger. But almost at the same moment, Cassio arrives from the Ducal Palace to beckon Othello to an audience with the Duke (the Doge of Venice), and other Senators. They have just learned that the Turkish invasion of Cyprus has begun. Cassio refers to the urgent search underway to find Othello, saying "Being *not* at your *lodging* to be found." (Emphasis mine) In the face of this plain statement by Cassio, I find it surprising that the *Pelican* edition of *Othello* has an editor's footnote for Scene 2 which says it takes place "Before the lodgings of Othello" in direct contradiction to Cassio's words.

There is more. Othello tells Cassio:

> 'Tis well I am found by you:
> I will but spend a word here *in the house*
> And go with you.   (Emphasis mine)

Can it not be inferred from this that Othello is going inside a house to take leave of Desdemona? With Othello absent for a moment, Cassio questions Iago, "Ancient, what makes he here?" And after a typically nasty remark about Othello, Iago says: "He's married." One more time, then, the playwright has indicated, has told us, that Scene 2 must be necessarily set at "the Sagittary," — where the search is now completed, and where Othello is found at a house there. The Sagittary must then be a street or a square, or perhaps a district, lined with houses, and not an inn with a sign and not a military lodging. It is, in fact, if the playwright can be trusted, a specific place in Venice that has this unusual name, "Sagittary."

~

Only a tiny portion of the place names and street names of Venice describe literally what can, or once could, be found there. They are names that would be immediately helpful to strangers. Such names identify the things most commonly sought by using the essential noun onto which "-eria," or "-ria," — meaning "place of" or "workshop of" — is attached. Thus: *Corderia* (rope); *Erberia* (vegetables); *Fonderia* (foundry); *Merceria* (dry goods); *Pescaria* (fish); *Spadaria* (swords); and *Spezieria* (pharmacist or grocer). There is no "Sagittary" in any modern map listing, but there is a *Frezzeria*, the name for arrows and arrowsmiths, those arrows being enough reason for coming to Venice to obtain them in quantity. And being made in that famous and sophisticated city, those arrows very well could have had superior qualities.

In the seventh *Arden* edition of *Othello*, the one prepared by the prominent scholar M.R. Ridley, his footnote to "the Sagittar" [*sic*] has this, in part, to say:

> Miss V. M. Jeffery, in MLR [*Modern Language Review*]
> for January 1932, advanced the view that the word was
> Shakespeare's equivalent for the word Frezzeria, the street of
> the arrow makers. But the trouble with that prima facie attrac-
> tive explanation is that the locality to which Iago is thereby
> made to indicate *is not specific enough*.   (Emphasis mine)

From Violet M. Jeffery's incisive 1932 work,[2] I offer the following quotation from her *Shakespeare's Venice*. Ms. Jeffery found that the Sagittary:

> ... is none other than the Frezzeria [the Venetian version of the
> Italian word *frecciaria*], a narrow dark street which runs from
> the Salizzada San Moise just off Piazza San Marco (St. Mark's
> Square), takes a right-angle turn, and ends on the Ponte dei
> Barcaroli near Campo San Fantino. The Frezzeria was so
> called because the makers of arrows had their shops there. In
> 1271 the guild of smiths was divided up into distinct and spe-
> cialized groups, arrow-makers, armourers, sword-makers,
> cutlers, makers of scabbards and smiths proper, and their
> workshops gave their names to various streets in the city.

Earlier in her article, Jeffery noted:

> Nor is this identification of the Sagittary with a street in
> Venice mere conjecture. Records show that the street [by that

name] existed in the thirteenth century, [and] Marin Sanuto noted in his diary that a fire broke out there [calling it the Sagittary] during the night of 12 July 1518, causing great damage. The street was a busy thoroughfare in Shakespeare's time, and Giacomo Franco, the celebrated engraver, had his shop there at the sign of the Sun.

And subsequent to the above quotations, Jeffery states:

> In Shakespeare's time the word arrow could be expressed in two ways in Italian. One is *frezza*, and the other is *sagitta*.
>
> ...
>
> It is true that Shakespeare would have the authority of Marco Antonio Sabellico for his Latinized adaptation of the name, for in the *De Situ Urbis Venetae* this very street is spoken of as the *vicus sagittarius*.[3]

~

The location of Senator Brabantio's house (no doubt a palazzo) isn't given, but it's safe to assume that Desdemona boarded that gondola very close to (if not a part of) her residence. It was an unusual Senator's home that did not have its own landing. The other end of her secret trip, where she would disembark, ought to be a place right by her destination, the street which now we know has three versions of its name: *Frezzeria* in Italian, *Sagittarius* in Latin, and when the latter is englished, "Sagittary."

Was there a suitable place for Desdemona to arrive in her gondola at the Sagittary? Could I continue to trust the playwright for Venetian accuracies? I went to have a look. The Frezzeria-Sagittary is not *on* a canal but, to be sure, there is a canal parallel to it and only a few steps away: the Rio Orseolo, with its own landing, the Fondamento Orseolo. The Rio now flows into a large turning basin, the Bacino Orseolo, where gondolas from a number of "rios" congregate to serve tourists coming from the adjacent St. Mark's Square; but in the sixteenth century there was no Bacino, only a simple right-angle turn that is now called Rio del Cavaletto. It was easy for me to picture Othello waiting for Desdemona on the Fondamenta Orseolo, then bringing her safely the remaining few steps to the house of their rendezvous.

The first measure of Othello, the man, is provided as soon as he appears on stage in Act I Scene 2. Here Cassio is speaking to him in front of that house in the Frezzeria-Sagittary, just as Roderigo arrives along with Brabantio, his servants, and some officers of night. Those servants would be armed with "weapons" of various sorts, which would likely be clubs, hatchets, and kitchen knives: swords were against the law. On arriving, Roderigo says to Brabantio, "Signior, it is the Moor," and Othello, seeing them all fitted out and coming his way, commands them: "Holla, stand there!" With this, however, the furious Brabantio shouts, "Down with him, thief!" And here in many modern editions we find the unfortunate stage direction: *They draw on both sides.* (Emphasis mine)

The playwright did not furnish this stage direction. It does not exist in either the Quarto or the First Folio. It was added to the play's text in the eighteenth century by Nicholas Rowe, the man usually called the first editor and first "authoritative" biographer of "William Shakespeare," meaning, of course, William Shakespeare of Stratford. Rowe, unlike the playwright, was ignorant of the rule in Venice against the carrying of swords. Only persons of privilege or authority were permitted to do so, and then only on defined occasions. Persons authorized to carry swords included military offi-

Frezzeria–Sagittary.
The Venice street called Frezzeria, which in Othello *is called the Sagittary. The house where Desdemona and Othello rendezvoused was on this street. (Author's photos)*

cers, when in uniform, as both Iago and Roderigo are. Rowe inserted his stage direction in the wrong place, and for the wrong people.

If Rowe's instructed action were to complement the playwright's lines, it should have been in connection with a subsequent line: the one snarled at Roderigo by the tricky Iago, who wants to appear hotly loyal and quick to defend Othello. Iago says: "You, Roderigo! Come, sir, I am for you." This is a clear challenge to a duel. It is here where swords would be drawn.

By the playwright's dialogue, the persons to "draw" are but two: Iago and Roderigo. Iago's declaration to Roderigo is something a sixteenth-century adult, English or Continental, would instantly recognize: a challenge to death, and a challenge made to Roderigo alone, not to anyone else. Iago draws his sword to verify the challenge, whereupon Roderigo reflexively responds by drawing his, too.

Rowe's stage direction, if followed, makes the Sagittary-Frezzeria into the site of an impending general melee, and makes Othello appear to be a sword-drawn and willing participant, when that is exactly what Othello is not. The direction deprives him of the dignity and composure that the playwright has afforded him by the lines he wrote for him. Unarmed and in command above the rash dramatics of Iago and hence Roderigo, as Gerald Eades Bentley, editor of the *Pelican Othello* has observed, Othello says to Iago and Roderigo,

like a veteran to excited boys, "Keep up your bright swords, for the dew will rust them." What Elizabethans meant by "keep up" we now mean by saying "put away." And calmly, Othello continues, turning in a respectful manner to say to Brabantio:

> Good Signior, you shall command more with years
> Than with your weapons.[4]

When Brabantio is told at the beginning of Act I Scene 1 that Desdemona has run off, his first utterance is "How got she out?" Desdemona, only daughter of that Venetian nobleman, was locked in at night, an accepted practice that the author knew. Regardless of what fathers did in other places, or on other social levels, this was done in Venice, at least in its noble households: especially in a Venice with its libertine ways, a worry to parents.[5] If there was a common denominator in the lives of Venetian women, especially those of the upper classes, it was boredom: physical confinement; the company of no one but family and servants; chaperoned outings to church for prayers; and supervised visits by approved nominees for a possible marriage to one of those fellows whom Brabantio describes in Scene 2 as "The wealthy, curled darlings of our nation." The author knew that the Venetian young men had their hair curled with a lock falling onto their foreheads. And who else to come visit? Tutors, dressmakers, and visiting relatives. Surely, fathers thought, this was more than enough to keep "the little dears" content, and usually it was. But not for Desdemona, not for Jessica, and not for a few others. Desdemona would have long since devised a way to escape.

*A*t least one other real life Venetian daughter, the scandalous Bianca Capello (1548–1587), was one. She was the daughter of Bartolomeo Capello, a member of one of the richest and noblest Venetian families. She was famed for her beauty, especially for her remarkable blue eyes. At age fifteen Bianca fell in love with a young Florentine clerk employed at that time in Venice. They eloped to Florence, but soon she became the mistress of Francesco, son and heir apparent of Grand Duke Cosimo I de' Medici. Ultimately, with the deaths of Cosimo I and then of Francesco's wife, and of course, her husband, Bianca, in turn, became the Grand Duchess of Tuscany (see Chapter 12).

Rather than Bianca Capello, I see Desdemona's exact counterpart in the younger of the two Venetian noblewomen in the painting by Vittore Carpaccio (c. 1465–c. 1522) done about 1520. In the nineteenth century, John Ruskin mistakenly thought this painting to be the picture of two courtesans, a label that persisted for a long time.

Rather recently, however, it was determined that the two women depicted carry all the signs of nobility and wealth. Indeed, from the coat-of-arms on the vase on the balustrade, the name of their noble family has been identified. In *Venice Art and Architecture*, the art historian Augusto Gentili has this to say about Carpaccio's painting (translated here from his Italian):

> Their clothes and hairstyles are elegant and fashionable, not showy or ostentatious, and their demeanor is suited to the balcony, a place in a noble home of honest rest and leisure … Apart from the reality represented—the double portrait, clothes, balcony, and crest—the painting is arranged using deliberate symbolic codes, following a consciously mapped-out itinerary that clearly outlines the stereotypical morality for women: chastity for single and widowed women, restraint for married women, modesty and shyness for all, and a discreet vigilance regarding the irrefutable facts of desire, to be converted immediately into virtue … The younger woman, with a melancholy gaze straight in front of her, is either about to be or recently was married; only such as she can wear pearls around her neck.

Due Dame Veneziane *by Vittorio Carpaccio (c. 1465– c. 1522). Rendering (on wood) of a bored mother and daughter of a Venetian noble house passing the time on the rooftop terrace of their palazzo. The painting confirms the adage: "An idle mind is the Devil's workshop." The painting depicts the circumstances in which Desdemona lived.*

(The older and milder-featured woman in the foreground is considered to be the mother.)

As informative as the above extract is, I found it remarkable for what Gentili does not say. It is a graphic portrait of the crushing idleness, isolation, and boredom to which Venetian noblewomen were made subject. It is no wonder that they might yearn for excitement, sometimes taking a secret vengeance through peccadilloes of one sort or another, even—though rarely—of running away.

I include this picture here for another reason: these women have their very blonde hair—perhaps bleached—done up in that same Venetian style described for Portia's hair by Bassanio in *The Merchant of Venice* at the end of Act I Scene 1:

> ... her sunny locks
> Hang on her temples like a golden fleece
> Which makes her seat of Belmont Colchos' strond,
> And many a Jason come in quest of her.

And again, the style is described in Act III Scene 2, of *The Merchant*, in the midst of Bassanio's speech about false beauty:

> ... Look on beauty,
> And you shall see 'tis purchased by the weight,
> Which therein works a miracle in nature,
> Making them lightest that wear most of it:
> So are those crisped snaky golden locks,
> Which maketh such wanton gambols with the wind ...

~

In Scene 3 of Act I of *Othello*, once Othello and Desdemona have explained to the Duke, Brabantio, and the assembled councilors that their marriage deserves acknowledgment, Brabantio surrenders his wrath, if not his heartbreak. In his speech, which begins with the line: "God be with you, I have done," he turns to Desdemona to say:

> ... For your sake, jewel,
> I am glad at soul I have no other child,
> For thy escape would teach me tyranny
> To hang clogs on them ...

Clogs. It is a word with several different meanings. In *The Oxford English Dictionary*, the sixth definition is "a wooden-soled overshoe or sandal worn (chiefly by women) in some localities to protect the feet from wet and dirt." For people, then, a clog is a wooden shoe, a sabot, a patten. For cattle, however, it is a fetter, a shackle, a pastern, to impede the movement of grazing livestock, as in an open pasture, for example. The Italian word for this animal shackle is *pastoia*, but the name of the clog — the wooden or otherwise elevated shoe worn by a person — is *zoccolo* (*zoccoli*, plural), having nothing to do with herdsmen and cattle. Clogs for people don't ordinarily impede movement, but in Venice they did. They were extraordinary. For Desdemona they would be *both* an impediment *and* elevated.

Zoccoli had been introduced sometime in the fourteenth century due to the mud and standing puddles in the many streets and squares that were then unpaved, including St. Mark's Square. The zoccoli grew to absurd heights and continued to be worn well into the seventeenth century, becoming an item of ostentation among the wealthy. The wealthier the woman, the higher her clogs, some so high she couldn't walk in them without placing her hands on the shoulders or heads of servants walking along on either side of her. Examples of zoccoli can be seen today in the Museo Correr in Venice. Zoccoli eighteen and even twenty inches high were not uncommon.

Even as late as June 1645, when John Evelyn began a stay in Venice and described many things in his *Diary*, one of his descriptions is of these extraordinary shoes which he calls "choppines." Evelyn wrote:

> It is ridiculous to see how these ladies crawl in and out of their gondolas, by reason of their *choppines* [clogs]; and what dwarfs they appear when taken down from their wooden scaffolds; of these I saw nearly thirty together, stalking half as high again as the rest of the world.

Horatio Brown in his *Studies in Venetian History*, in commenting on the continuing use of these high clogs observed:

> The story in St. Didier's *La Ville et la Republique de Venise* ... appears to throw light on Shakespeare's intention in this passage. The French traveller relates that the Ambassador of France, in conversation with the doge, remarked once that shoes would be much more convenient; whereupon one of the ducal councillors broke in severely, "Yes. Far, far, too convenient."

～

Using an event of recent history, or current events on which to base a fiction tale, lends it credibility. The playwright uses this device in *Othello*, in a way that grows out of events about Cyprus in 1570, soon after Cinthio's earlier story was published in 1565. The story of "the Moor" in Cinthio's collection thus had an immediacy to it that is

Ladies on terraces bleaching their hair, with their zoccoli at their feet. (Watercolor)

often unrecognized. A Venetian reader of Cinthio in 1565 would be aware of the reason for the Doge and Signoria to send a military commander, along with troops and war galleys, to their island colony of Cyprus. There had been steady Turkish advances in Europe, North Africa, and the Mediterranean ever since Süleyman the Magnificent (1494–1566) had become Sultan of the Ottoman Empire.

For Venice to add new forces to its garrisons on Cyprus, not far from the western coast of Turkey, was only prudent. Or so it seemed, especially when exactly one year later, the great Süleyman was dead. He was succeeded by his son, Selim II, who had the reputation of being a drunkard and was often referred to as "the Sot." Early in 1570 an ambassador of Selim II's departed from Istanbul for Venice. On arriving in Venice on 28 March 1570, the ambassador requested an audience with the Doge and his six councillors, called the *Collegio*, and delivered this message from the Ottoman Sultan. The message opened with a typical oriental flourish:

> Selim, Ottoman Sultan, Emperor of the Turks, Lord of lords, King of kings, Shadow of God, Lord of the Earthly Paradise and of Jerusalem, to the Signory of Venice:

We demand of you Cyprus, which you shall give us willingly or perforce; and do not awake our horrible sword, for we shall wage most cruel war against you everywhere; neither put your trust in treasure, for we shall cause it suddenly to run from you like a torrent.

Beware, therefore, lest you arouse our wrath ...
— from Norwich, *A History of Venice*

In a matter of months, this crisis would have been heard of in faraway England. It was the promise to clip the Venetian imperial wings, the outcome of which might make Cyprus more freely accessible for trade. And so it did in 1573, when English trading ships began coming through the Straits of Gibraltar, after an absence of twenty-five years. Using this background, and weaving in his own adaptations, the playwright begins his *Othello* with the time when the Turkish fleet appeared off the coast of Cyprus on 1 July 1570, and two days later, dropped anchor at Salines — modern Larnaca — and the attack on Cyprus began.

This segment of Cyprus history in fact occurred five years after Cinthio's publication. It is one of the author's methods to take a recognizable event in history — just distant enough in both place and time — and embellish and compress it in order to impart an urgent air for his own plays.

Now, four centuries later, the playwright's anachronistic techniques have laid him open to charges of historical ignorance, his allegedly "doctored" events being condemned as inaccurate. But like so many incidents in the Italian Plays (for example, the date of the visit of Charles V to Milan), this one looks very

Zoccoli. *The elevated shoes, or "clogs," worn by Venetian noblewomen or women of fashion in 16th-century Venice. (Photo courtesy of Sylvia Holmes) [See also the previous two illustrations. In* Due Dame Veneziane *note the pair of red zoccoli at the middle left of the painting.]*

like many Italian affairs that happened not in, but near that significant year of 1573. In any case, by that year, English merchant ships had begun touching the Cyprus shore.

~

Cyprus had been so harshly ruled by its Venetian governor that the Greek population, although Christian, widely welcomed the Muslim invaders, in hope of a more lenient, less avaricious, rule. It so happens that Venice actually gave its ruler of Cyprus the title of "Lieutenant." In *Othello* it will be remembered that Iago was quite bitter that Cassio, a "foreigner," was appointed Lieutenant to serve on Cyprus, and to be second in command in case of Othello's absence. But Cassio may have worn two hats: both a military hat and an economic hat, the latter of greater importance to the merchant princes of Venice.

Iago criticizes Cassio as unfit to make war, complaining in Scene 1 of Act I:

> And what was he?
> Forsooth a great arithmetician,
> One Michael Cassio, a Florentine,
> A fellow almost damned in a fair wife
> That never set a squadron in the field
> Nor the division of a battle knows
> More than a spinster — unless the bookish theoric,
> Wherein the toged consuls can propose
> As masterly as he. Mere prattle without practice
> Is all his soldiership …

It just may be that by a Venetian policy — which seems hinted at in Iago's lines — someone with the sixteenth-century equivalent of an MBA or CPA would be a Lieutenant more capable of looking after imports, exports, taxes, and so on at Cyprus, rendering Cassio a far better candidate for the post there than a mercenary soldier such as Iago. Through Iago's carping, the playwright had taken the trouble to describe just where Cassio's talents lay.

On Cyprus, Lieutenant Cassio shows himself to be both guileless and without direction, easily deceived by Iago, vacillating, and crippled by his adoration of the beautiful Desdemona. The real life

Lieutenant of Cyprus at the time of the Turkish invasion was, in fact, one Niccolò Dandolo, whom John Julius Norwich describes in his *History of Venice* as "Uncertain, timid, forever vacillating between bouts of almost hysterical activity and periods of apathetic inertia."

And so, the tragic Othello helps us realize that the playwright was fully aware of the complex affairs that could affect England's Mediterranean plans for trade and power.

NOTES

1. "Officers of night" were authorized protectors of property who would sometimes extend their services to aid individuals. It is the First Folio that has this quoted phrase, the one now used in most modern editions; though in a few others the Quarto is followed, where the erroneous phrase is "some special officers of might." Stratfordian scholars have found a description of those singular officers of Venice in *The Commonwealth and Government of Venice*, published in England in 1599, being a translation by Sir Lewis Lewkenor of *Della Republica et Magistrati de Venetia*, written by Cardinal Gasparo Contarini (1483–1542), and published in Venice much earlier on. These officers were stationed in all six of the *sestieri* (districts) of Venice for the protection of property — and incidentally of persons — during hours of darkness.

2. *Modern Language Review*, Vol. XXVII.

3. Jeffery's footnote to the above statement informs that: "Marco Antonio Coccio Sabellico da Vicovaro wrote his history of Venice in 1487...", her quotation being from the 1560 edition of *Opera Omnia*, Basilea, IV.

4. Those weapons being that odd equipment his servants have brought to brandish. After seeing the remarkable care the author took in *The Merchant of Venice* in allowing Portia no more than a dagger to wear while in the city, I do not believe I have suggested more here than to expect he would consistently exercise the same attention to the wearing of swords in Venice, in his masterly *Othello*, as he had in the story of Portia going to defend Antonio, in *The Merchant of Venice*.

5. In contrast to Desdemona's gilded prison, when Shylock goes off to a supper in Act II Scene 5, of *The Merchant of Venice*, he hands his daughter, Jessica, the keys to his house, telling her to "Lock up my doors." But then, as it turns out, Jessica was even less trustworthy than Desdemona, stealing her father's ducats.

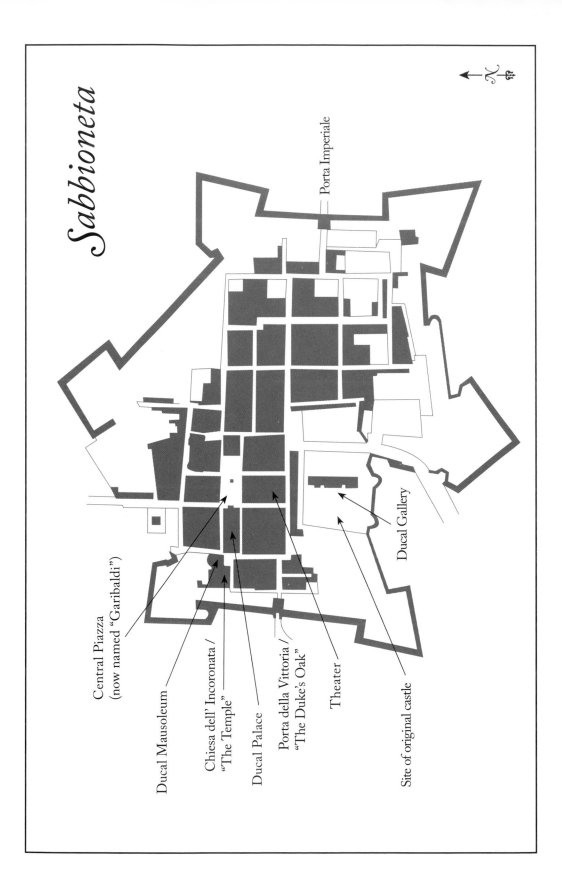

Sabbioneta

Porta Imperiale

Ducal Gallery

Central Piazza
(now named "Garibaldi")

Ducal Mausoleum

Chiesa dell' Incoronata /
"The Temple"

Ducal Palace

Porta della Vittoria /
"The Duke's Oak"

Theater

Site of original castle

8

A Midsummer Night's Dream
"Midsummer in Sabbioneta"

O n my way from Verona to Florence, I made a stop-over for a few days in Mantua, to see the many great works of Giulio Romano (c. 1499–1546).[1] It was a kind of pilgrimage: Giulio Romano is the only Renaissance artist ever named by the playwright. His name is spoken by the Third Gentleman in *The Winter's Tale*, Act V Scene 2:

> No: the princess hearing of her mother's
> Statue, which is in the keeping of Paulina, —
> A piece many years in doing and now newly
> Performed by that rare Italian master, Julio
> Romano, who, had he himself eternity and
> Could put breath into his work, would beguile
> Nature of her custom, so perfectly he is her ape …

On a Sunday morning, a few days later, when ready to continue on to Florence, I was chatting at breakfast with another traveler. He asked me if I had yet visited the unusual small city near Mantua called Sabbioneta. I had never heard of it. He said it was well worth a visit, being a showcase of idealistic architecture, and completely constructed in only one architectural style, the late-sixteenth-century style called "Mannerist." Moreover, it was entirely built during the reign, and under the personal supervision, of its sixteenth-century duke, Vespasiano Gonzaga, a man of singular erudition.

He mentioned this to me, he said, because on Sundays, this very day, escorted tours were offered to the visiting public, since Sabbioneta had recently been restored to be almost as it was when originally built in the sixteenth century. I was intrigued. It would be only a bit of a detour, and though I assumed Sabbioneta wouldn't have anything to do with the Italian Plays, I realized it would have been under construction, with some of it completed, at the very same time — around 1573 or 1574 — when many events described or alluded to in the Italian Plays were happening. In any case, I thought, no matter what, I could experience being in a perfect chunk of what had become my favorite Italian century. So I went there.

❦

Sabbioneta is about forty kilometers — only twenty-five miles — southwest of Mantua, on Highway 420, and is still surrounded by its massive walls. I eas-

The walls of Sabbioneta and the moat. The design and strength of its bastions represented the state-of-the-art in defensive techniques for the period. (Author's photo)

ily drove through the handsome fortified gate, Porta Vittoria, which stood welcoming on its western flank, noting the attractively paved interior streets, as I entered the little city. Straight ahead, I saw a small crowd of people standing in front of a building. I parked nearby. From the sign on the front of the building, I knew it was the local tourist office, and a smaller placard said this was the very hour for which a city tour was scheduled. I bought a tour ticket and was given a brochure entitled *La Piccola Atena* — "Little Athens." I also purchased a tourist guide in English, with full color pictures and a descriptive text of more than seventy pages.

Our guide explained the carefully planned layout of the city's streets and plazas, and she told us about the wealthy, enlightened duke who had built the city. He was Vespasiano Gonzaga Colonna (1531–1591), a member of the cadet branch of the powerful Gonzaga of Mantua. Vespasiano was born on 6 December 1531, in Forli, in the Papal State of Romagna. His father, Luigi Gonzaga, was an illustrious *condottiere* in the service of Emperor Charles V. Luigi, usually called "Rodomonte," died when Vespasiano was only one year old.

As a teenager, Vespasiano was sent to the Royal Court of Spain, there to acquire an education in both academics and military disciplines. In service to Philip II, he rose in rank to become experienced in warfare, then a commanding general, a viceroy, and builder in both

Left: **Vespasiano Gonzaga Colonna, 1st Duke of Sabbioneta,** *attributed to Antonio Moro. The portrait hangs in the Museo Civico, Como. (From Sabbioneta: Guida alla visita della città. Il Bulino edizioni d'arte, 1996, p. 68)*

Europe and North Africa. Vespasiano was an avid student of Vitruvius, the Roman architect and engineer who wrote *De Architectura* — the only surviving Roman treatise on the subject — which he carried with him at all times, even during battle.

Right: **The Ducal Palace** *is the oldest of the buildings constructed by Vespasiano Gonzaga. The front of the building overlooking the square, pictured here, has retained part of its original appearance. (Author's photo)*

*A*long our guided way, we visited the interiors of a number of impressive buildings, including the once-elegant ducal palazzo, the summer palace, and other structures housing the duke's galleries, museum, personal church and ducal mausoleum, an elegant small theater, and even his long gallery for exercise, traditional for noblemen of his day. I remembered that in other ducal or royal palaces I had visited, such facilities were included as *part* of the palace. Here, however, the *city itself* was largely the palace of the duke. Indeed, his guards, physician, aides, and servants were accommodated in various edifices *within* the city. In every case, all designs, materials, and the details of their execution had been subject to the approval of Vespasiano Gonzaga. His walled town was his brainchild and a one-of-a-kind masterpiece.

Some of the buildings in Sabbioneta were originally commodious quarters for the duke's invited guests, his pleasure having been in inviting the erudite among both Italy's, and other western Europe's, nobility and intelligentsia for a visit to his model city. While there, they would admire his rich collections of paintings and sculpture and take part in the festivities, salons, and scholarly lectures that he sponsored during his lifetime. Thus, in addition to the name "Sabbioneta," Vespasiano Gonzaga's guests—and then its steadily increasing numbers of visitors—gave it a second name, *La Piccola Atena*—"Little Athens"—not because of its architecture but because of its immediate reputation as a hospitable gathering place for scholars and intellectuals.

With Vespasiano's passing in 1591, all this ended. Only since the latter half of the twentieth century—a hiatus of some 400 years—have many of these same kinds of events been offered again, with prominent Italian scholars of relevant arts, histories, and literature participating.

Toward the end of the tour, as we stood in the shade of the arched Porta della Vittoria, the architectural main gate of Sabbioneta, our guide explained that this passageway was also known as "*il Quercia dei Duca.*" Not understanding the word "*Quercia,*" I questioned one of our group. "Oak," he said,

Equestrian statues of the Gonzaga. Of the original ten statues completed by Venetian artists in 1589, only four full figures on horseback remain. Fire in the early part of the 19th century destroyed The Hall of the Horses (in the Ducal Palace) where the statues were displayed. All Gonzaga figures in the series were rendered wearing full armor to emphasize Vespasiano's descent from a long line of military leaders. (Author's photo)

"the Duke's Oak." I gasped in disbelief. Thinking I had misunderstood, he repeated, "The guide said, 'the Duke's Oak.'" My breath nearly left me, and I steadied myself against the wall. The Duke's Oak? Could this be true?

A Midsummer Night's Dream! The playwright had been in Sabbioneta! A world of understanding burst in my brain. Of course. It made so much sense. I reached my parked car and collapsed. I grabbed my dog-eared paperback of *Dream* and quickly leafed through it. Indeed, the play was set in Athens. It was so designated, not only at the beginning of Act I, but I counted more than thirty references throughout the play to "Athens" or "Athenian"—though tellingly, no references to Greeks, Greece, Grecians, Attica, or Atticans: only "Athens" and "Athenians." It was no accident. The playwright had wanted his *Dream* to take place only there, in "Athens." But it was increasingly clear that *there* was actually *here*—in Sabbioneta, La Piccola Atena—"Little Athens." Here in Italy.

And the Duke's Oak? Gears clicked into place.

In Act I Scene 2 of *A Midsummer Night's Dream*, in admiration of its own Duke Theseus and his beautiful bride, Hippolyta, six of its rustic characters—Quince, the carpenter; Snug, the joiner; Bottom, the weaver; Flute, the bellows-mender; Snout, the tinker; and Starveling, the tailor—decide to put on a play. It is to be their rendition of *Pyramus and Thisbe*, an ancient love story. They meet to discuss their preparations and to be assigned their roles:

Bottom: We will meet, and there we may rehearse
            Most obscenely, and courageously. Take
            Pains, be perfit: adieu.

Quince: At the Duke's Oak we meet.

It has been assumed over the years, that the Duke's Oak, as mentioned in *Dream*, is some mighty oak tree on the outskirts of Athens, in Greece. What little commentary there has been merely suggest it is an oak tree in the wood close to a town of such characteristics as to merit being named for the Duke. But by now, having seen in preceding chapters the playwright's allusions to unusual things in Italy, this reference to the Duke's Oak should, especially since it is a proper name, give thoughtful pause. It should never have been dismissed in such an offhanded way. Indeed, the playwright has gone a bit out of his way to bring attention to it.

No ransacking of the legend-history of the hero Theseus reveals such a place or name. Nor were there any dukes, *per se*, in ancient Athens, Chaucer notwithstanding.[2] "Duke" (*duc* in French; *duca* in Italian; *Herzog* in German) is a Western European title. In French and Italian "Duke" is derived from the Latin word *dux*, and while there were none in Greece, there were plenty of them in Renaissance Italy.

~

The second and only other allusion to something that is unique in *Dream* (and located in "Little Athens") is not recognized as noteworthy in modern editions of the play, due in large part to the zeal of modern editors. But it is significant, and one further piece that fits perfectly into the puzzle of the setting for *Dream*.

This unique reference — the word "temple" with a lower case "t" — appears in Act IV Scene 1 of *Dream*, in the wood. Near the ending of this scene, "temple" appears in typical modern editions, in the following lines:

*Porta della Vittoria was, for many years, the sole entryway into Sabbioneta. It was also known as **the Duke's Oak** since it opened onto an oak forest which in the 16th century was the Duke's hunting ground. The name does not refer to a specific door but to the passageway. (Author's photo)*

Theseus: Fair lovers, you are fortunately met.
             Of this discourse we more will hear anon.

             Egeus, I will overbear your will,
             For in the temple, by and by, with us
             These couples shall eternally be knit ...

Shortly afterward, the following exchange occurs:

Demetrius: Are you sure
             That we awake? It seems to me
             That yet we sleep, we dream. Do not you think
             The Duke was here, and bid us follow him?

Hermia: Yea, and my father.

Helena: And Hippolyta.

Lysander: And bid us follow to the temple.

In the Duke's Oak.
This modest studded
door leads up to the
loggia above the
central archway and
crest of the Porta
della Vittoria, the
Duke's Oak.
(Author's photo)

*I*n both the Quarto and First Folio editions, the word "temple" is capitalized. There it is spelled accurately, "Temple." It is a small matter, to be sure, but as was demonstrated in Chapter 3 and will be demonstrated again in Chapter 9, it is a matter of no small significance when seeking to confirm the true location of the playwright's "Athens." In Sabbioneta, "Little Athens," there exists a "Temple." It is the church abutting Vespasiano Gonzaga's mausoleum, known as *La Chiesa dell' Incoronata* (The Church of the Crowned Virgin). More simply, however, that little church was referred to only as "the Temple." With capital "T."

*I*t would come as no surprise if, during his travels, the playwright was captivated by this perfectly designed little town, Sabbioneta. He may well have been invited here. Giving free reign to his imagination, it would have been a short leap to create a dream sequence with a title describing what he had written.

Moreover, it is commonly acknowledged that the playwright's education included Greek language and history, so perhaps he was remembering the ancient Greek love story of Pyramus and Thisbe, and the legendary hero of ancient Greece, a king named Theseus who captured the queen of the Amazons, Hippolyta, and made her his wife. Perhaps. But it is abundantly clear that the romance in *A Midsummer Night's Dream* is a romance between two people who are very different from heroes who are Greek.

By "cracking the codes" of three small elements — Little Athens, the Duke's Oak, and the Temple — it is certain that the playwright visited Sabbioneta. Through complete serendipity, I had come upon yet another Italian setting for a Shakespearean play; and it was in Italy, not Greece, as the world has supposed.

NOTES
1. Though best remembered historically for his paintings, Giulio Romano was also a celebrated sculptor and architect in Mantua during his day, demonstrating, yet again, that the playwright knew more than is acknowledged by orthodox academia.
2. In his *The Knight's Tale*, Chaucer also entitles his Theseus "Duke," but for a different reason.

Left: **"The Temple,"** **la Chiesa dell' Incoronata** *(the Church of the Crowned Virgin). One must pass through this modest church to reach Vespasiano Gonzaga's octagonal mausoleum, which was built up against the church in order to be on hallowed ground. (From* Sabbioneta: A Tourist Guide to the City, *Il Bulino edizioni d'arte, 1992, p. 23)*

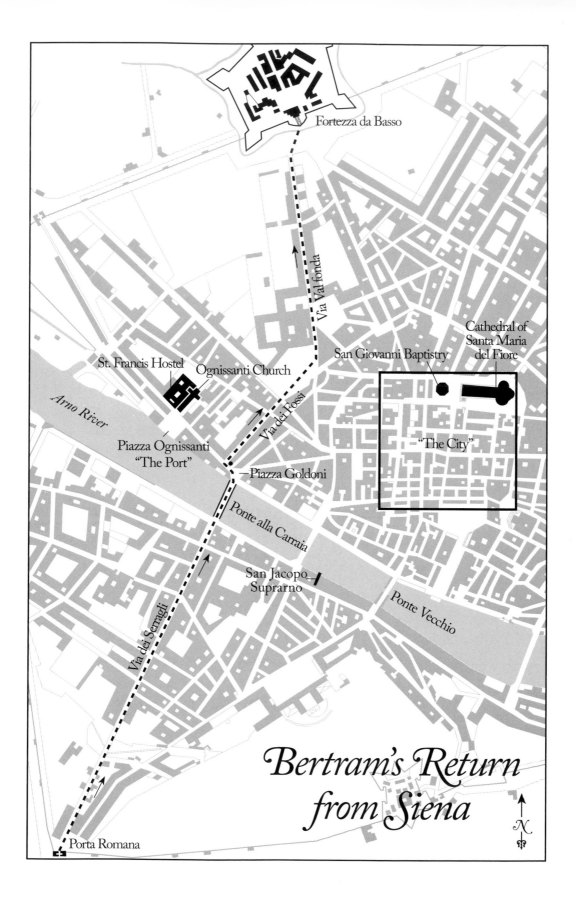

Fortezza da Basso

Via Val fonda

Cathedral of
Santa Maria
del Fiore

San Giovanni Baptistry

St. Francis Hostel

Ognissanti Church

Arno River

Via dei Fossi

"The City"

Piazza Ognissanti
"The Port"

Piazza Goldoni

Ponte alla Carraia

San Jacopo
Suprarno

Ponte Vecchio

Via dei Serragli

*Bertram's Return
from Siena*

Porta Romana

N

9

All's Well That Ends Well
"France and Florence"

*A*ll's Well That Ends Well begins and ends in France, with four scenes set in Paris and eleven in a place the playwright calls "Rossillion" (an earlier English spelling of Roussillon). There are eight scenes in or near an Italian city, however; in this case, supposedly intriguing Florence.

There are no topographical details for the places in France, and seemingly none for Florence either, but that will change as the lines of the play are carefully read. Indeed, an alert reading — while keeping in mind that the author was devious and ingenious at double meanings and had a quirky way of alluding to places in Italian cities — demonstrates his deep personal knowledge of Florence and its environs. It is knowledge he deliberately wove into his story, and for this reason I have counted *All's Well That Ends Well* among the Italian Plays.

As to France, while it can be assumed that the four scenes set in Paris take place in the Louvre, the geographical location of the play's Rossillion is less certain. Commentators have said the Rossillion of the play is an old province in the southwestern part of France, next to the Pyrenees Mountains. This Spanish province, however, would not become part of France until 1659,[1] which is about seven decades *after* this play was written. *The Shakespeare Name Dictionary* has remarked that "Sh[akespeare] overlooks the Spanish orientations of the Roussillonais," which simply furthers the myth of a geographically ignorant playwright.

Searching for some clue as to where the playwright's Rossillion actually might be, I turned to his source for *All's Well*, the story of Beltramo de Rossiglione and Giglietta de Narbone in *The Decameron* of Giovanni Boccaccio (1313–1375). Although Boccaccio did not furnish a specific location for Rossillion either, he did write, at the story's opening:

> In the kingdom of France there once lived a nobleman
> who was called Isnard, Count of Rossiglione ... (Italian for
> Rossillion or Roussillon)

Thus, Boccaccio's Count of Rossiglione was a resident of France, not Spain. This was a good start. But other than eliminating Spain, Rossillion, Roussillon, or Rossiglione's location still remained undetermined. I needed more facts. I knew that there are now, there were when this play was written, *and* there were even when Boccaccio's tale was composed, *three* places with that same name: indeed, a territory which was then part of Spain, and two towns which were solidly in France. Boccaccio had helped me cross off Spain altogether, so my investigations then focused entirely on France.

At the very beginning of *All's Well*, the playwright tells us that Bertram, the young Count of Rossillion, is a vassal of the King of France, because Bertram's father, the old Count of Rossillion, has just died and Bertram, heir to the title, hasn't yet reached his majority. Consistent with the feudal law that still obtained in the playwright's day in both England and France — as well as other parts of Europe — Bertram has automatically become a ward of his overlord, the King of France. He will remain so until he is at least twenty-one. At the beginning of Act I Scene 1, Bertram says to his mother, the dowager Countess of Rossillion:

> ... I must attend his majesty's command,
> To whom I am now in ward ...

With this, Bertram departs for Paris to begin his mandatory wardship. Through these lines of the play, we indirectly glean some substantial, though perhaps inconclusive, information about just where Rossillion might be; Bertram's journey alone hints at a better fit with one of the two towns in France, rather than any territory in Spain. Fortunately, a bit of outside research, along with a little travel, can help narrow the field even more.

One of the French Roussillons is a strikingly situated medieval village in the region of Vaucluse, in a mountainous area north of the Luberon, not too far from the town of Apt. This Roussillon is built in red and ochre stone quarried from the cliffs on which it is perched. The village is dazzling in the sunshine and a very pleasant tourist destination. Its former ruler, however, would have been a Count of Venaissin, not a Count of Roussillon: not a good fit.

The other of the two French Roussillons is in the Department of Isere, and once it did have counts with the correct name. Those Counts of Roussillon existed as early as the tenth century, although by the time *All's Well* was written, the line had died out. This Roussillon is on the east side of the Rhône River, about forty kilometers south of Lyon, on the ancient highway that in more modern times became the National Route N7.

Today, the high-speed Autoroute A7, which is parallel to N7, has physically cut the old town in two: the western section — adjacent to the Rhône — is now called Le Péage-de-Roussillon, and the other section, on the east side of the Autoroute, is simply Roussillon.

It is in this eastern section that both the old castle ruin and the existing Château of Roussillon, now the Hôtel de Ville (City Hall), are situated. The château was not built by a count, but by the Cardinal of Tournon. He acquired the estate of Roussillon by purchase, after there were no longer any Counts of Roussillon, and constructed the château in 1552.

Attractive and commodious, the château was frequented by traveling royalty and nobility, both French and foreign. Henri III stayed there on his way from Avignon to Paris in 1574. Ten years prior to that, on 16 July 1564, Charles IX, on a grand tour of France as its new king, lodged in the château for a month, along with this mother, Catherine de' Medici. While there, Charles IX issued the important Edict of

Château of Roussillon, 16th century, Bertram's home in France. Today the complex is the Hôtel de Ville (City Hall) of Roussillon. (Author's photo)

Roussillon, which proclaimed that thenceforth, the civil year in France would begin on the first day of January of each year. This was eighteen years before the reform published by Pope Gregory III would institute the Gregorian Calendar to the same effect. By the king's edict, France had proudly reformed the old Julian Calendar, a major event that took place in this Roussillon and was widely noted abroad. The Edict gave the town a taste of fame that would linger for years.

The final piece of evidence that this Roussillon on the Rhône is the very best candidate for the Rossillion of *All's Well* comes near the end of the play, where the King of France is reported to have been in Marseilles (called "Marcellus" in the play). The King has left that city and can be reached at "Rossillion," the town, *this* town, directly *en route* from Marseilles to his capital, Paris. Neither a digression to the distant Pyrenees region in a less-than-friendly Spain made by a French king for a social visit, nor a detour to a tiny and out-of-the-way village in a mountainous Vaucluse where its counts had another name, makes any sense. This King is on his way to his capital, and this Roussillon is on his way.

Helen,[2] the heroine of *All's Well*, is a commoner and the orphaned daughter of a learned man named Gerard de Narbon, who had been physician-in-residence to the old Count and Countess of Rossillion. On her father's death, Helen came under the guardianship of the dowager Countess, Bertram's mother. As the Countess says in Act I Scene 1, Helen was "bequeathed to my overlooking." Thus, Helen and Bertram have grown up in the same household, with Helen quietly in love with Bertram most of her young life.

Before Helen's father died, he taught her some of his medical secrets. One of these was how to cure an affliction called a "fistula"—in those days meaning a severe tubercular abscess—fatal unless treated. True to one of those happy coincidences frequently encountered in *The Decameron* and other medieval tales, it just so happens the King has one, and no physician, no matter how skilled, has been able to heal him.

Early in Act I, Bertram, now a ward of the suffering King, leaves for Paris. By Act II Scene 1, Helen has arrived there as well, coming to offer her secret fistula cure to the monarch, though she admits to herself that her motive in coming is not wholly without self-interest; after all, Bertram is present and that's not exactly a coincidence.

In Act II Scene 3 Helen's treatment has been a success. As her reward, the King gives her the right to marry any unwed noble at his court. No surprise to the audience, Helen selects Bertram who exclaims: "A poor physician's daughter to my wife! Disdain / Rather corrupt me ever!" At the King's command, despite Bertram's objections, the marriage takes place. Bertram is furious, and at the end of this scene he vows: "I'll to the Tuscan wars and never bed her."

❧

The Tuscan wars. What are these? What does Bertram mean?

At the beginning of Act I Scene 2, before the happy cure and the unhappy marriage, there is a conversation between the King and two of his nobles, where we learn more about these "Tuscan wars"—and get a history lesson, too.

King: The Florentine and Senoys are by th'ears;
          Have fought with equal fortune, and continue
          A braving war.

1 Lord: So 'tis reported, sir.

King: Nay, 'tis most credible; we here receive it
          A certainty, vouch'd from our cousin Austria,
          With caution, that the Florentines will move us

```
                 For speedy aid; wherein our dearest friend
                 Prejudicates the business, and would seem
                 To have us make denial.

1 Lord:          His love and wisdom,
                 Approv'd so to your Majesty, may plead
                 For amplest credence.

King:            He hath arm'd our answer,
                 And Florence is denied before he comes.
                 Yet for our gentlemen that mean to see
                 The Tuscan service, freely have they leave
                 To stand on either part.

2 Lord:          It well may serve
                 A nursery to our gentry, who are sick
                 For breathing and exploit.
```

Using contemporary language, the King might have said that the Florentines and the Sienese are going at each other and have fought to a standstill, but they continue with their defiant war. In what would seem odd, or even traitorous today, the King remarks that it is all right with him if some of his nobles enter the war, even if they fight on opposing sides.

In the King's day, such conduct was, in fact, not all that unusual. Taking part in foreign wars was not regarded as disloyal; indeed, it was considered a glorious learning experience for young men, "a nursery," which later could be useful in service to their own ruler.

The Second Lord says the young nobles are "sick" (hungry) for "breathing" (excitement) and "exploit" (adventure). But notice the sarcasm with which "cousin Austria" is described. It is a powerful clue to the identity of that "fictitious person" when some real history is added to the pot. It was the practice of Europe's rulers to refer to each other as "cousin," and sometimes they really were. More to the point, however, when "our cousin Austria," the ruler of Austria, is described by the French King as "our dearest friend," and First Lord speaks of his "love and wisdom," Elizabethan audiences might chuckle, knowing that these mouthed compliments were sarcastic. The King and his lords roundly fear this "Austria," and so did the English. Who is he? History will tell us, but sooner so will I.

*T*here were so many skirmishes, battles, and all-out wars over the centuries between Florence and Siena that it is quite impossible in a practical way to count them all. Hostility began with a dispute over their common boundary — the earliest of the recorded conflicts dating to 1129 — resulting in a feud that was protracted and hopeless. Grievances were made more complex by outside alliances, such as those involving France and Spain — or Austria. Spasmodic truces were inevitably broken, creating a cycle of destruction and suffering. Finally, four centuries after that first confrontation, during the reign of Cosimo I de' Medici of Florence (reigned 1537–1574), the Florentine-Sienese feud was resolved. By April 1555, Siena had been completely subjugated.

One cannot say with assurance that this was the "Tuscan war" the playwright had in mind for Bertram, but it seems to fit. By now we are familiar with the author's propensity to allude to events that were just beyond the fringes of an audience's accurate recollection, so it would not be a stretch if the war in *All's Well* is indeed this final Tuscan war of 1555. After all, it took place only a mere generation before the play would have been written.

There is additional historical evidence for this view. The mid-sixteenth-century histories of Siena and Florence, mixed with that of France and Austria, better explain the undercurrent in the conversation between the play's King of France and his lords.

"Austria" refers to the Austrian Archduke and Holy Roman Emperor, Charles V (reigned 1519–1556), his Duchy of Austria being only one of the numerous Habsburg domains (see Chapter 3). It was this monarch, more than any other, whose vast power rendered both the English and the French apprehensive of his policies.

England had several "issues" with Charles V (see Chapter 3), which carried over to his son and heir, Philip II (1527–1598);[3] and as for France, it had some, too. Its kings had long been engaged in military adventures in Italy, all to the irritation of Austria and the Holy Roman Emperors who had ambitions there of their own. Added to the conundrum were the personal antagonisms of Francis I (reigned 1515–1547) toward his "cousin," which began in 1515 when Francis I renewed the French expeditions in Italy, one of which was the capture of Milan. Then in 1519, to the ire of Francis I, who was competing for the title, Charles V won the majority of the Electors' votes to become Holy Roman Emperor. In 1525 Charles V defeated Francis I at Pavia and had him imprisoned. And there was more: Francis I held the duchy of Burgundy, which Charles V claimed by descent from Charles the Bold; Francis I revived the French claim to Charles V's Netherlands provinces of Flanders and Artois; Francis I held Milan, which Charles V claimed as a fief of the Empire; Charles V ruled the kingdom of Naples, which Francis I claimed as the heir of the house of Anjou — and so on.

Wars continued, treaties were made and broken. When Francis I died, his son, Henri II (reigned 1547–1559) continued the hostile behavior — and this brings us to the final Tuscan war of 1555 during the reigns of both Henri II[4] and Charles V — the one which seems to fit best Bertram's comment about going off to "the Tuscan wars."

～

It also fits best when we listen again, more attentively, to that conversation between the King and his nobles in Act I Scene 2. Listen carefully as the King speaks:

> … A certainty, vouch'd from our cousin Austria,
> With caution, that the Florentine will move us
> For speedy aid; wherein our dearest friend
> Prejudices the business, and would seem
> To have us make denial.

The King is speaking about the "caution" (the threat) in the message he has received from "Austria." "The Florentine," in this case, would be Cosimo I de' Medici. The message would be Charles V ("Austria") saying to Henri II (model for the French King in the play): "If Cosimo asks you for troops or money, you'd better say 'No.'"

In effect, the message was a warning to the French king to stay out of this war. In giving his nobles leave to join either side, the French king in the play is politically feigning neutrality, but if wisdom is the better part of his nobles' valor, they would never side with the Sienese. (In real life, the situation was even more complicated: the French king, Henri II, was married to Catherine de' Medici, who was born and raised in Florence and was a genuine blood cousin of Cosimo I.)

The bits and pieces of history that have been laid out here are not, by any means, a fully rounded accounting of the hostilities and the bewildering side-changing of the Houses of Valois and Habsburg in the sixteenth century. While history can serve to bring the Tuscan war that ended in 1555 into focus as the probable war of the play, it is only my opinion that its events serve, in fact, as the basis for *All's Well*, updated from the Tuscan war in Boccaccio's *Decameron*. *All's Well* was not printed or published until its inclusion in the First Folio in 1623, and there is no record of any public performance of it during the reigns of either Elizabeth I or James I. Moreover, it probably includes parodies of, and allusions to, certain Elizabethan nobles and courtiers. This suggests it may have been privately performed — perhaps only for Elizabeth I and her court.

∼

By the time we reach Act III Scene 2, Bertram has gone off to Florence in a huff and has sent two letters to Rossillion — one to his mother, the Countess, and the other to Helen. To his mother he writes, "I have wedded her, not bedded her, and sworn to make the 'not' eternal." To Helen, he writes:

> When thou canst get the ring upon my finger, which
> Never shall come off, and show me a child begotten of
> Thy body that I am father to, then call me husband; but
> In such a "then" I write a "never."

Here it is: Bertram's challenge to Helen. It is the foundation of the play. Now Helen knows what she has to do to call Bertram "husband." She says Bertram's letter is her "passport" — for indeed, it is her authorization to set out. At the end of this scene, as though speaking to him, she says, a little wistfully (and we worry about what she means by invoking "angels" and "paradise" and being "gone"):

> … come thou home, Rossillion,
> … I will be gone;
> My being here it is that holds thee hence.
> Shall I stay here to do't? No, no, although
> The air of paradise did fan the house
> And angels offic'd all, I will be gone.

*T*he next scene, Scene 3 Act III, has only ten lines. It is somewhere in Florence. In it, the Duke of Florence, in front of the assembled soldiers, declares to Bertram: "The general of our horse[5] thou art." Bertram has been in Florence at least long enough to present his credentials to the Duke and offer himself and his men for service.

As Bertram has not reached his majority and therefore, is "under age," this appointment has sometimes been criticized as unrealistic. However, age alone did not impede such decisions in the sixteenth century. When quite young, nobles in that period became skilled horsemen and were often schooled in warfare. As related in the Eleventh Edition of *The Encyclopedia Britannica*, concerning Robert Devereaux, second Earl of Essex (1566–1601):

> In 1585 [aged nineteen] he accompanied his stepfather, The Earl of Leicester, on an expedition to Holland and greatly distinguished himself at the battle of Zutphen. ... In 1587 [aged twenty-one] he was appointed master of the horse and in the following year was made general of the horse and installed as a knight of the Garter.

There were several like careers on the Continent, such as that of Gaston de Foix, Duc de Nemours, a contemporary of both Francis I and Henri II. By the time Gaston reached his majority, he was already an outstanding military commander.

∾

In Scene 4 Act III, Helen has left a message for the Countess that reads, in part:

> I am Saint Jaques' pilgrim, thither gone.
> Ambitious love hath so in me offended
> That barefoot plod I the cold ground upon
> With sainted vow my faults to have amended.

Her message has an ominous ending:

> He is too good and fair for death and me,
> Whom I myself embrace to set him free.

From these lines it could be assumed that Helen has gone on a pilgrimage from Rossillion to Santiago de Compostela in Spain, the great shrine there dedicated to Saint James the Greater (*Santiago* in Spanish, *Saint Jacques* or *Jaques* in French, and *San Jacopo* in Italian). There is no evidence in the play, however, that she did so, no matter how briefly, and we can soon doubt that she would have had enough time to make such a lengthy journey.

In fact, as soon as Bertram goes to Italy, Helen goes there too; on an undercover, fact-finding mission and determined to resolve her marriage. It will not be long before she will re-surface, having learned everything she wants — and needs — to know; and she will have surprises for everyone.

∽

The many subtleties, circuitous descriptions, and allusions about Florence found in Scene 5 Act III are what persuaded me to include *All's Well* in my listing of the Italian Plays. It is in this scene, especially, where the playwright displays his most precise knowledge of that city. His descriptions are a first-person testament to his having walked its streets, visited its sites and learned of its colloquialisms — and also of having acquainted himself with a most ordinary local building located near a most ordinary square, which itself once had a particularly local name.

∽

But before investigating that local building, there is something bothersome in this scene. In two instances, early in Scene 5, there are stage directions for a "tucket." Directions state: "Florence. Without the walls. A tucket afar off." Or something similar. A second tucket is indicated at Line 7 "[*Tucket*]." A tucket[6] is a run of tuneful notes, generally on a trumpet.

We can comfortably accept this first tucket, not only because of the actors' verbal response to it, but because it is indicated in the First Folio. The second tucket, as we will see, is, however, problematic.

As that first tucket[7] sounds, four women — Widow, her daughter Diana, one named Violenta and another named Mariana — along with other folk, have made or are making their stage entrances. The playwright has neatly postponed giving his audience any clues as to where the group is standing because there has only been the sound of this "tucket afar off." While the meaning of a tucket would escape a modern audience, it would get the immediate attention of Elizabethans — and Florentines, too. They, like all medieval and Renaissance peoples, were conditioned to react to a tucket because they knew exactly what the sound of one meant, and they would suspect that this was the tucket of the young Count of Rossillion, now of reputation in Florence.

Since his tucket is not followed by a trumpeted military command of any sort, it would indicate to the Florentines — Widow and the others — that Bertram is probably at a Florence gate where his harbinger,[8] according to custom, has announced his arrival.

In all modern editions of the play, there is another tucket at Line 7. This "tucket" is the disputed *second* tucket. It is misleading. Worse, it is incorrect. [*Tucket*] was added to the play 145 years after it was written, by the industrious Edward Capell, and has been repeated by editors ever since. There is no such stage direction [*Tucket*] in the First Folio. The scene's second trumpet sound is *not* a tucket: it is a trumpeted "signal," a military command; and there is a sea of difference between the two.

The Oxford English Dictionary describes a tucket as "a *flourish* on a trumpet; a *signal* for marching used by cavalry troops." (Emphasis mine) The *OED* also supplies the definition of a "flourish." It states: "In music, a flourish is the execution of profuse but *unmeaning* ornamentation." (Emphasis mine) The problem with these *OED* definitions is that no trumpet sounding can be simultaneously a signal with a meaningful message and an unmeaning ornamentation. These two definitions are mutually exclusive. The *OED* is incorrect — a statement that many will consider a sacrilege.

A "signal" on a trumpet is a brief, identifiable series of notes or tune that broadcasts a specific command. Nearly always it is a military command directing soldiers to mount, march, charge, retreat, etc.

The trumpeted tune called a tucket, on the other hand, was a musical declaration sounded by a harbinger to announce a personage of high rank at a city gate or castle or palace. Each personage had his or her own distinctive, personalized tucket (sometimes called a "touch").

On hearing the distant tucket (or trumpet touch) at the beginning of Scene 5, the audience would guess that Bertram was nearby. And since his tucket is not followed by a trumpeted military command, they would infer that the young Count is probably at a Florence gate.

Diana gives credence to the idea that indeed it is Bertram who has been announced by his harbinger when she says, "They say the French count has done most honorable service." Widow replies, "It is reported that he has taken their great'st commander, and that with his own hand he slew the duke's brother."[9] Her verb tense ("reported," "slew") tells us that the events are past. Widely known and victorious Bertram has thus returned to Florence, and on hearing his tucket, everyone knows they'll be seeing him soon.

∽

After the tucket sounds, Widow says:

> Nay, come; for if they do approach *the city*,
> We shall lose all the sight.   (Emphasis mine)

"… if they do approach the city …" What does Widow mean? If the stage directions are correct, Widow need not have said "if," because the men *are* approaching the city. Aren't they?

Ever since Edward Capell's 1768 tinkering with the play, editors have concluded — erroneously — that Widow and the others are standing "Outside the walls of Florence." We think so, too; after all, that's what it says in the stage directions. But in fact, Widow and the others are standing well *inside* the walls of Florence. The editorial insertion, "Without the walls of Florence" stems from ignorance about what Widow's "city," in reality, was.

∽

In the First Folio, Widow's wording has a capital "C" for "city." There it is written "the City," not "the city." The early spelling should be restored. It makes more sense for Widow to be saying "if they do approach the City," because that's what she means. A capitalized "C" alters the sense of Widow's remark — indeed, a capital "C" alters *everyone's* understanding of the history of Florence, and what Widow is fretting about so much.

For Florentines, "the City" has a specific meaning. Even today the expression "la Città" (the City) can be overheard from conversations, in a context that *does not* refer to Florence as a whole. Its meaning in the play is erased by the editorial reduction of the First Folio capital "C" to a lower case "c." A proper name has been changed into an ordinary noun making it mean *all* of Florence when it does not.

Capitalization can be of significance in Shakespeare. In Chapter 3, for example, concerning the north gate of Milan, "North-gate" in the First Folio should *not* have been capitalized. (The hyphenation there was to indicate that "north-" was an adjective describing where, among all the gates of Milan, that particular gate stood.) "North Gate" or "Northgate" was never its proper name. The opposite treatment should be used in Widow's case. The First Folio capital should be resurrected. "The City" refers to a specific district which was — and still is — *within* the walls of Florence.

The City, in Florence, is a delineated area north of the Arno River which had once been the walled Roman colony of Florentia. Consistent with Roman design, Florentia was rectangular, with straight streets laid out on a grid pattern. It included a large central plaza or "forum," which today is the "Piazza della Repubblica." With some relatively minor modifications during the Middle Ages, this nucleus of Florentia expanded into the Florence of today's modern Italy. The perimeters of that original settlement, though, can still be discerned today. They are defined by Via de' Cerrentani on the north, Via Tournaboni and Via Rondinelli on the west, and Via del Proconsolo on the east. On the southern perimeter there was a wall which was close to, but set back from, the Arno River to allow space for ships to dock and load and unload their cargoes. This is "the City" of which Widow speaks.

Just as "the City" in London is capitalized for the proper name that it is — defining London's origins much like those of Florence — so too, the word should be capitalized in Italy, where the Florentine "la Città" speaks of the very same thing.

When she hears Bertram's tucket, Widow says she fears they may not be in the right place to see "all the sight." But from Diana's remark about "the French count," combined with Widow's comment, the audience would be certain that Bertram and his cavalry had already arrived at one of the gates to the city.

Where would this gate be? Where are the men coming from and where could they be heading to in Florence? Because Diana and Widow speak of Bertram's *past* service, he and his men are most likely coming from the direction of Siena, seventy kilometers — forty-odd miles — to the south. This would mean that they will be entering Florence through its southernmost gate, the Porta Romana, which lies on the outskirts of Florence on the ancient road from Siena. The massive portal is still there.

But Widow is worried. She says, "if they do approach the City," which we now understand to be within the walls of Florence, she is telling us that she feels she might be standing at the wrong place. If Bertram goes to the City, the parade will march from the Porta Romana, over the Arno on the Ponte Vecchio and into the City; while Widow is waiting two bridges away. She is standing near the Ponte alla Carraia (the Bridge of the Carts). If the procession heads to the City, Widow will indeed miss the exciting spectacle.

Again Widow frets:

> We have lost our labor; they are gone a contrary way.
> Hark! *You may know by their trumpets.*   (Emphasis mine)

Widow hears the trumpeted fanfare. This is not a tucket. The procession is coming; the men are somewhere not far off. But where are they? She exclaims: "Hark!" (Listen!) — to enlist the ears of the people around her to determine in which direction the warriors are marching through Florence.

It is easy to understand Edward Capell's stage direction here — *[Tucket]* — when Widow speaks of hearing trumpets. But at this point in the story, were the trumpeted sound truly a tucket, it would be a *second* declaration that Bertram has arrived at the city gate — and the Elizabethan audience already knows this. Even though Capell's is an "honest mistake," his addition to the text is very confusing to those who are familiar with tuckets.

The Porta Romana. This is the southern entrance (exterior shot) to Florence from the Via Romana, the principal road between Florence and Rome. It is the gate through which Bertram entered the city with his cavalry on their victorious return from Siena.

The Porta Romana seen from the interior. (Photos courtesy of Sylvia Holmes)

here are Bertram and the men going? Why would they go to the City? If they headed into the City — to today's Piazza della Repubblica — for an "official welcome," we can imagine the soldiers dismounting, going across to Piazza San Giovanni, and entering the great Florence Duomo, Santa Maria del Fiore, for a stately ceremony of thanks. Then what? These men are tired, filthy, hungry, and thirsty — and so are their mounts. Surely there is a better place in Florence for them to go — to rest, to wash, to nourish themselves, to change their clothes — before going to any official welcoming event by the Duke.

Indeed there is, and it would be the colossal Fortezza da Basso, the enormous citadel in the north of Florence. The citadel was constructed in 1534 under Alessandro de' Medici, and with its stables, kitchens, armory, hospital, barracks, officers' quarters, etc. — all facilities battle-weary soldiers of any era require — Bertram and the men would find rest, water, food, wine — everything they desired, following their long April day of riding and marching. And it was all in one spot.

It would be a fairly straight shot for the weary warriors making their proud progress back to Florence. Entering the city through the monumental Porta Romana, the cavalcade would march straight up the Via dei Serragli, cross the Arno on the Ponte alla Carraia, jog slightly left on the Borgo Ognissanti at Piazza Goldoni,[10] then continue straight as two arrows into the main entrance of the Fortezza da Basso, first along the Via dei Fossi and then along the slightly longer Via Valfonda. The route was pretty much a direct path. Is this the route they took? It is indeed. And it is the shortest possible route from Porta Romana to the most sensible goal in Florence for exhausted soldiers and their tired steeds.

But there is more: much more. There is solid evidence that Piazza Goldoni, by whatever name it had in the sixteenth century, is not only where Bertram will pass by, but is where Widow, her group, and the other onlookers are standing. Widow may already know from experience that military parades through Florence used this route, but more concretely, the spot where she is standing is only a short distance from the lodging place she sometimes calls her "house." Soon, Widow will clarify why this *exact* location is the one in the story; but first, we get a surprise.

The Fortezza da Basso. This vast military complex built by Alessandro de' Medici in 1534 was the destination of Bertram and his cavalry when they arrived in Florence. (Photos courtesy of Sylvia Holmes)

❧

A pilgrim arrives on the scene. We quickly recognize that it's Helen, dressed in pilgrim garb. Neither is she in Spain nor is she dead. Helen's arrival at this moment in the play — and at this exact spot where Widow is standing — is often thought of as a happy coincidence fashioned by the playwright in the trusty old way of folk tales. But it is not. For one thing, a stranger such as Helen pretends to be, with a plan to execute, is better served by striking up a conversation in a public place than by knocking on a local door to chat.

Of far greater significance for the events of this play, however, Helen has been in Florence long enough to do a thorough sub rosa investigation of Bertram's whereabouts and local behavior. In this and ensuing scenes, what Helen has found out becomes apparent. It was only after she had acquired the information she sought that she donned her pilgrim outfit and made her way to Piazza Goldoni — to "bump into" Widow and Diana. Helen already knows what Bertram has been up to, who Diana is, what Widow does for a living, and other facts necessary to trick Bertram.

Her plan for him is called "the bed trick." It is not new with the playwright; it is a ploy that was known and had already been used in medieval and Renaissance stories. Since this bed trick does not involve the author's knowledge of Italy, it will not be pursued further in this chapter. Suffice it to say, Helen knows it and is going to use it to prevail over Bertram's angry challenge.

～

When Widow sees Helen, she says:

> Look, here comes a pilgrim. I know she will lie at my house; thither they send one another. I'll question her: God save you pilgrim! Whither are you bound?

Helen replies,

> To Saint Jaques le Grand.[11]
> Where do the palmers[12] lodge?

Widow's answer is the most important, and consistently the most misunderstood, line in the entire play. Widow responds:

> "At the Saint Francis here *beside the port*."   (Emphasis mine)

～

The port. What is Widow talking about now? A port in Florence?

There was indeed a kind of "port" in Florence. Once again, though, its capital letter in the First Folio needs to be restored. The correct spelling is "Port," and it makes a very important difference in the play.

While I've emphasized only part of Widow's remark, every single word in her one quoted line should, in fact, be emphasized. If there is one sentence in this play that demonstrates definitively that the setting of the Italian portion of *All's Well* truly is Florence; if there is one sentence that reveals the playwright's quite amazing knowledge of this particular Italian city — not just its topography, but its history, too — it is this one line spoken by Widow in Act III Scene 5.

"Port," with a capital "P," is the ancient name for an area that was located between the southern wall of Roman Florentia and the Arno River. The word lost its capital because of ignorance about just what the Port in Florence was. Nor did I know until I was rescued by my learned friend Professor Gino Corti of Villa I Tatti, The Harvard Center for Renaissance Studies in Florence. It was through Dr. Corti's tutelage that I learned exactly what "the Port" was — and "the City," too.

In Italian, in simplest terms, *porta'* means "gate" or "door," and *porto'* means "port" or "harbor." It has already been discussed elsewhere in this book (Chapter 2) that a port does not need to be on a seacoast — a decent-sized river in Italy will do very nicely. In Roman days, Florence was also quite near to the coast of the Tyrrhenian Sea. When these two different words — porta' and porto' — are used in English, their ending vowels disappear, and ambiguity arrives, ready for the playwright's clever use.

In modern English, again in simplest terms, we do not usually use "port" to mean a gate or a door, though it's possible. In fact, the playwright used the word in this, and in other ways, and often.[13] Here in *All's Well*, his use of "Port" recalls his use of "time," "tide," and "tied" in *The Two Gentlemen of Verona* (see Chapter 2) where, as here, he takes pleasure in introducing not just a double, but a triple, ambiguity. To wit: gate, port, and the Florentine Port.

In Roman times, an area between the City's wall and the Arno River was the port of Florentia. Its principal purpose at that time was for deliveries of iron ore shipped from the mines on the island of Elba. Trees on the slopes above Florence were cut to make charcoal for smelting.

By the Middle Ages, the principal import had become raw wool, there to be beaten, picked, de-greased of its lanolin, washed, combed, carded, and spun. It was then woven, burled, shorn while still damp, and stretched out to dry in huge sheds. Next the wool might be dyed, using the excellent dyes made by the Franciscan monks.[14] The industry continued to expand.

The raw wool came from everywhere in the Mediterranean, but the finest came from faraway England. By standing agreements with the monasteries in the English Cotswolds, an entire year's wool might be bought in advance, sight unseen. By far, woolens were the most important commodity in the Florentine economy, and the foundation of its wealth. At one time, one-quarter of the population of the city was involved in the wool industry, and it was the powerful Wool Guild of Florence that commissioned — and paid for — Brunelleschi's colossal dome crowning Santa Maria del Fiore, the Duomo of Florence. Arriving raw from all over Europe, the wool was worked by the Florentines into the world's best cloth, then sold as far away as the Middle East. The industry grew so large that another open space, the Piazza Cestello, almost directly across the Arno from the Port, was made available for the wool trade.

Carts were everywhere, moving products and tools for craftsmen and merchants, shifting wool and woolens to and from each place of processing, and, at the large paved area that had been the old Roman port, receiving each year's bales of raw product while delivering bolts of finished cloth for export. The name of the bridge, Ponte alla Carraia (the Bridge of the Carts), where Widow is waiting, speaks of this city-wide activity. So vital was the Port to Florence and the surrounding towns — so deeply stamped on the psyche of its citizens — that ever after, even when vessels could not always ply the river all the way up to Florence, it continued to be called — or one might say "nicknamed" — the Port. ⁓

Both the Port and the Ponte alla Carraia were overseen for several centuries by monks of a Benedictine Order called the Umiliati. In 1256, the Order constructed a large church, a monastery, and other facilities, beside the Port. The monks named their church "Ognissanti," meaning "All Saints." It is still the name of the church today. As the Port fell into disuse, the name of the church, Ognissanti, came to encompass the adjoining area, and thus the Port acquired what is its official name now, the "Piazza Ognissanti." But all through the centuries, to local folk anyway, the area continued to be referred to as "the Port."

With this in mind, I went again to investigate the area — Piazza Ognissanti as well as the nearby Piazza Goldoni, the small piazza presently graced by the statue of the Italian dramatist Carlo Goldoni (1707–1793), reached by the Ponte alla Carraia.

From the Piazza Goldoni there radiate six streets. Of special importance is the one named "Borgo Ognissanti," which leads into Piazza Ognissanti. I already knew that Bertram and his cavalcade would pass through the Piazza Goldoni on their direct way to the Fortezza da Basso, so I asked myself, "Where would Widow and her company stand so Widow could both watch the parade and easily indicate to Helen the location of the Saint Francis pilgrim lodge?"

I positioned myself around the Piazza Goldoni and looked this way and that. Then I had it. All the elements fit. Were Widow to stand at the corner of the Piazza Goldoni and the Borgo Ognissanti, she could both view the oncoming parade *and* direct Helen. In that exact spot, by pointing her index finger, Widow could accurately inform her that the pilgrim lodging was "here beside the Port." And it was, indeed: that ordinary local building near that ordinary local square mentioned many paragraphs ago.

~

For reasons lost in time, Cosimo I began to dislike the Umiliati. In 1561, he banished them from Florence, whereupon the Franciscans acquired the Ognissanti Church, its monastery, and all its other parts and privileges. Still today, Ognissanti belongs to the Franciscans.

When only a few people could read, signs and symbols were used to identify places — such as a coat of arms, a crown, a rose, an elephant, and so on. You could tell someone to meet you, for example, at the sign of the Crown, at the Blue Boar, at the Elephant, or, in Florence, at the Saint Francis. When Widow says "at the Saint Francis," "at the sign of" is implied.

Before traveling to Florence, I attempted, without much success, to research ways to identify "the Saint Francis," if I actually managed to locate it at the Port. I searched high and low to see what such a sign would look like until it dawned on me that all I needed to do was ask a Franciscan. I telephoned a Franciscan monastery not far from where I live in California, and graciously in the next day's mail, I received a small stylized sketch of the sign of Saint Francis. On my next trip to Florence, as soon as I learned from Professor Corti that "the Port" was an ancient

Above: **The Piazza Ognissanti,** *called the Port, showing the Ognissanti (All Saints) Church. To its left is the entrance to the cloister, and farther down the street (in obscurity) is the entrance to the St. Francis pilgrim's hostel.*

Right: **Entrance portal to the St. Francis pilgrim's hostel.** *Note the sign of St. Francis directly above the door. Helen stayed here dressed as a pilgrim. (Photos courtesy of Sylvia Holmes)*

name for Piazza Ognissanti, I hurried there to track down my prey. I looked systematically and carefully at all the buildings facing Piazza Ognissanti, worrying that mine had been razed to make way for one of the two grand hotels. Frustrated in my fruitless quest, I opened my companion paperback copy of *All's Well* to check, yet one more time, Widow's lines. Widow does not say "here *within* the Port"; she says: "here *beside* the Port." (Emphasis mine) "Beside" also means "next to."

Could the playwright have been so precise about something so far away and foreign? I widened my search. A few steps beyond the far corner of the Piazza Ognissanti, just past the Franciscan monastery's wall, there was a plain building with a large door — and my eyes popped when I saw what was embedded directly above it. There was the sign of Saint Francis, exactly where it had been since the building changed hands in the late sixteenth century. The carving was far more realistic than the modern symbol I had brought with me, but the schema was exactly the same: a cross at the top and beneath it, two crossed arms. In the foreground, Christ's unclothed arm displays the wound of his crucifixion. Behind Christ's

arm is the arm and hand of Saint Francis, bearing the stigmata.

Four centuries ago the author of *All's Well That Ends Well* stood in front of this same building where I was standing now. He may not have known that the sign was placed above its door only about six years after "the Tuscan wars" had ended and the Franciscans had settled in; but I knew that that would not matter at all. More than once the playwright had pushed events together to tell a good story — and did it whenever it pleased him.

*A*s soon as Widow tells Helen where the Saint Francis is, a distant trumpet sounds. It's a military order, "A march afar," and the stage direction for it in the First Folio has resisted tampering over the years. Widow, no doubt with relief, says to one and all, "Hark you! They come this way." Bertram is indeed heading straight for the Fortezza da Basso through the Piazza Goldoni. As the stage direction instructs: "Drum and colors. Enter Bertram, Parolles, and the whole army" — and so they appear, marching past excited Widow and the expectant crowd, in all their triumphant glory.

Line drawing clearly showing the Franciscan "stemmee." (Courtesy of the St. Joseph of Cupertino Friary, Conventual Franciscans, Arroyo Grande, California)

Left: **The Sign of St. Francis.** *This is the plaque above the entrance to the St. Francis pilgrim's hostel beside the Piazza Ognissanti. It shows the symbol of the Franciscans, the "stemmee," composed of the crucified hand of Christ (foreground), crossing the hand of St. Francis (sleeved arm background) with its stigmata. (Photos courtesy of Sylvia Holmes)*

16th-century soldiers on parade. *This cavalcade of fully armed horses and knights decked with festive plumes is how Bertram and his troops would have looked as Bertram's tucket sounded and the men paraded through Florence, victors over Siena.*

NOTES

1. By the Treaty of Pyrenees.
2. The First Folio edition of *All's Well That Ends Well* calls her Helena once, Helen once, and Hellen in all the remaining fourteen instances. Modern editions almost always change Hellen in the play's text to Helen, but not to Helena, although in all scholarly commentaries, critiques, and such, she is consistently referred to as Helena, instead of Helen, despite its solitary use in the play's text. Barbara A. Mowat and Paul Werstine, editors of *All's Well* in *The New Folger Library Shakespeare*, are the only ones I know of who call her Helen. To me, modernized "Helen" is the more fitting name; she is a very different kind of person than the Helena in *A Midsummer Night's Dream*.
3. Becoming Philip II of Spain in 1556.
4. It is much to be doubted, though, that Henri II ever had a fistula.
5. The word "cavalry" does not appear in Shakespeare; the military word was simply "horse."
6. "Tucket" is the English version of the Italian word toccata, from toccare, meaning to touch. In Renaissance Italy a "toccata" was also the royal or noble declaration. Its attention-getting style—so tuneful and attractive—was soon to be adopted in the early seventeenth century, in compositions of music, such as those of Corelli and Bach.
7. The word "tucket" appears only once in Shakespeare *dialogue*, in *Henry V*, Act IV Scene 2, a scene in the French camp where the leaders, including the Dauphin, are present and his Constable orders *two* successive trumpet calls: "Then let the trumpet sound / The tucket *sonance* (sound, i.e., the tucket tune, to inform the listener that something royal or noble is about to be announced) *and* [then] the signal *to mount*." (Emphases mine) It seems that these lines in *Henry V* have been interpreted as describing one single thing, instead of two, upon which the definition for "tucket" in *The Oxford English Dictionary*, may have been based. Constable's instruction to the trumpeter was for a tucket (to identify the royal or noble who is issuing the ensuing military order), and *then* the specific order itself—in this case to the cavalry to mount up. The signal to mount would be only one particular cavalry order out of a number of possibilities. This difference is made clear in *All's Well* since the tucket *and* the command—in this case, to march—are separated by thirty lines of text. The First Folio itself makes the distinction by a stage direction in *The Merchant of Venice* (Act V Scene 1): "A tucket sounds," whereupon Lorenzo says to Portia, "Your husband is at hand; I hear his trumpet." It is information, and contains no order in and of itself. This is identical to the stage direction at the opening of Scene 5 of Act III of *All's Well*.

Church of San Jacopo sopr'Arno (*"St. James overlooking the Arno"*). *This was the church and hostel in Florence for the pilgrims of St. James—pilgrims from southern Italy en route to Spain and pilgrims en route to Rome. The cockleshell-shaped windows in the photo are located at the rear of the church. They can be seen clearly from the Piazza Goldoni when looking diagonally across the River Arno. The cockleshell (*"Coquille St. Jacques"*) is the symbol of St. James. Until today, only those who have made the long pilgrimage to Santiago de Compostella in Spain on foot have the right to display it on their clothes. The author of* All's Well *clearly understood which hostels in Florence welcomed which type of pilgrims. (Photo courtesy of Sylvia Holmes)*

8. As an example of a harbinger being considered essential to a noble entourage, when Edward de Vere, the seventeenth Earl of Oxford, went to Paris in January 1575, he took a remarkably small company for such a wealthy nobleman: two gentlemen, two grooms, one payend, a housekeeper, a trencherman, and a harbinger. This was the bare minimum of attendants.

9. According to *Blue Guide — Northern Italy*, Cosimo I "entrusted the final suppression of the Sienese to the bloodthirsty Marquis of Marignano, who took the city in 1555 after a disastrous siege of 18 months." Did the playwright have the marquis in mind in writing Widow's lines about Bertram? Widow means here not the brother of the Duke of Florence, but rather, *a* brother of *a* duke in Siena.

10. In those times, there was no boulevard called Lungarno along the edge of the river that passed the Piazza Goldoni, as the modern Lungarno Amerigo Vespucci does today. The walls of buildings along the north side of the Arno from Piazza Goldoni extended right to the water's edge. If one wanted to see from a public place a parade that was approaching from across the bridge (the Ponte alla Carraia), it could only be seen from the Piazza Goldoni. For an idea of why Widow is so anxious to see the parade, visitors to Florence today can get an excellent impression of one from the life-size cavalcade of sixteenth-century soldiers and their horses—fully armed, armored, and plumed—in the Great Hall of the Stibbert Museum, located in the Montughi District of Florence, a photograph of which has been included in this chapter.

11. There is more here than might be realized and Helen's appearance as a pilgrim of "Saint Jaques le Grand" has, for someone standing where these women are, a redoubled credibility. Looking across the Arno from Piazza Goldoni, at an angle of sight to one's left (south-southeast), the apse of a Romanesque church can be seen above the river's edge. Its

two large windows overlooking the river are in the shape of the famous cockleshell of "Saint Jaques le Grand," whose name in Italian is "San Jacopo." This church building, appropriately named San Jacopo sopr'Arno, was a pilgrims' church. Its front portico faces on Via San Jacopo and was added in 1526.

12. By the sixteenth century, "palmer" and "pilgrim" were used as synonyms.

13. The word "port" is used twenty times in the Canon: seven times to mean personal comportment, bearing, carriage, or demeanor; five times clearly to mean harbor, or the like; five more times where it could mean harbor but could alternately mean a gate or door, depending on one's interpretation; and two times to mean city gates.

14. "Many of the necessary artisans and the places where they worked have left their names on the city's (Florence's) streets; *Lavatoi, Saponai, Tintori, Cimatori* (wash-houses, soapers, dyers, and shearers)." — Borsook, *The Companion Guide to Florence.*

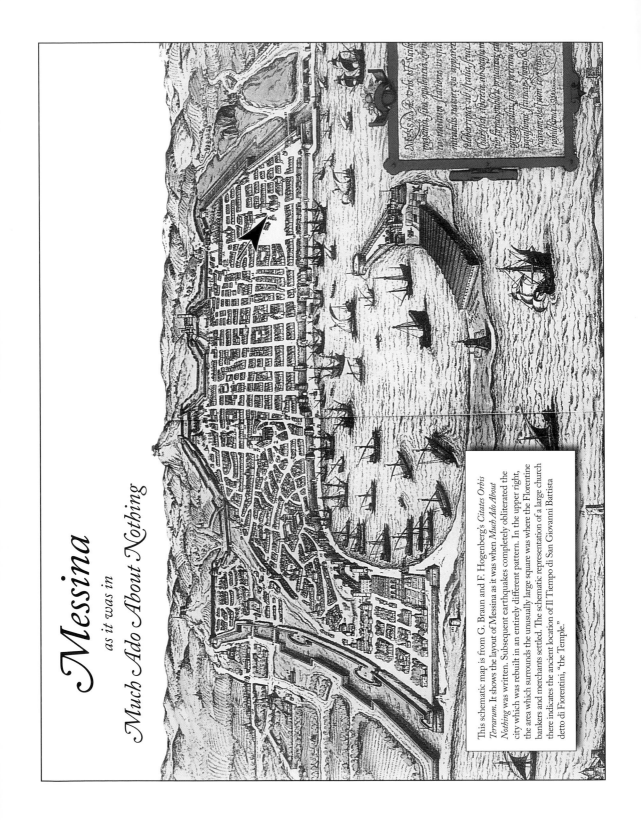

Messina
as it was in
Much Ado About Nothing

This schematic map is from G. Braun and F. Hogenberg's *Citates Orbis Terrarum*. It shows the layout of Messina as it was when *Much Ado About Nothing* was written. Subsequent earthquakes completely obliterated the city which was rebuilt in an entirely different pattern. In the upper right, the area which surrounds the unusually large square was where the Florentine bankers and merchants settled. The schematic representation of a large church there indicates the ancient location of Il Tiempo di San Giovanni Battista detto di Fiorentini, "the Temple."

10
CHAPTER

Much Ado About Nothing
"Misfortune in Messina"
PART 1

uch Ado About Nothing is set in Messina, a city in northeastern Sicily facing the important strait which bears its name. The harbor at Messina is one of the deepest and safest in the Mediterranean, and it has been a resource for merchants and mariners throughout the centuries, both for the transit of cargoes, and as a haven for ships and sailors when the Mediterranean is angry. Yet *Much Ado About Nothing* has no scenes at Messina's famous harbor: all but one take place in the city, and the lone scene that does not is set somewhere on the lowest slopes of the Peloritani Mountains—a natural barrier separating Messina from the rest of the island.

In March 1282, a time when Sicily was ruled by the French king, Charles I of Anjou, brother of Saint Louis, a harrowing event took place in Palermo, almost as though prearranged by the island's inhabitants. This event, remembered in Italy even today, came to be known as the "Sicilian Vespers," as it broke out at the hour of Vespers on Easter Tuesday. All at once, the entire population of Palermo, the island's splendid capital, rose up to slaughter their French oppressors. The uprising then quickly spread throughout the island. And though never confirmed, it is said that thousands of French men, women, and children were butchered to death. It was a frightening, violent event. By the end of April, the whole of Sicily was in the hands of the insurgents, who proclaimed a republic.

The widening rebellion was thorough, but the new free communes of the Republic were so inept that a vacuum in Sicily's government rapidly developed. To restore some type of administration, the parliament at Palermo offered the crown to Peter (Pedro) III (1240–1285), King of Aragon and Catalonia, who had a distant, though legitimate, claim to the Sicilian throne.[1] Pedro III arrived immediately and proceeded to drive out the French. Once the island was subdued, Aragonese rule commenced, and from 1296 to 1402 the Sicilian branch of the Aragon dynasty retained power — which devolved to the Spanish crown and lasted until 1713.

Messina figured strategically in all this. While Pedro III had begun his campaign against the French in Sicily's west, Messina, well to the east, was their last remaining stronghold. The city was Pedro's ultimate battleground, and the site of his final victory over Charles I and the French oppressors.

This is a very generalized description of the events surrounding the "Sicilian Vespers," but it is the atmosphere in the tale of *Timbreo and Fenicia*, a story set in Messina. This tale is in the collection composed by Matteo Bandello (1480–1562) entitled *La Prima Parte de le Novelle del Bandello*, first published at Lucca in 1554. In Bandello's story, a young noble, Timbreo, is a favorite of King Pedro, and Fenicia is the daughter of a Messina nobleman named Lionato de'Lionati. The young people are in love but there is trouble afoot. Scholars have pointed out that from ancient days forward, there have been numerous stories such as *Timbreo and Fenicia*, where a virtuous young woman such as Bandello's Fenicia (and the playwright's Hero), is made to appear involved in an affair with a man other than her betrothed.

Scholars have also compared Bandello's tale to the playwright's *Much Ado About Nothing*. It is clear that the playwright, in crafting his play, was inspired by Bandello's story, but not surprisingly, he expanded his own story into something more complex and nuanced. Though the playwright's young heroine in *Much Ado*, Hero, is comparable to Bandello's Fenicia, and young Claudio in *Much Ado* comparable to Timbreo, the playwright added elements to his story not found in Bandello, such as the ever-amusing love war of the feisty pair Beatrice and Benedick, and the comic speeches of Messina's bumbling constables.

The fathers of the wronged Fenicia, and the wronged Hero, also have similar names — Lionato and Leonato — though they lead quite different lives. Bandello's Lionato is an impoverished nobleman, while the Leonato of *Much Ado*, far from being impecunious, is the important Governor of Messina.

~

For much of history, most of the island of Sicily has been involved in extensive agriculture and fishery, with its capital at Palermo. The Arabs, who arrived in the ninth century, had brought with them superior irrigation techniques and introduced many new crops to the island — plants now closely associated with Sicily, such as date palms, melons, oranges, lemons, sugarcane, and even rice — all of which thrived in the island's rich soil.

The economy of Messina, unlike the rest of the island, however, focused almost entirely on maritime commerce and naval activities. For this reason, Messina was separately governed for the Spanish kings[2] by a different kind of nobleman than those appointed elsewhere on the island. The "Governor of Messina" was (at least) supposed to have experience in administrative and financial affairs. In *Much Ado*, its Governor holds the office in the last half of the sixteenth century, three hundred years after the Governor in *Timbreo and Fenicia* held that same post.

~

The opening scene of *Much Ado* is set where most editors have set it, that is, in Messina, in front of the Governor's palace. No such palace exists today, but if it did, it would have been the "Royal Palace," which did exist. That Royal Palace faced onto the square still called "Piazza del Governolo," at the confluence of the Corso Garibaldi and Viale della Libertà, and overlooked the entrance to the harbor and the Lanterna, the ancient lighthouse there. Today, the *Prefettura*[3] of the District of Messina occupies the spot where the Royal Palace once stood.

Unlike the playwright's other settings in Italy, where many of the buildings and places can still be found, Messina today has few traces of the city as it was in the playwright's day. Over the years, Messina has been subjected to several severe earthquakes, and in 1908 one of them almost completely destroyed the entire city. That earthquake, one of the most astounding earthquakes in recorded human history, shook the city into a pile of rubble twenty feet deep. The disaster, compounded by fire, brought swift death to 84,000 people. Only the Cathedral and a few other landmarks remained, all of them heavily damaged. Restoration — what could be done — was almost hopeless, and Messina to this day has never really recovered from the shattering event.

Thus, although nearly all of the places alluded to in the playwright's *Much Ado About Nothing* no longer exist, for the purpose of the present chapter their actual sixteenth-century locations, nonetheless, have been fully verified.[4]

While the "unidentified background event" in Bandello's tale (the Sicilian Vespers) took place in 1282 in Messina the similarly "unidentified background event" for *Much Ado* took place in 1573 — in Tunis. (It will be described in detail in Part 2 of this chapter.) When the latter event drew to a close, the participants in it in the play made their way to Messina.

Neither Bandello, nor the playwright, would need to detail what we would call the "back story" of their tales, because their audiences would already know, or have heard, what happened. For modern audiences, however, the back story of *Much Ado* is somewhat murky, and one of the reasons the play's meaning is poorly understood.

Italians today are still aware of the historical Sicilian Vespers; but for the Elizabethan English, the events behind *Much Ado* — and their potential consequences — were of immediate concern. As noted in the examination of *The Merchant of Venice* (Chapters 5 and 6), 1573 was a defining year for the English. In that year, the English renewed their mercantile ventures in the Mediterranean, with far-reaching repercussions. The moment that Act I Scene 1 of this play begins, when the playwright makes an oblique reference to "this action," he has prompted his audience to keep those interests firmly in mind.

~

In that Scene 1, the individuals on stage are Governor Leonato; his daughter, Hero; his niece, Beatrice; and a man simply called "Messenger." Leonato is holding a piece of paper, and this is what is said:

Leonato: I learn in this letter that Don Pedro of Aragon[5] comes this night to Messina.

Messenger: He is very near by this, he was not three leagues off when I left him.

Leonato: How many gentleman have you lost in this action?

Messenger: But few of any sort and none of name.

These lines — generally overlooked — are not spoken without purpose. What the audience understands by them — albeit a little vaguely — is that some sort of battle or war[6] has taken place somewhere, but that Leonato and Messenger are not too concerned about it. A modern paraphrase of Messenger's remark about losses might sound something like: "Hardly anyone of whatever rank, and no one worth mentioning." But by now we should be familiar with the playwright's methods: we should pay more, not less, attention to the Governor's words, for indeed, he is telling us something important.

Leonato's almost offhand reference to "this action," downplayed as he remarks on Don Pedro's pending arrival and inquires about the casualties, is, in fact the back story of this play. Moreover, the play's subsequent outcome largely explains the behavior of a person — seemingly a minor character — who will be entering the stage momentarily with his brother, Don Pedro. This is the man called "John the Bastard."

~

The next conversation in this opening scene takes place between Messenger and Hero's cousin, the sassy Beatrice. We learn about some of the men who are "of name," all of whom are safe and sound, and who will soon arrive as part of Don Pedro's entourage. One of them is Claudio, a young Florentine count upon whom — pointedly mentioned — Don Pedro has bestowed "much honor," and who is destined to become Hero's betrothed. Another young gentleman is Benedick, a noble from Padua. We can conclude that these two young men are representative of the young nobles of that age, who left home to seek glory in a foreign war.[7] Also present is a commoner named Balthasar, a professional singer, who provides Don Pedro's entertainment.

~

Throughout *Much Ado*, as in his other Italian Plays, the author has woven elements into his story which demonstrate firsthand knowledge of places, things and comportment unique to Italy.

For example: "pleached alley."[8] The playwright has sprinkled this unusual garden feature all over his play, referring to it many times, as though it had been something in Messina that had especially caught his fancy. Indeed, the author uses a pleached alley more than once to further his storyline in *Much Ado*.

In Act I Scene 2, Leonato's brother Antonio, reveals to Leonato the young Count Claudio's love — and pursuit plans — for Hero. In Antonio's description, he mentions the "thick-pleached alley in mine orchard," where he overheard Don Pedro and Claudio — who were unseen inside it — discussing this personal matter. Later, in Act II Scene 3, the playwright again refers to this dense arbor, when Benedick says, "I will hide me in the arbour," which he does to eavesdrop on the deliberately staged conversation just outside it among Don Pedro, Leonato, and Claudio — a prearranged conversation where Benedick is supposed to "overhear" about Beatrice's love for him.

Again in Act III Scene 1, Beatrice is tricked to hide in a pleached alley to eavesdrop on a different invented conversation, this time between Hero and Ursula (affectionately called "Ursley"). As Hero says to Margaret:

> … And bid her [Beatrice] steal into the pleached bower
> Where honeysuckles, ripen'd by the sun,
> Forbid the sun to enter …

The women stroll outside the arbor conversing loudly, while Beatrice is unseen inside and "by chance overhears" their gossip about Benedick's love for her. Hero also calls it "this alley," and Ursula refers to it as "the woodbine coverture."

Pleached alley.
Seen today at the University of Messina. (Author's photo)

In *Much Ado*, the author has brought this leafy outdoor feature — indeed it is impressive and he certainly has his fun using it — to our attention no fewer than *five* times: "the thick-pleached alley" in Act I; "the arbour" in Act II; and then three more references to it in Act III: "pleached bower"; "this alley"; and "woodbine coverture."

Both on the Continent and in England, gardens commonly included arbors — and still do — on which roses, honeysuckle (or woodbine), or other attractive vines climb. Climbing vines afford beauty, fragrance, and a mottled shade — all very desirable on a summer's day. In Messina, where the summer sun can be brutal, such arbors are a dark and cool refuge. In Messina, vines were "pleached," that is, woven together in such a dense manner to "forbid the sun to enter," as Hero says.

Not only were pleached arbors made of vines, but often of trees, too. The trees were planted in two rows, with a walkway in between, and their branches were bent and intertwined overhead again and again to make a dense construction looking like a large green tunnel.

Such thick-pleached alleys, an example of which is pictured above at the University of Messina, are striking. As Father Santino Buontempo, Director of its Central Library, said to me, "I love them, the coolest possible places in the summer, but there are not too many of them left in Messina anymore."

In some of the conversations in *Much Ado*, especially those of Hero, Margaret, and Ursula, the author simulates a singularly Italian style of master-servant interaction. Such easy banter as we witness among these three females would, in Elizabethan England, never have been tolerated. Margaret and Ursula would have been considered impertinent. The easy relation between classes observed in Italy was comportment unusual for travelers from the north, where class relations were far more formal.

Who are Margaret and Ursula? Designated as "gentlewomen" in the Quarto edition — though not so in the First Folio — a theatre director would understand they be cast and costumed as serving women; but women both of good family and decent upbringing. It would be made quite evident, however, that they were *not* the same social class as Hero, their mistress.

In Act II Scene 1, first Margaret has a conversation with Balthasar, the singer, which implies social equality. Then a little later Ursula has a brief, rather impudent chat with Hero's Uncle Antonio, an important noble. Her comportment, too, implies social equality. Who is whose "equal?"

The two women also appear in Act III Scene 1, in Leonato's orchard, and though Margaret exits the scene early on, Ursula chats at length with Hero around the "pleached bower." In that scene, both attendants converse in a surprisingly frank way with a governor's daughter, but Hero doesn't seem to mind at all. In fact, it seems quite natural to her.

Then there is the dialogue in Act III Scene 4, a scene that takes place in the private apartment of Hero. Hero, with Margaret and Ursula's assistance, is dressing for her wedding. Listen to their conversation:

Hero: Good Ursula, wake my cousin Beatrice,
          And desire her to rise.

Ursula: I will, lady.

Hero: And bid her come hither.

Ursula: Well. [*Exit*]

Margaret: Troth, I think your other rebato were better.

Hero: No, pray thee, good Meg, I'll wear this.

Margaret: By my troth, 's not so good; and I warrant your cousin will say so.

Hero: My cousin's a fool, and thou are another; I'll wear none but this.

Margaret: I like the new tire within excellently, if the hair were a thought browner; and your gown's a most rare fashion, i'faith. I saw the Duchess of Milan's gown that they praise so.

Hero: O, that exceeds, they say …

What kind of behavior is this? Isn't Margaret a little cheeky?

Of the demeanor and remarks of Margaret and Ursula, Charles Cowden Clarke (1787–1877), a prominent Shakespeare scholar and author of *Shakespeare's Contrasted Characters, Chiefly Those Subordinate*, and other works — which include his own edition of the plays — had this to say:

> These two [Margaret and Ursula] may come under the denomination of "pattern waiting women," — that is, the patterns [of behavior] somewhat surpassing the order of the women. Margaret has, perhaps, too accomplished a tongue for one of her class; she, however, evidently apes the manner of Beatrice, and like all imitators of inferior mind, with a coarse and exaggerated character. She forms an excellent foil to her mistress from this very circumstance; and both domestics are samples of that *menial equality that exists between mistress and dependent still common in Italy*.   (Emphasis mine)

Margaret and Ursula's interaction with Hero is the kind of comportment between master and attendant that would surprise a class-conscious Englishman visiting in Italy, as it did Charles Clarke in the late nineteenth century. A playwright, on the other hand, might view such unusual local manners with interest and, in fact, even make a few mental notes. Incorporating such singular Italian behavior in his story would lend yet more credence to a play set in Italy.

*A*nother item of dress in this same Scene 4 of Act III is described by Hero when she says: "These gloves that Count sent me, they are an excellent perfume." There is only one other reference to perfumed gloves in Shakespeare. It is in *The Winter's Tale*, Act IV Scene 4. It is the scene set in front of the Shepherd's cottage in Bohemia, and where that peddler, pickpocket, and rogue Autolycus enters—after the first two hundred twenty lines or so—singing of his merchandise for sale, including "Gloves as sweet as damask-roses." At the end of his song, Clown, old Shepherd's son, decides to buy a pair for his love, Mopsy, who calls them "sweet gloves."

In 1576, Edward de Vere, the Earl of Oxford, returned to England after a lengthy visit in Italy. At the time, it was much noted that one of his gifts for his young queen, Elizabeth I (1558–1603), was a pair of perfumed gloves. It was a rare gift, yet elegant enough for the most important lady in the land. At that period in England, perfumed gloves were a singular novelty.

Then, as today, people loved fashion, and among the privileged wealthy, word of this enviable, elegant gift would have spread, and the desire to own such a pair of perfumed gloves like the queen's would have mushroomed.

I see something wrong with dating here. According to scholars of Shakespeare, *Much Ado* was not written before 1598, which is twenty-two years after Elizabeth I would have been given her perfumed gloves from Italy. By 1598, however, possessing such gloves was commonplace, as demonstrated in *The Winter's Tale*. The juxtaposition of these two, and very different, allusions to perfumed gloves, with the Queen's gloves thrown into the equation, suggests that *Much Ado* was written nearer to 1576, perhaps 1578, at a time when perfumed gloves were still a happily received "luxury item" and would still have been a gift worthy of the noble Hero. By 1598, however, such perfumed gloves were commonplace, and even a shepherd clown could afford to purchase a pair from a roving peddler.

Near the end of Act III Scene 3, the drunkard Borachio,[9] says Hero's wedding will take place, according to the spelling of modern editions, "next morning at the temple."

In the First Folio, and in the Quarto, however, Borachio's "temple" is capitalized; it is spelled "Temple." In some of the other Italian Plays in the First Folio and the Quarto, the word is sometimes capitalized, and sometimes not. We have addressed the playwright's use of spelling elsewhere in this study and have seen that it requires a specific knowledge of Italian cities to realize the importance his spelling makes.

For example, when a word such as "temple" is used as a synonym for "church" or "chapel," the word has not been capitalized, neither in the First Folio, nor the Quarto, and should not be today.[10] But when the word refers to a specific building, such as the Temple in Messina, it is a proper noun, and its capital "T," as originally written, should be retained.

This difference between "t" and "T" according to context is particularly significant in *Much Ado*. In Messina, there was an ancient — and throughout many succeeding centuries — important place of worship. It was built in Doric style by the Greeks in 98 B.C., if not earlier. Intended for the worship of Hercules, it was so perfectly executed that it became famous throughout the known world. Called the "Temple of Hercules Manticles" (Tempio di Ercole Manticolo), when the Roman author Marcus Tullius later wrote of its virtues, ancient visitors came from as far away as Britain, Flanders, France, and Germany to admire it.

When the first Christians took possession of the Temple of Hercules Manticles, they dedicated it to Saint Michael and designated it as a parish church. Some centuries later, when Florentine bankers and merchants came to do business in Messina, they settled in the precincts of that Saint Michael's parish, located in what was then the northernmost sector of the city. To appeal to these important Florentines, and garner their wealthy support, the Church complimented them by renaming the parish church in honor of their own favorite saint, John the Baptist.[11] Services were conducted in Florentine Italian, rather than the Italian of Messina.

The building's renown continued to expand. In 1572, Prince Marco Antonio Colonna, distinguished commander of the Papal forces at the Battle of Lepanto, was appointed Viceroy of Sicily. Because of the Temple's great beauty, the Prince publicly declared that the Temple/Church of St. John the Baptist in Messina, though admittedly not as large, was comparable to the Pantheon of Rome. The pronouncement of the Viceroy was noted far and wide.

In 1580, again in deference to the Florentines, the parish church of St. John the Baptist was elevated in importance from a parish church to a full-fledged Florentine — as distinguished from Messinan — church. It was officially renamed "Il Tempio di San Giovanni Battista detto di Fiorentini." The meaning of this is not easily translated into English, but would be something like "The Temple (Church) of Saint John the Baptist so-called of the Florentines."

For the intended marriage between the noble Hero and Claudio — a *Florentine* count — it is singularly noteworthy that the playwright selected Messina's most appropriate church for their union ceremony.

But no matter to whom the building belonged, throughout its entire pagan and Christian history Messinans have referred to it simply as il Tempio, the Temple. In spite of all successive name changes over the centuries, the word of its original name was retained. It was a designation that continued throughout the Christian era as well, when, in fact, the name it had been originally given, Tempio di Ercole Manticolo, lived on. No other church in Messina has had the word Tempio — Temple — as part of its name.

~

Act IV Scene 1 opens inside that very Temple. The most important members of the cast are assembled for the marriage of Count Claudio and Hero, with Friar Francis officiating. When the friar asks the traditional question, whether either of the pair knows of "any inward impediment why [they] should not be conjoined," Claudio bursts out with his litany of insults aimed at Hero, and her alleged lack of virtue, "… she knows the heat of a luxurious bed," he exclaims, for all to hear. Claudio has been completely taken in by the counterfeit tryst planned by Don John, earlier in Act III Scene 2, which was staged on the night before this wedding. Unfortunately, even tragically, Leonato believes Claudio's terrible accusations.

Stunned by this rain of falsehoods, Hero collapses and appears to have dropped dead. In a huff, Claudio, Don Pedro, and Don John stomp out of the Temple, leaving Hero and her family, along with Friar Francis and Benedick, to regroup. Hero is then revived, and a plan of recoupment is arranged at the recommendation of Friar Francis, who is certain of Hero's innocence.

The calming friar says, in part, to Leonato:

> Pause awhile,
> And let my counsel sway you in this case.
> Your daughter here the princes left for dead,
> Let her awhile be secretly kept in,
> And publish it that she is dead indeed;
> Maintain a mourning ostentation
> *And on your family's old monument*
> *Hang mournful epitaphs,* and do all rites
> That appertain unto a burial.   (Emphasis mine)

This is to be done, as the friar next counsels, to convert Claudio's anger toward Hero into remorse.

Traditional rites of Hero's passage to the next world would include posting notice of the funeral mass at the church, the mass itself, the procession to the burial place, and the ceremony of interment, a process as well known to the English by their prayer books as was known to the Messinans by theirs. Since Hero is the daughter of the Governor of Messina who had died under unusual circumstances, her death, and the formalities surrounding it, would be widely known. But the playwright gives us more when he writes "your family's old monument."

~

"Your family's old monument …" What could this be? It must be something Friar Francis knows about—possibly all Messinans know about. The friar may even have seen this "old monument" himself, so it must be somewhere in Messina. What is Friar Francis talking about here?

In both England and parts of Italy, a notable person might have a special monument or tomb in a churchyard, or even inside a church,[12] but generally they would be buried in a single grave. In Italy, the tradition was the family tomb or monument, where all family members would eventually find their eternal rest together. A single grave, with headstone, was not customary.

Of course, graves and tombs everywhere are most often located in sanctified places, but in Messina, they were built at one single place: an enormous burial place that throughout history has been especially noteworthy. This is the immense walled enclosure called the *Cimiterio Monumentale*, the Monumental (or Great) Cemetery, located just outside the southwestern boundary of the old city, on the slopes above ancient Via Catania.

The Cimiterio Monumentale was, and still is, so extraordinary, that a visit to Messina today is not complete without spending a little time there. The *Blue Guide* for Sicily, for example, describes the Cimiterio as "a luxuriant garden built in terraces on the slopes of the hill, commanding a lovely view of Calabria." It is filled with row upon row of impressive and old family monuments.

Little damage to the Cimiterio was done in the colossal earthquake of 1908, save for its now restored "Pantheon"; and almost all of the family tombs there have remained intact. Over the centuries, it has grown larger, coming to embrace not only thousands of victims of the 1908 disaster, but graves transferred from the former British cemetery nearby, which had been established during the Napoleonic wars. The transfer took place, ironically, in 1940, just after World War II had begun.

This ancient and unusual cemetery is neither named for any saint, nor is it exclusive to any religious doctrine. As its name implies, the Cimiterio Monumentale is entirely ecumenical, and has been a vital part of Messinan life — and death — throughout the ages.

Just outside the gates of the Cimiterio are a variety of vendors hawking flowers, religious articles, food, drink, and other necessities for a visit to family inside. Even on an ordinary weekday, there is much coming and going, not just by one or two come to honor their dead, but entire families who've made the journey to pass part of their day at the family's collective final home. The Cimiterio is virtually the Messina common, and the family tomb there is the essential place to post epitaphs, tributes, and poems to the deceased, not only in their memory, but also because it is the place where most Messinans can be expected to see them. Thus, in accordance with ancient custom, the playwright has Friar Francis advise Leonato, "And on your family's old monument / Hang mournful epitaphs." All of Messina will know of Hero's death.

⁓

At the close of this sorry Scene 1 of Act IV, after Friar Francis, and the horrified attendees have left the Temple, Benedick and a distraught Beatrice remain together on stage. The lovers share an important, almost hurried, conversation. Trying to soothe his weeping sweetheart, Benedick implores her: "Come, bid me do any thing for thee." Beatrice responds without hesitation: "Kill Claudio."

In neither the Quarto, nor the First Folio, is there an exclamation point after these two startling words. Most modern editions have adhered to this punctuation, but occasionally an editor, unaware of the "tradition" of blood vengeance in Messina, embellishes Beatrice's words with an exclamation point. The playwright appears to have been aware of this cultural phenomenon, perhaps even personally overhearing such a shocking order expressed in such a businesslike way. To be taken seriously, such a nefarious deed — basically an execution — would be neither spoken loudly nor with any kind of emotion. This type of murder — eliminating another human being — was to be taken care of as swiftly as possible, and without drama of any kind.

It is only a little later, when Benedick has responded, "Ha! Not for the wide world," that Beatrice's rage boils over. She cries out:

> … O that I were a man! …
> O God, that I were a man!
> *I would eat his heart in the market place!*   (Emphasis mine)

When I read these lines to a native Messinan, he explained that such an utterance was a variation on the most dire of Messinan expressions:

> "No, not an expression, more like a threat — an event that is bound to happen. It wouldn't need to be done 'in the marketplace,' but it would not be done in secret, either. This is how it is said in our dialect: *'Ti manciu 'u cori*: I will eat your heart.'"

PART 2

Toward the beginning of Act I Scene 1 of *Much Ado*, in *the playwright's stage direction* for the order of entry onstage of the returning warriors, something odd would have been noticed by sixteenth-century *readers* of the play (though not by an audience, who would not hear any of those stage directions). In both the First Folio and the Quarto, this stage direction presents the entering company in an order which is somewhat disturbing: Don Pedro first, then Claudio, Benedick, and Balthasar; and *lastly*, "John *the Bastard*." (Emphasis mine) It is the *playwright himself* who has ranked "John the Bastard" last — and without any title. In the *Dramatis Personae*, "John the Bastard" has also been listed *after*, meaning *beneath*, the commoner Balthasar. Who is this person? We only know, at this point in the story, that John is a bastard (meaning born out of wedlock).

Elizabethans, either upon reading the play, or attending a performance, would have sensed early on who this John the Bastard, in the real world, is meant to be. They would assume, correctly, that here was a personification of the historical Don John of Austria (1547–1578). Knowing this, the events and people portrayed in *Much Ado About Nothing* begin to come into focus, suggesting a much larger dimension to the story that otherwise is not revealed through the characters' spoken words.

The deprecation of Don John originates in the Quarto, is repeated in the First Folio, persists in one form or another throughout the entire play in both these editions,[13] and is faithfully repeated in subsequent editions of the play even today. It would be difficult in the sixteenth century to contrive a more thorough debasement and personal insult of any individual, much less a person of royal blood, especially when repeated again and again, as it is in the stage directions of *Much Ado*.

For anyone so widely admired on the Continent — as well as by many in England — these affronts toward Don John of Austria would be astonishing, notwithstanding the unfortunate sixteenth-century notion that bastards were synonymous with evil. Apart from the stage directions regarding the order of scene entry, there are only two verbal insults for him in the play's text itself. They occur late in the play, when Benedick, furious with Don John for the harm he has caused Hero in Act IV Scene 1, refers to him as "John the Bastard." And in Act V Scene 1, again it is Benedick, speaking to Don Pedro, who refers to John as "your brother the bastard."

There are other slights to Don John in *Much Ado*, but they are indirect. For example, at the very beginning of the play, in Act I Scene 1, following his entry onstage with the others, John is not included in the conversation. And when Don Pedro announces "Signior Claudio and Signior Benedick, my dear friend Leonato hath invited you all," he includes Don John in no such nicety. It is Leonato who attempts a tardy effort to mend this violation of protocol — and simple courtesy — by turning to John and saying, "Let me bid you welcome, my Lord, *being reconciled*[14] *to the Prince your brother*: I owe you all duty." (Emphasis mine) Only in these lines given to Leonato is John's presence acknowledged.

If John hadn't already come to despise all these people for their constant snubs beforehand, at this point in the play he couldn't be blamed for detesting them now. And if Elizabethan readers and viewers of *Much Ado* hadn't already figured out who this "Don Pedro" represents, they would — or should — have deduced it from the words spoken by Leonato: Don Pedro is a thinly disguised personification of Philip II, King of Spain — half-brother of Don John of Austria.

~

Don John of Austria was the illegitimate son of Holy Roman Emperor Charles V (1500–1558), also King of Spain (from 1519 until 1556). Charles, "every inch an emperor" and "a model of continence, temperance and moderation," who had "tenderly loved his wife,"[15] fathered John well after his wife's death. The Emperor had difficulty recognizing the boy as his child, but made sure John was well cared for. John was brought to Spain when quite small, and Charles had him looked after and educated by guardians who did not know who he was.

But as the Emperor aged, he put his affairs — both state and personal — in order. Two years before his death, he handed his Spanish crown and its world-wide domains — which, not incidentally, included the Lowlands — to his only legitimate son, Philip, who, as Philip II,

Don John of Austria (left), Supreme Commander of the fleet of the Holy League at the Battle of Lepanto 7 October 1571. With Don John are two of his lieutenants, Marco Antonio Colonna, Viceroy of Sicily (center), and Doge Sebastiano Veniero of Venice (right). The third lieutenant, Gian Andrea Doria, Commander of the Genoa squadron, because of his unseemly conduct at the battle was not included in this painting. Artist unknown.

reigned over Spain and his Spanish empire, until his own death in 1598. Charles V also publicly recognized John as a member of the royal family, ordering that henceforth, John be known as "John of Austria."

A mature John, while living in Spain at the court of his half-brother, was increasingly admired for his outstanding military and naval successes on behalf of Philip. But this was just the beginning. On 7 October 1571, John became world-famous. On that date, Don John, now twenty-four and Supreme Commander of the entire fleet known as "the Holy League," became heralded as the victor of the Battle of Lepanto,[16] and the savior of Christendom from the supremmacy of the Turks. John's command consisted of the combined squadrons of Spain, the Papacy, Venice, and Genoa. The battle was waged against the Turks, under the command of Ali Pasha.

The Battle of Lepanto is considered one of the most famous naval triumphs in all of history, and the last great battle in which both sides used vessels propelled by oars. The Turks were completely routed, losing their entire fleet with 25,000 of their soldiers killed, while the Holy League lost fewer than 8,000 men. Naval historians have ranked the Battle of Lepanto alongside Octavian's victory over Mark

Antony at nearby Actium in 31 B.C., and Horatio Nelson's victory over the French off Cape Trafalgar in 1805.

Less than twelve months after Don John's success, the grateful citizens of Messina, where the forces of the League had assembled before the battle, commissioned a bronze statue in his honor. The statue, with Don John holding the triple truncheon of the Holy League, stands in the piazza facing the now-restored twelfth-century church of Santa Maria Annunciata. Even now, Don John of Austria is remembered as a hero, and his handsome statue, though its gilding has disappeared, can still be admired in Messina today.[17]

Gregory XIII, who became Pope in 1572, eight months after Lepanto, spoke of John in this unrestrained accolade:

> That young chief has proved himself a Scipio in valor, a Pompey in heroic grace, an Augustus in good fortune, a new Moses, a new Gideon, a Samson, a new Saul, a new David, without any of the faults of these famous men; and I hope to God to live long enough to reward him with a royal crown.[18]

Many shared this hope. But even long before Lepanto, Don John was ambitious, dreaming of a throne of his own. It was a dream that became an obsession.

❧

Prior to the great battle of Lepanto, the military prowess of Don John had come to the attention of Rome — and of London, too. Early in 1570, Pope Pius V (1566–1572), Gregory's predecessor, developed the idea for an invasion of England. It was to be led by Don John, with his half-brother, Philip II's support. The plan was to rescue Mary Queen of Scots, Elizabeth I's prisoner, the notion being that John would then become

Don John of Austria, victor of the Battle of Lepanto (1571). This statue, once gilded, by Andrea Calamech of Carrara, was erected in Messina in 1572 by its grateful citizens. An exact copy was erected in Regensburg (Ratisbon) in Bavaria between the house of Don John's father, Emperor Charles V, and the house of Don John's mother, Barbara Blomberg. (Photo courtesy of Sylvia Holmes)

King of England and make Mary his queen. In February of that year, Pius excommunicated Elizabeth I and purported to depose her, two actions obviously intended to set this scheme in motion. Philip II opposed the whole idea, and John's hopes for a crown of his own were dashed.

A similar plan called "the Ridolfi Plot" was also advanced in 1571. That scheme was concocted just after Lepanto, but by then, John already had a new plan in mind.

The decimation of the Turkish fleet at Lepanto did not signal the end of Turkish ambitions. Replacement of the destroyed Turkish military vessels was promptly undertaken, and by the spring of 1572, the Grand Vizier could boast 150 galleys and eight galleasses, ready for battle. The Holy League's plan for this resurgence was simple: destroy the rebuilt Turkish fleet. The newly constructed warships, anchored at Nauplia, on the eastern side of the Peleponnesus, gave John the idea of carving out a kingdom of some sort for himself in Greece.

The Holy League was misnamed: though it was a league, it was never holy. Its members were self-centered and bickering, and Philip II constantly equivocated. Finally, regarding this new plan against the Turks in Greece, Philip made a decision: he withdrew from the Holy League. Philip claimed he had no interest in profiting Venice at the expense of Spain. With this, Don John's dream of a kingdom in Greece evaporated.

Though now truly bitterly disappointed, yet another possibility for a kingdom for Don John appeared. This time, concerned that the expansion of Turkish power westward in the Mediterranean would eventually connect with the large population of disgruntled Moriscos residing in Spain, Philip ordered John to set about assembling a Spanish invasion force to conquer Tunis. The assembly point for the Spanish force was not Messina, however; it was to be closer to North Africa, on Sicily's southern shore, ninety miles across the sea from the target.

John's orders were to destroy Tunis completely. In Philip's view, only total destruction of the city would deny the Turks a base from which to operate. Don John set to work. Some thought his assemblage of vessels on Sicily's southern shore was astonishing, especially given that Spain already had possession of Goletta, the port for Tunis; but

John gathered together 104 galleys, 44 large ships, 12 barges, 23 frigates, and 12 feluccas, creating a fleet about the size of the enormous combined fleet of the former Holy League. In addition to the mariners, there were to be some 20,000 infantry. It was an enormous show of force. On 7 October 1573, John set out on his mission. It was an especially auspicious date for him: the second anniversary of the Battle of Lepanto.

On the evening of October eighth, Don John's force landed at Goletta, and two days later, Tunis capitulated. This was the result of the bloodless "action" that Leonato asks about at the opening of *Much Ado About Nothing*.

Philip II knew what John had in mind. Not only had John landed an unnecessarily powerful force in Tunis, he proceeded to disobey Philip's order to raze the city to the ground. Although John had promised Philip that he would do as commanded, instead he proceeded to strengthen Tunis's fortresses and bastions.

In the play, there is no mention of any of this, but the frostiness between Don Pedro and Don John, from the outset of *Much Ado*, demonstrates there's a serious problem between these two brothers; and Leonato's remark about John "being reconciled to the Prince" is pure presumption.

In point of fact, there was an ongoing exchange of letters between Don John in Italy and "the Prince" (Philip II) in Spain (never actually in Messina). The correspondence reveals the serious disagreement between the siblings on strategy: John insisting Tunis be a permanent military and naval barrier to Turkish expansion; Philip replying that the destruction of Tunis would deny the Turks an essential springboard at much less cost, and so on. John sought unsuccessfully to persuade his half-brother to his point of view; they reached an impasse.

Pope Gregory shared John's opinion that a permanent barrier to Muslim expansion in Tunis was a good idea. Trusting to John's proven prowess, he sent a memorandum to the papal nuncio in Spain, which was finally delivered to Philip in January 1574. In it, the Pope suggested that the monarch reconsider the razing and abandonment of Tunis. Concerning John, he wrote:

It might be well to consider whether it would not add to his power and authority were he invested with the title of King of Tunis, so that Your Majesty might evince your gratitude to God for the conquest, after the manner of your ancestors, by founding a new Christian realm.[19]

The Pope's advice was not well received. Instead, Philip assured him that he need not concern himself that Don John's services would go unrewarded. He added that the Pope's proposed reward of a kingdom for Don John was not good enough; and besides, Philip asserted, even if it were, he didn't have the power to grant it.

It was only a matter of time. The Turks attacked again, capturing the neglected Goletta. Finally, on 13 September 1574, all of Tunis fell into their hands. What had appeared to be John's final opportunity for a crown of his own—a crown which, ultimately, would have dovetailed with Spain's aspirations—was irrevocably lost. Now, as before, his imperious, though evasive, half-brother Philip had destroyed his fondest hope.

*T*he play describes a Don John who is profoundly bitter. His entire effort, not only in Tunis, but as historians acknowledge, at Lepanto as well, turned out to be *much ado about nothing.* John understands that despite his having the world at his feet, he will always be Philip's prisoner dressed in silk. Accordingly, Scene 3 of Act I begins with a conversation between Don John and Conrade, his companion. It is an eloquent depiction of John's confrontation with his fate. Despite the Elizabethan acquaintance with Don John's ambition, this is a conversation that has been consistently misconstrued throughout history; a consequence of not having thoughtfully considered the personal history of Don John of Austria and his private ongoing battle between institutions and personal ambition.

Conrade opens the conversation with a question, and his query to Don John might be the single most important question in the play. Conrade asks John: "What the Goodyear, my Lord, why are you thus *out of measure* sad?" (Emphasis mine) John's answer emphasizes the singularity of this sadness. He responds: "There is no measure in the *occasion*[20] that breeds, therefore the sadness is without limit." (Emphasis mine)

In history, the profitless consequences that followed the "action" were not only due to Philip's waffling decision, but to his jealousy toward the mature and highly acclaimed John. And John, helpless against his brother, is deeply embittered, as he says in Act I Scene 3:

> ... I cannot hide what I am.[21] I must be sad when I have cause, and smile at no man's jest, eat when I have stomach, and wait for no man's leisure; sleep when I am drowsy, and tend on no man's business; laugh when I am merry, and claw no man in his humour.
>
> ...
>
> I had rather be a canker[22] in a hedge than a rose in his grace, and it better fits my blood to be disdained of all than to fashion a carriage to rob love from any.
>
> ...
>
> I am a plain-dealing villain. I am trusted with a muzzle and enfranchised with a clog; therefore I have decreed not to sing in my cage. If I had my mouth I would bite; if I had my liberty I would do my liking.

Throughout his entire adult life, Don John was Philip's glorified prisoner. He could do nothing without Philip's financial and military support. Even before the Turkish conquest, Don John thought he had earned — had even somehow been promised — a kingdom of his own. He slowly came to the painful realization it was all a hopeless dream.

Unless the audience knows the back story of *Much Ado*, it is difficult to comprehend this character, John the Bastard, and the great emotion he expresses in his deeply poignant speech. The historical sources of John's anger are never mentioned, and never taken properly into account. Instead, John's hostile behavior is explained by his illegitimacy; that he's angry because he's a bastard. It is wrongly concluded that such behavior in the play was a *lifetime* situation for John, rather than one produced only in his maturity by Philip's denial of a kingdom — first in Greece, then in Tunis. Here are some academic views:

From *The Riverside Shakespeare*:

> The fact that Don John was born a bastard becomes an all-sufficient explanation of why it is he is treacherous, scheming, savage, and morose. A thing of darkness, out of step with his

society, he hates the children of light simply because they generate radiance in a world that he prefers to see dark.

Another example, *The Arden Shakespeare* 1981 edition of *Much Ado*, has this to say:

> Don John's malevolence and unsociability, marked by images of sickness, festering poison, and incompatibility (the canker-rose, the thief of love, the muzzled dog, the caged bird) and by themes of resentment and moroseness, are defined by his being a bastard.

The history behind this play does not agree with the above-stated views; nor did the playwright. But why the playwright's repeated insults, his attacks on John's character?

∽

Despite Philip's expressed disinterest, Don John's role in a conquest of England in 1570 was not forgotten in that country, nor was the Ridolfi Plot, one year later. Moreover, for nearly two years after the Tunisian fiasco, Don John had little to do with his brother, other than see to some diplomatic tasks for him in northern Italy. But in February 1576, Philip's Governor General of the Low Countries suddenly died, and in April, Philip appointed Don John as his replacement. John was reluctant, protesting that the long efforts to suppress the Protestants there seemed a hopeless cause, but Philip sent him "pep letters," and made him more promises he would not keep.

John's obsession had never really died out, and his ambition blinded him to his sly brother's machinations once again. Soon, John suggested to Philip that the Spanish forces in the Low Countries should cross the English Channel and take England, thereby immediately depriving the rebellious Protestants in the Lowlands of Elizabeth's critical assistance.

Privately, Philip may not have agreed with this, but somehow John thought he did, and on 1 May 1576, John arrived in Brussels. England was enraged and alarmed. Her fleet was small, both in size and number of ships, while Spain's was large. The risks to England have been described as "infinitely greater"[23] than they would be twelve years later, when the Spanish Armada arrived. But the threat was real, and the time had come for the Queen to warn all Englishmen of the trouble brewing on the horizon. In 1576, she had two effective ways to do it: from the pulpit, and in the theatre.

In 1578, while campaigning for Philip in the Lowlands, Don John, aged thirty-one, died. His death was long and painful.

~

It has been asserted that *Much Ado About Nothing* was written in 1598. Why would a playwright wait until 1598 — twenty years after "John the Bastard" had died — and ten years after the defeat of the Spanish Armada — to write a play specifically designed to arouse the English against him in 1576? It makes no sense. Perhaps this dating should be revisited.

NOTES

1. Pedro III's kingdom of Aragon and Catalonia also included Valencia, Montpellier, and the Balearic Islands. His claim to the throne of Sicily was through his marriage to Constance, the last Hohenstaufen, daughter of Manfred, briefly a King of Sicily, and granddaughter of the celebrated Frederick II, both King of Sicily and a Holy Roman Emperor.

2. Throughout the Spanish reign, from 1282 until 1713, Messina enjoyed special privileges not available to the rest of Sicily due to its different — and lucrative — affairs.

3. Meaning the offices and official residence of the governor of a district.

4. Thanks to Father Santino Buontempo of the Faculty of Letters and Philosophy and Director of the Central Library of the University of Messina, and Doctor Francesca Campagna Cicala, Director of the Regional Museum of Messina.

5. "Don Pedro of Aragon" is a title that the playwright has contrived to amuse his English audience. "Don" is a broad Spanish address for someone of high honor or distinction, and "Pedro" could tend to evoke some memory, perhaps, of the medieval King Pedro, but it is a characterization of Philip II, ruler of vast regions of the world, and both feared and despised in England.

6. Later, in her first lines in this scene, Beatrice refers to "this action" as "the wars," but in light of what the action was, as discussed in Part 2, she is being sarcastic.

7. As remarked by Panthino in *The Two Gentlemen,* and in the behavior of Bertram and the other young nobles in *All's Well,* service in a foreign war was a frequent desire. *And,* when the young men returned home, they should have had some battle experience to better serve their overlord and advance their own ambitions.

8. Meaning entwined, entangled, or plaited.

9. It is interesting to note the playwright's choice of name for his character Borachio, the drunkard. In Spanish, the word for a drunkard is "un borracho."

10. In *The Merchant of Venice,* Act II Scene 1, "temple" is used generically, and has always been in lower case. In *The Winter's Tale* the word—though in plural—refers to specific temples, those of Apollo and Segesta, and it was capitalized. In *A Midsummer Night's Dream,* it is lower case only once, when it is used generically in Act II Scene 1, but when referring to a specific place that the playwright had in mind in Act IV Lines 180 and 197 and in Act IV Scene 2 Line 15, it is a proper noun, and thus is capitalized.

11. Thus, *Il Tempio di San Giovanni Battista detto di Fiorentini.* Although the name of the Florence cathedral is "Santa Maria del Fiore," its baptistry, "San Giovanni Battista," is considered by Florentines to be the place of their spiritual birth.

12. In Act V Scene 3, Claudio, Don Pedro, Balthasar, and others are at the monument. *The Riverside Shakespeare* puts the scene in "a churchyard"; the 1989 *Signet* edition in "a church." The 1981 *Arden* offers a perceptive footnote: "Conventionally, following [Alexander] Pope, a church, though [sometimes admittedly it] indicates a monument out of doors. Wherever situated, an impressive tomb ... is essential ..."

13. In the First Folio Act I, and at the same place in the Quarto, he is "John the Bastard," and then, "Sir John the Bastard"; in the First Folio Act II, and in the Quarto, the entry direction includes him, strangely, as "Balthasar, or dumbe John" (although he will speak), and then merely as "John"; in the First Folio Act II, he is again "John the Bastard"; and in the First Folio Act IV, he is simply "Bastard." Thus also in the Quarto.

14. "Reconciled," of course, means "restored to friendship or compatibility," which is exactly the opposite of Don Pedro's consistent treatment of his brother throughout the play.

15. *Encyclopedia Britannica,* 1962, v. 5, p. 264.

16. The battle is named for the harbor where Turkish fleets were then assembled, now called Navpaktos, on the Gulf of Patras, an arm of the Adriatic Sea. It actually took place a mile or two east of Cape Scropha, at the entrance to the Gulf. The combined Turkish fleet consisted of

273 galleys, and the Holy League fleet, commanded by Don John, consisted of 208 galleys, six galleasses, and twenty-four ships. In the single day of battle, the Turkish losses were 113 galleys sunk, 117 captured. The League losses were twelve galleys sunk and one captured. The battle lasted five hours. Twelve thousand Christian captives were rescued from slavery at the oars.

17. A second one stands in the Tendergasse at Regensburg, next to his birthplace.

18. Sir Charles Petrie, *Don John of Austria*, pp. 221–222.

19. Sir Charles Petrie, *Don John of Austria*, pp. 233–234.

20. Dictionaries define "occasion" as a particular event, hence the antithesis of a permanent situation, such as John's bastardy. The occasion here is the falling together of circumstances which have ruined his hope of becoming the king of Tunis.

21. This remark is interpreted as a reference to his bastardy, but he knows he is a proven, heroic conqueror, and a richly deserving one, and everybody else knows it, in spite his brother's elusiveness. He also knew that fawning courtiers at Philip II's court had "suggested" that he was already ungrateful to his king.

22. A wild rose, blooming unattended.

23. *Encyclopedia Britannica*, Eleventh Edition, v. 28, p. 293.

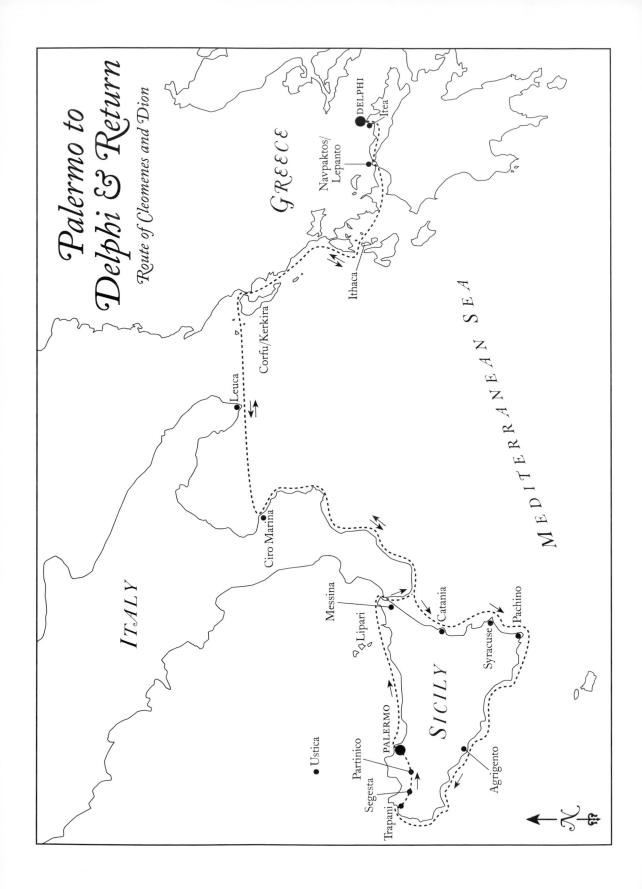

Palermo to
Delphi & Return

Route of Cleomenes and Dion

GREECE

DELPHI
Itea
Navpaktos/
Lepanto
Ithaca

Corfu/Kerkira

Leuca

Ciro Marina

ITALY

MEDITERRANEAN SEA

Messina
Lipari
Catania
Pachino
Syracuse

PALERMO
SICILY
Partinico
Segesta
Trapani
Ustica
Agrigento

N

The Winter's Tale
"A Cruel Notion Resolved"

*T*he *Winter's Tale* is a story of love turned to hate, of journeys afar, of pride and redemption. It is almost a tragedy, but with the use of anachronisms, the playwright gives us a joyous ending.

This play has the most widely diverse geographies of any of the Italian Plays. Some are in a medieval Sicily, just west of the toe of the Italian boot, and others are set in a medieval Bohemia, the once-great kingdom in Central Europe with its royal capital at Prague, a remnant of which is now part of the Czech Republic.

For the play, the two kingdoms — Sicily and Bohemia — are as they were in the thirteenth century. But the playwright weaves into his drama other events that occurred at other times, though he treats them as though happening in that same medieval period. In this, the author has also invoked historical figures of other eras, as though they were living during the play's ostensible time. *The Winter's Tale* is then, an inspired creative mix of events, periods, places, and people that coalesce into one final aspiration.

The first scene is laid in Sicily, somewhere in, or near, the palace of the play's fictional King Leontes. There are two important nobles on stage. One is a Bohemian royal attendant named Archidamus; the other is his Sicilian counterpart, called Camillo. Archidamus speaks:

> If you shall chance, Camillo, to visit Bohemia, on the like occasion where on my services are now on foot, you shall see, as I have said, great difference betwixt our Bohemia and your Sicilia.

This is a statement of both geographical and cultural fact. There were distinct differences between these two early kingdoms.

~

Sicily, the largest island of the Mediterranean Sea, is a land of sunshine, and at one time was also a land of abundance in great variety. Its history of civilization began with Greek colonization in about 750 B.C. Its topography, however, differs greatly from that of Bohemia. Most of Sicily's terrain is relatively easy to cross, while Bohemia has a series of steep and snowy mountain ranges and large rivers, most of which lacked bridges. Defined roads and highways in Bohemia were rare, while Sicily still retained most of its Roman roads and bridges. In fact, many Roman roads are still there, although now mostly concealed under modern tarmac.

Camillo responds to Archidamus' opening lines saying:

> I think, this coming summer, the King of Sicilia means to pay Bohemia the visitation which he justly owes him.

Here, "Bohemia" refers to the play's Polixenes, a fictional King of Bohemia, who is presently in Sicily visiting King Leontes, his close boyhood friend. Archidamus then tells Camillo of a specific concern he has about such a proposed visit:

Archidamus: Verily I speak it in the freedom of my knowledge: we cannot with such magnificence — in so rare — I know not what to say. We will give you sleepy drinks, that your senses, unintelligent of our insufficience, may, though they cannot praise us, as little accuse us.

Camillo: You pay a great deal too dear for what's given freely.

Archidamus: Believe me, I speak as my understanding instructs me, and as mine honesty puts it to utterance.

~

All but one of the scenes located in Sicily can be assumed to take place within, or near, its royal palace. Even in faraway England, some may have heard what a marvelous place this palace was. One or two at court may even have been there, but few could have imagined its splendor. Like all medieval kings, the kings of Sicily had dotted their kingdom with strategic garrison castles. But there was only one royal palace. It still stands in Palermo today. It is frequently called "the Norman Palace," or *Palazzo Normani*,[1] but is known more widely as the *Palazzo Reale*. A visit there today, to admire its magnificent chambers, especially its Royal Apartments and chapel, Capella Palatina, both substantially the same now as when completed in 1140, will reveal why they are rated among the grandest of their kind in all of Italy.

Sicily's medieval kings were the wealthiest of Europe's rulers, and Palermo was one of the largest and most important cities of the known world. It was a place of elaborate parks, fountains, nobles' palaces, and religious establishments, and its culture reflected successive centuries of Greek, Roman, Arabic, Norman, and Christian imprints. During much of the thirteenth century it was the cradle of Italian poetry, and a fountainhead of scientific learning.

~

Not only does the playwright avoid using proper names for Palermo and its Norman Palace, he also withholds the name of both Bohemia's capital, Prague, and that of its royal residence, then known as either "Prague Castle," or *Prazsky hrad*. What is now left of that thirteenth-century castle in Prague has become a part of a later and larger structure called the "Old Royal Palace," or *Stary Kralovsky Palac*.

In the thirteenth century, Prague Castle was, in fact, a great fortress of early Romanesque construction. It stood inside high and thick walls, which also enclosed the adjacent royal church, a pre-Romanesque rotunda. In his day, although Bohemia's important

Residence of the fictional King Leontes, the Palazzo Normani. The monumental building, known also as the Palazzo Reale, was the seat of the Norman and Swabian kings. Restored in the 16th century, it was subsequently used as the residence of viceroys and royalty of different European houses. Since 1947, it has been the seat of the Sicilian Regional Assembly. This photo shows the interior of the Palatine Chapel, richly decorated with mosaics and multicolored inlaid marble. [From Art and History of Sicily (English Edition), Casa Editrice Bonechi, p. 18]

thirteenth-century king, Premsyl Ottakar II (1230–1278),[2] was the wealthiest, and most admired monarch of Central Europe, he did nothing to relieve the castle's austerity. Instead, he concentrated on its fortifications, and the expansion of his city.

~

Near the close of Act I Scene 1, Camillo describes the background of this visit of Polixenes to see Leontes:

> Sicilia cannot show himself over-kind to Bohemia. They were trained together in their childhoods, and there rooted betwixt them then such an affection which cannot choose but branch now. Since their more mature dignities and royal necessities made separation of their society, their encounters, though not personal, hath been royally attorneyed with interchange of gifts, letters, loving embassies, that they have seemed to be together though absent; shook hands as over a vast; and embraced as it were, from the ends of opposed winds. The heavens continue their loves!

Camillo's appeal will not be heard.

~

In the next scene, Scene 2 of this first act, we witness the increasingly suspicious Leontes deciding aloud that Polixenes "hath touch'd his queen / Forbiddenly." He orders Camillo to poison Polixenes.

Instead, Camillo quietly informs Polixenes about this shocking turn of events, and an alarmed Polixenes responds, "My ships are ready, and / My people did expect my hence departure …" To escape Leontes' wrath when he discovers that Camillo has disclosed his nefarious plan to Polixenes, Camillo decides to flee with Polixenes to Bohemia.

When Polixenes says his "ships are ready," it is the first indication we have that he plans to sail from Palermo back to Bohemia. From this it can be inferred that he came to Sicily—some nine months before—the same way: by ship. By extension, it can then be inferred that the inland kingdom of Bohemia actually has a coastline from which Polixenes embarked, and will now return. This seemingly odd geography—an invention of the playwright?—has been ridiculed for centuries. Old landlocked Bohemia with a coastline on the Adriatic Sea? What fantasy!

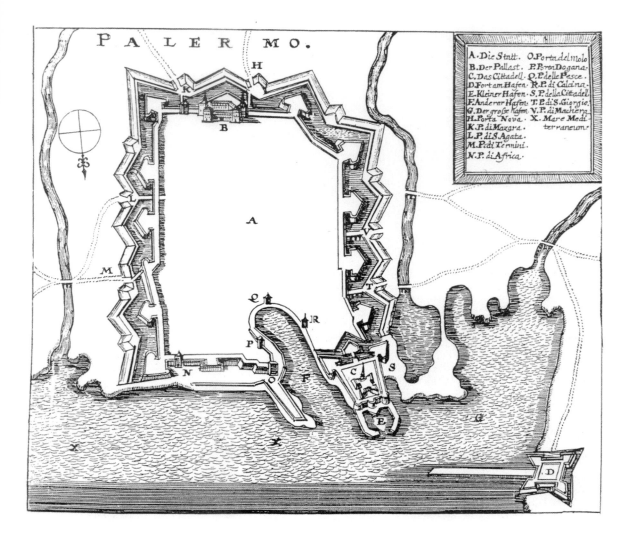

PALERMO.

A. Die Statt.   O. Porta del Molo
B. Der Pallast.   P. Port Dogana.
C. Das Cittadell.   Q. P. delle Pesce.
D. Fort am Hafen.   R. P. di Calcina.
E. Kleiner Hafen.   S. P. della Cittadell.
F. Anderer Hafen.   T. P. di S. Giorgio.
G. Der grosse Hafen.   V. P. di Machera
H. Porta Nova.   X. Mare Medi-
K. P. di Mazara.   terraneum.
L. P. di S. Agata.
M. P. di Termini.
N. P. di Africa.

Palermo in the 16th century. This map shows the fortified walls of the city and its moats, along with a key to the major features in German. (From Italiens, *Francoforte e Lipsia, 1693. Author's collection)*

However, as we will see, once again the playwright knew something unusual—and significant. And with a little digging, we can discover it, too. He certainly knew some special things about Palermo.

The Palazzo Normani, or Palazzo Reale, was situated inside the city walls at its southernmost area, while the city's official port was at the other end, on the north. This port was guarded around the clock, and its traffic and uses would seem to have been generally limited to routine mercantile traffic and naval functions. But it would not have been ample enough to harbor a foreign naval fleet, especially one anchored for nine months or so. However, such a fleet could easily have sat at anchor in the large natural bay, then outside the western city walls, and there would occupy only a fraction of the wide area without discommoding any other vessels.

In the play, a substantial Bohemian naval complement, sailors and naval officers who had accompanied their King Polixenes to Palermo, evidently stayed at various locations within the city. Thus, in an escape in the dead of night, these men would need certain city gates to be unlocked. It just so happened Camillo had command of those keys.

~

In 1251, Ottakar II, before he became King of Bohemia, secured his election as duke of Austria, the adjacent duchy to the south of Bohemia. It, too, was landlocked, and far from the coastline of the Adriatic Sea. In 1253 Ottakar inherited the throne of Bohemia, whereupon his new kingdom was considered to have included the duchy of Austria. Now he was ruler of an even larger landlocked kingdom. It continued to expand. Through a series of events, Moravia, Silesia, Lausitz, and Styria fell to him — all of which were also far from the Adriatic Sea. But then things changed. In 1269, under the will of the childless Ulrich III, Duke of Carinthia and Carniola, Ottakar inherited his two adjoining domains, which lay south of the Austrian part of the thus-expanding Bohemia. Carinthia served as a stepping stone to Carniola, which in turn touched the Adriatic Sea on either side of the Peninsula of Istria, at that time a Venetian possession.

The westernmost of Carniola's two separated waterfronts was a stretch of coastline that ran westerly from the boundary of the medieval Commune of Trieste, across to Duino, a fishing village on the Adriatic Sea's Gulf of Panzano. This stretch would have provided a base for the King of Bohemia's fleet. Part of it was sandy beach and dunes, inhabited only by wild animals in the thirteenth century, and still largely so in the sixteenth century, when this play would have been written. (*The Winter's Tale* first known publication — as distinguished from its composition — was inexplicably delayed until its inclusion in the 1626 First Folio.)

In 1278, in a battle over the succession of Rudolf of Habsburg, founder of the Habsburg dynasty, to the German crown, Ottakar II was slain. Carniola and Carinthia were absorbed into the Habsburg possessions. In historical fact, then, the seacoast to which the playwright referred was in Bohemian hands for nine years. While in the play it is sixteen years or so, no one has ever faulted the imaginative playwright for squeezing, or stretching, time to fashion his story's needs.

*I*n Act II Scene 1, the ire of Leontes is so great that he casts his pregnant queen Hermione into prison. Though certain himself of the truth of Hermione's infidelity, he nevertheless wants sacred affirmation, acknowledgment from a "higher authority," so that the entire court will agree with him. Leontes announces:

> ... I have dispatch'd in post
> To sacred Delphos, to Apollo's temple,
> Cleomenes and Dion, whom you know
> Of stuff'd sufficiency. Now from the oracle
> They will bring all, whose spiritual counsel had,
> Shall stop or spur me.

In some of his other plays, the playwright indulges in anachronisms with aplomb. But the insertion of such an ancient and long-gone oracle in faraway Classical Greece into a story with a thirteenth-century setting, is admittedly bizarre. In fact, Delphos, by the thirteenth century, had been a ruin for 1,000 years. It had been pillaged by the Emperor Nero, furious because the oracle had castigated him for murdering his mother; stripped by Constantine; and finally, closed down in 392 A.D. by Theodosis, a Christian Roman emperor. After this, it became a quarried wreck. This strange resurrection of such a distant, ravaged place is routinely dismissed as a quirk of the playwright. But as we will see, it was no quirk, but rather a pillar of his plot.

~

In Act II Scene 2, we learn that Hermione, now in prison, "is something before her time deliver'd" of a daughter. The noble Paulina, Hermione's close friend, brings the infant to Leontes, hoping the sight of the perfect babe will soften his stony heart. Instead, Leontes rages that the infant is the bastard of Hermione and Polixenes, and delivers this command to his trusted Lord Antigonus (ironically, the husband of Paulina):

> … We enjoin thee
> As thou art liege-man to us, that thou carry
> This female bastard hence, and that thou bear it
> To some remote and desert place, quite out
> Of our dominions; and that there thou leave it
> (Without more mercy) to it[s] own protection
> And favour of the climate …

The Temple of Apollo at Delphi (Greece), with Mount Parnassus rising in the background. This is where Cleomenes and Dion were sent to consult the renowned Oracle. (Author's photo)

Skipping to Act III Scene 3, we find it opens on a deserted beach. The obedient Antigonus is standing there with the infant child cradled in his arms. Beside him is the Mariner of the ship they have just traveled on. Antigonus asks, "Thou art perfect [certain], then, our ship hath touched upon / The deserts of Bohemia?" The Mariner says it has. There can be no doubt here: the playwright has described a Bohemian coastline.

A storm is threatening, and Antigonus sends the Mariner back to the ship, saying he will soon follow. Almost overcome with grief and guilt — and having dreamed that Hermione told him to name her babe "Perdita" — Antigonus leaves that name in the baby's bundle of things, along with his own box of gold coins. Thunder sounds and he says, "The storm begins." After another short speech, he cries, "I am gone forever!" As he runs from the scene, a stage direction indicates: "He exits, pursued by a bear."

Just then, a shepherd appears searching for lost sheep browsing on seaside ivy.[3] He is soon followed by his son, who reports seeing a ship being "swallowed with yeast and froth," and that "the sea flap-dragoned it." Also, he saw a man being torn by a bear; that "the bear tore out his shoulder-bone; that ... he cried to me for help, and said his name was Antigonus, a nobleman." He adds: "The men are not yet cold under the water, nor the bear half dined on the gentleman. He's at it now." The shepherd, seeing the beautiful infant with her elegant blankets, and all the gold, takes the baby home to raise as his own child.

In Act II Scene 3, we return to Sicily's royal palace. Leontes is arguing with Hermione's intimate friend and defender, the noble Paulina, and then with some of his lords. Almost at the end of that scene, a servant enters with some happy news:

Servant: Please your highness, posts
           From those you sent to th'Oracle, are come
           An hour since: Cleomenes and Dion,
           Being well arriv'd from Delphos, are both landed,
           Hasting to th'court.

Lord: So please you, sir, their speed
           Hath been beyond account.

Leontes: Twenty-three days
           They have been absent: 'tis good speed; ...

By the fact of specifically numbering the days of the messengers' trip so exactly, Leontes' words make us certain that the playwright knew about this route, having traveled it himself. And knowing the route, he also knew how long it took: ten days of sailing, three days at Delphi, then ten days back to Sicily and the royal palace: twenty-three days. Not fifteen or forty or twenty: exactly twenty-three.

Both the outbound and the return voyages of Cleomenes and Dion can be traced on a map with confidence. Mediterranean routes have not changed for millennia. Departing from the harbor at

Palermo, an eastward course would be taken along the rugged northern coast of Sicily, with the wind at their backs and a well-known easterly surface flow in their favor. In time they would make a hard starboard turn of some 150 degrees and head southerly, straight through the Strait of Messina. They would pass the jaws of Scylla on the mainland on their left, and the opposite whirlpool of Charybdis, close to the coast of Sicily on their right. These names and descriptions were given to us by Virgil, in *The Aeneid*,[4] and Odysseus passed this way, too.

Once through the Strait, and around the toe of Italy, their eastward course would resume along the arch. Keeping the shoreline in view, they would come to Italy's heel. From there, at a propitious dawn, the helmsman would steer eastward, straight toward the rising sun. Turning south and hugging the coastline, they would pass the long island of Kerkira (Corfu), and then slip into the Gulf of Patras, just after Ithaca. Sailing past Lepanto, they would soon dock at the then-little north-shore harbor called Itea.

Disembarking at Itea, a climb up a winding mountain track on the rugged slope of Mount Parnassus would bring Cleomenes and Dion to Delphos and its Temple of Apollo. Here, they might need three days or so, making necessary arrangements, purchasing the proper offerings, waiting their turn, and putting the question of Hermione's fidelity to the famous oracle. Allowing ten days out, plus three at Delphos, the Sicilian King's emissaries would have another ten days to return to Palermo: twenty-three days. Just as Leontes had said.

∽

In contrast to Italian sailors, the English sailed both day and night. To do so, they used the lodestone, augmented by the star Polaris. Mediterranean sailors could have done this too, but they didn't. Nor would they sail in hours of darkness. They sailed close to the shore and put in at nightfall safely near it, to eat and get a little sleep. As Mediterranean sailors, Cleomenes and Dion would have sailed like this too, as had all Mediterranean peoples throughout history. It was called "coasting," and Fernand Braudel described it clearly in his history of the Mediterranean:

The [Mediterranean] sea in the sixteenth century was an immensity of water: man's efforts had only conquered a few coastal regions, direct routes, and tiny ports of call. Great stretches of the sea were as empty as the Sahara. Shipping was active only along the coastline. Navigation in those days was a matter of following the shoreline, just as in the earliest days of water transport, moving crab-wise from rock to rock, "from promontories to islands and from island to promontories. This was called *costeggiare*, avoiding the open sea."

⌇

Cleomenes and Dion's return voyage would retrace the route of their outward journey, until they came to the toe of the Italian boot. There, although it appears on a map to be a much shorter trip to Palermo, they would not turn north into the Strait of Messina. This was never done. The possibility of Mediterranean sailors sailing north into the Strait — going *counter*-clockwise around the great island of Sicily to reach Palermo, in a sailing ship without oarsmen — was unthinkable. Modern yachtsmen sail through the Strait of Messina, but are admonished not to attempt it without a strong engine. Even today, tidal streams run in this strait for six and one-quarter hours each way at daunting strength. Spring tides run through it at about four and one-half knots, and neaps at two and one-half, cutting down significantly on northward speed. Moreover, strong erratic winds can occur in the Strait.

The ship of Leontes' messengers would take a southwesterly course, in the direction of Syracuse. From there, they would proceed in a *clockwise* circuit around the great island: "the long way," as it is called in *The Aeneid*. To complete their return in the described time would require "good speed." In the right seasons, the winds on this clockwise course are usually favorable. Moreover, the surface of the sea along the southern coast of Sicily has a westward flow of about four knots, to help speed a vessel along. What was true in the time before Virgil had written *The Aeneid* would have been true for these two Sicilian nobles.

And true to ancient custom, then, Cleomenes and Dion would continue their sea voyage along the southern shore of Sicily. At a point on Sicily's western coast they could land, and from there gain greater speed to Palermo by posting — traveling on horseback. That point of disembarkation on the western coast of the island would be the harbor at Trapani — *Drepanum* for the Romans.

Trapani is a port that could have been known to some in England, because it was at Trapani in 1272 where a returning English Crusader named Edward found his men kneeling before him, and was informed he was now King Edward the First of England.[5] For the scholarly, there could be another recollection of Trapani: at the close of Book III of *The Aeneid*, Drepanum is the harbor where Aeneas and his Trojan warriors land, and where, to Aeneas' lasting grief, Anchises, his beloved father, dies in his arms.

Trapani would offer Cleomenes and Dion a safe harbor under royal protection, proper post stables, and the Roman road — the Via Valeria — over easy rolling country all the way to Palermo. Royal messengers would have been scanning the sea approaches daily, waiting to spy a mast flying the flags that would telegraph that these two nobles were arriving. On that exciting sighting, those messengers would speed to Palermo to report the news to their king.

～

It is about ninety miles (150 kilometers) by this old Roman road from the quay at Trapani to the Norman Palace in Palermo. An overland trip by post horses would be divided into three legs, each about thirty miles long, more or less. If riding at a canter gait, or a bit faster, a Sicilian posting horse, which had never eaten oats, would tire in two or three hours on a road like the Via Valeria. Hence, there should be a first change of horses about thirty miles or so east of Trapani. After walking about to get the kinks out, fresh horses would be mounted, and Cleomenes and Dion would set out on the second segment of approximately thirty miles. It is not difficult to identify their next stopping place; a glance at a map of Sicily reveals Partinico, Roman *Partinicum*. From Partinico, their third set of fresh mounts could easily complete the remaining distance of about thirty miles into Palermo, and the palace of Leontes.

In Scene 1 of Act III, only twenty-two lines long, we see the two nobles hastening to their king with the anticipated sacred message in hand. This short scene is usually presented in front of the stage's

Approaching the Temple of Segesta. The road, although now paved, is ancient, with the dramatic view of the temple, located on the western slope of Mount Barbaro, in the distance. (Author's photos)

curtain, though it's an opportunity for some astounding scenery. Cleomenes and Dion are chatting as they post along on the Via Valeria. They discuss where they are, where they've been, and about the hoped-for result of their mission. Cleomenes speaks first, and his pretty words describe their exact location:

The climate's delicate, the air most sweet,
Fertile the isle, the temple much surpassing
The common praise it bears.

They have arrived on Sicily, the most fertile island in the entire Mediterranean Sea. The countryside through which they are riding yielded — and continues to yield — figs, almonds, sugarcane, apples, plums, melons, and pomegranates and is dotted with vineyards and row crops of vegetables. In open spaces, and along the roads, native blackberries, lavender, rock roses, narcissus, ranunculus, and calendulas grace the route. One can truly say the air is "most sweet."

And what quickens the traveler's pulse on the Via Valeria? Just twenty-six miles beyond Trapani? There ahead, gloriously crowning a high hill, gleaming in the sun, stands the Temple of Segesta in majestic solitude, one of the grandest monuments of Doric architecture in all the Mediterranean world. All thirty-six columns of the famous temple stand silently intact, with its tall trabeation of alternating triglyphs and plain metopes, on both its façade and posterior, still in their original places; all of it in perfect grace and proportion. And, as Cleomenes has remarked, the Temple of Segesta is:

> … much surpassing
> The common praise it bears.

Tomasso Fazello (1498–1570), a dedicated scholar and historian from Palermo, who was also a priest, made one of the earliest — if not the very first — accurate archeological studies of this magnificent temple. Fazello's study was published at Palermo just before his death, and for the very first time, someone had accurately described the history of the Temple of Segesta. Fazello's publication caused a great stir of interest among the literate of Palermian society, and by extolling the temple's beauty, he fostered a new source of pride and curiosity among his fellow Sicilians. Sixteenth-century people did not often sightsee far from home, and the Temple of Segesta, ignored for centuries, at last came to be acknowledged for what it was, and what it represented: the tangible presence of a civilization existing two thousand years earlier, now newly understood. It was a place to admire, to visit, and to bring guests, such that within subsequent years, the magnificent Temple of Segesta had indeed become an object of "common praise."

As the two trot along, their conversation in this short scene continues. First Dion, then Cleomenes, are remembering the experience of visiting the oracle:

Dion: I shall report
        For it most caught me, the celestial habits
        (Methinks I should so term them,) and the
        reverence
        Of the grave wearers. O, the sacrifice!
        How ceremonious, solemn and unearthly
        It was i'th'offering!

The Temple of Segesta, one of the most significant examples of extant Doric architecture and among the best-conserved temples in Italy, dates to the second half of the 5th century B.C. This photo was taken before the unfortunate addition of tourist facilities and a gift shop, and the planting of oleanders that now obscure the view. [*From* Art and History of Sicily *(English edition),* Casa Editrice Bonechi, p. 66]

Cleomenes: But of all, the burst
And the ear-deaf'ning voice o'th'Oracle,
Kin to Jove's thunder, so surpris'd my sense,
That I was nothing.

Their conversation in this scene concludes with their hopes that the results of their mission will prove favorable to Queen Hermione:

Dion: If th'event o'th'journey
Prove as successful to the queen, — O be't so! —
As it hath been to us, rare, pleasant, speedy,
The time is worth the use on't.

Cleomenes: Great Apollo
Turn all to th'best! These proclamations,
So forcing faults upon Hermione,
I little like.

Dion: The violent carriage of it
Will clear or end the business: when the Oracle
(Thus by Apollo's great divine seal'd up)
Shall the contents discover something rare
Even then will rush to knowledge.
Go; fresh horses!
And gracious be the issue.

*A*ct III Scene 2 opens on a court of justice called by Leontes to present an indictment against the Queen. Hermione speaks at length on her own behalf, saying that the loss of her three greatest blessings: Leontes's love, the company of her son, and her precious infant daughter, leave her with no desire to live. She wishes that her father, the Emperor of Russia,[6] could be alive to offer her pity.

Officers usher Cleomenes and Dion into the courtroom, and and prepare them for their disclosure:

Officer: You here shall swear upon this sword of justice,
              That you, Cleomenes and Dion, have
              Been both at Delphos, and from thence have brought
              This seal'd-up Oracle, by the hand deliver'd
              Of great Apollo's priest; and that since then
              You have not dared to break the holy seal
              Nor read the secrets in't.

Cleomenes
and Dion: All this we swear.

Leontes: Break the seals and read.

Officer: Hermione is chaste: Polixenes blameless;
              Camillo a true subject; Leontes a jealous tyrant, his innocent
              babe truly begotten;
              And the king shall live without an heir, if that which is lost be
              not found.

Leontes, stunned, refuses to accept the Oracle's pronouncement, claiming it's "mere falsehood." At this moment, a servant rushes in:

Servant: My Lord the King, the King!

Leontes: What is the business?

Servant: O Sir, I shall be hated to report it!
              The Prince, your son, with mere conceit
              and fear
              Of the Queen's speed [fate] is gone.

Leontes: How! Gone?

Servant: Is dead.

Leontes suddenly realizes his tragic misjudgments and is plunged into tortuous remorse. Hermione collapses and is declared dead. She isn't dead, but sixteen years must pass before this truth is finally revealed.

Act IV, the longest in the play, opens with a Chorus named "Time" informing us that those sixteen years have passed, that now we are in Bohemia, that Polixenes has a son named Florizel, and that Perdita, daughter of a shepherd, has grown in grace.

Polixenes, accompanied by Camillo — still his faithful companion — goes in disguise to the shepherd's pasture to see why Florizel, so often absent from his princely duties, spends his time there. They arrive during the festive Sheepshearing Fair.

At this point, we also meet the scoundrel Autolycus, a new character in the story, who remains in the play to the end. We see him cheating his way through the entertaining complexities of the Fair, finally intimidating the simple shepherd and his son into entrusting him with the package holding proof of Perdita's identity.

We will also see the confrontation of Polixenes with his son, who declares his fixed intention to wed lovely Perdita, even though, by marrying a commoner, he will sacrifice his right to the Bohemian throne. In a fury, his father threatens the two young lovers.

In response, Florizel whisks Perdita aboard his own sailing vessel and takes her to Sicily, armed with Camillo's surreptitious sailing instructions, and a letter of introduction to Leontes.

Autolycus arranges passage for himself, and for the Shepherd and his son, aboard Florizel's vessel, just before it departs.

The five of them arrive at Leontes's palace in Palermo, just ahead of Polixenes and Camillo. Polixenes, having learned where Florizel and Perdita are heading, has sailed after them, to prevent the marriage of his only son to the young girl of falsely assumed low birth.

After all the grateful greetings among them, Perdita's true identity is revealed, with the certain proof. We do not witness the ensuing universal blissful joy, but it is described for us by three gentlemen of the court. Then follows, in a final scene, the climax of Paulina's dramatic presentation of the still-living Hermione.

We have learned a number of extraordinary things from our playwright, and as for his characters, their joy knows no bounds.

NOTES

1. The Norman Palace was originally built by the Saracens, and later enlarged and heavily embellished by the Norman kings of Sicily, notably by Roger II de Hauteville during the period 1132–1140.
2. His name is spelled variously in history, including Otakar, Otacar, and in Dante's *Purgatorio*, Canto VII, he is Ottacchero. He has also been called Primislaus. (Ottakar I was his grandfather.)
3. Varieties of ivy grow along the seaside in many places in Europe and North Africa. As for being edible, one might recall the line from the once-popular song: "Mares eat oats and does eat oats but little lambs eat ivy." Ivy that grows on the ground is not toxic to sheep, though it is to horses and some species of deer.
4. "… the whirlpool of Charybdis, who thrice swallows the vast flood down into her swirling throat and spews it upward again, lashing the sky with water. And Scylla is poised in the hidden recesses of her cavern, thrusting forth her mouths and drawing ships upon the rocks … Better to steer for the goal of Trinacrian Pachynus [three-cornered Sicily] for all the delays, and fetch a long circuit in thy course, than to catch sight of the grotesque Scylla deep in her dreary cavern, and of the rocks that resound in her hounds that are the color of the sea."
5. This Edward, nicknamed Longshanks, was one of England's greatest kings. Although his rise to the throne did not happen until 1272, when he was thirty-three, he served before that time as *de facto* king due to the muddles of his sire, Henry III. He was long remembered for his beneficial kingship of thirty-five years, which included the establishment of England's constitutional parliament.
6. In 1570, the Emperor of Russia had sought the hand of Queen Elizabeth in marriage, an event that worried her subjects, and with good reason: he was Ivan the Terrible (1530–1584), a ruler of evil and tyranny.

Water Route to Vulcano

Milan

Adda

Po

Genoa

Livorno • Florence

ITALY

ADRIATIC SEA

TYRRHENIAN SEA

IONIAN SEA

Vulcano

SICILY

0   100   200 km
0   100   200 mi

N

12
CHAPTER

The Tempest
"Island of Wind and Fire"

*T*he *Tempest*, at first a tale of terror and then of magic, takes place on an actual Italian island in the Tyrrhenian Sea just miles off the northern shores of Sicily. This island is a singular place, being endowed with a particular combination of characteristics found nowhere else on earth. Visitors to this island are surprised and intrigued by its remarkable properties, and the creative mind of a discovering playwright was deeply inspired. Those properties were such that this island was never deemed permanently inhabitable until the dawn of the twentieth century.

In all but *The Tempest* and one other Italian Play,[1] the actual locations are identified through a proper name. In *The Tempest*, however, the playwright gives us only indirect clues as to our whereabouts, scattering them throughout his story through the words of his characters. When one listens carefully to those words, the colorful detail and poetic renderings of the world the characters inhabit, with its unique and surprising geology, topography, flora, and fauna, it becomes evident that we are on one specific island: a small island in the Tyrrhenian Sea.

The first scene in the play, one of great drama, opens with a ship trapped in a storm. The storm is so sudden, and so violent, that the single word "tempest" is a perfect description. Raging wind and crashing sea have forced this one ship, somehow singled out from a passing royal fleet, to be swept dangerously close to this forbidding island and its jagged cliffs. Officers and crew struggle to save the craft from sinking, or being wrecked. All is confusion and alarm. Excitement mounts.

This is the royal ship of King Alonso, the play's imaginary sovereign of the once-wide Kingdom of Naples. In addition to his sailors, whom we do not meet, there are a few men whom we will get to know: Prince Ferdinand, King Alonso's son; Gonzalo, his honest old counselor; and Antonio, a noble visitor to the Neapolitan royal court, who will turn out to be much more than that. Rounding out Alonso's group aboard are two Neapolitan lords, and two underlings: Trinculo, a jester; and Stephano, a drunken butler.

❧

In this play, contrary to the more common practice, it is in the second, not the first scene, where the dramatic tension of the story is divulged. It is in this second scene where we meet the four residents of this island and learn some of their personal history.

The first person — and principal character in the drama — is Prospero, the "Duke of Milan," the lawful, but deposed, ruler of that important Tuscan duchy. With Prospero is his lovely, and completely sheltered, now-fifteen-year-old daughter, Miranda. Next appears Ariel, a flying and diving rogue spirit of magical abilities; and finally, Prospero's slave-servant, a misshapen, coarse, menacing lout named Caliban.

Prospero is also a powerful magus, and during the play we see him perform startling feats of sorcery. We meet him, in fact, as the curtain rises on this second scene, just as he is believed to have conjured up this tempest. Miranda implores him:

> If by your art, my dearest father, you have put the wild waters in this roar, allay them ...

It all has frightened her terribly, but Prospero assures her she's quite safe:

> Be collected:
> No more amazement:
> Tell your piteous heart there's no harm done.

Then, after promising his daughter this for some time, Prospero begins to recount the story of how the two of them came to be on this remote island. He tells Miranda that as a "prince of power" and the "Duke of Milan," he had indulged in his passion for "liberal arts" and "secret studies" (magic and astrology), to the exclusion of almost everything else. He became so absorbed in his keen interest that he delegated the administration of the duchy to his younger brother, Antonio—whom we have just met aboard that troubled royal ship.

Prospero explains that while he and Miranda were still in "Milan," the ambitious Antonio had gathered enough loyalties to overthrow, and then exile him, whereupon he and the then-three-year-old girl, were hustled:

> … aboard a bark,[2]
> Bore us some leagues to the sea, where they prepared
> A rotten carcass of a butt,[3] not rigged,
> Nor tackle, sail, nor mast …
> …
> … There they hoist[4] us
> To cry to th' sea that roared to us, to sigh
> To th' winds whose pity, sighing back again,
> Did us but loving wrong.

The "loving wrong" appears to be that, on the one hand, while Prospero and Miranda's lives were spared, on the other, they were cast upon this nearly uninhabited island where they have been living in exile many years.

~

But there is something wrong with Prospero's account. Something he said does not seem right—or possible. We have already seen in the preceding Italian Plays that this playwright was both exact and geographically correct in the details he gives about places and things. Indeed, if Prospero had literally taken the "route" he describes to Miranda, sailing from "Milan" to their present location on this island, their journey would have brought them down the wrong arm of the Mediterranean Sea. They would have come down the Adriatic Sea — on the *eastern* side of the Italian peninsula; whereas it has already been established in Scene 1 that this island, where King Alonso and his party have just now been stranded, is in its *western, Tyrrhenian*, segment.

What is going on here? Something does not fit.

Never, in all the history of the Italian peninsula, was there a continuous navigable waterway linking Milan with the Mediterranean. The massive Apennine Mountains prevent this. That chain forms the spine of Italy, standing high between Milan and the sea.

Prospero and Miranda's watery trip to Vulcano, had it originated in Milan, would have been possible, but very complicated, and extremely lengthy. The "some food" and "some fresh water" the noble Gonzalo had provided them "out of his charity," might not have lasted through such a time-consuming, quite hazardous voyage. To undertake such a trip from Milan, Prospero and Miranda would first have sailed in their "bark" by canal to the long, meandering Adda River; then connected to the even longer Po; and then, after traveling the length of the Po, transferred to their "carcass of a butt," and finally cast off into the Adriatic Sea. Only then would they have begun their voyage on the Mediterranean: down the length of the Italian peninsula — in a boat that "rats [would] instinctively have quit" — then up and around the island of Sicily to at last, run aground on Vulcano's "yellow sands." Such a trip does not accurately fit the words Prospero has been given to speak. His description is far more concise.

Prospero and Miranda's credible route would have begun in Florence, on the Arno River. In their "bark" they would easily "continue some leagues to the sea" on the canal dug by Cosimo I de' Medici in the sixteenth century, which connected the Arno River to the port of Livorno.[5] At Livorno, transferred to their "rotten carcass of a butt," Prospero and Miranda would have been immediately propelled out into the Tyrrhenian Sea, there to be pulled by the currents and pushed southward by "th' winds, whose pity, sighing back again," led them directly to the sandy beaches of Vulcano — all in a handful of days.

But why this mix up? Why would Prospero and Miranda's watery itinerary matter? Why Milan and not Florence?

≈

A plausible answer can be found in England's then-current trade agreement with Tuscany,[6] whose seat of power was the city of Florence. We can strongly suspect that the departure-from-Milan route results from a "doctoring" of the original manuscript by high authority, *after* it was written, but *before* it was finally published for the first time, in the First Folio.

≈

Plays by popular playwrights were frequent entertainments at the court of Elizabeth I. The Queen, and much of her court, would attend them, and high-ranking foreign envoys would have been invited, such as those from the friendly Tuscany and the ducal seat at Florence. But a play depicting events in the presumed original version of this play, could have appalled the Tuscans. The unfortunate characteristics of *The Tempest*'s fictional Duke Prospero were very like those of their own problematic, but living, Grand Duke Francesco I de' Medici (1541–1587); thence, the consequences of staging the play in such an original form, could be politically disastrous. In Tuscany (and probably in England as well), such a scenario could easily be viewed as an affront to both Francesco I and his brother, Ferdinand I, who later replaced Francesco I as the Tuscan duke.

The invasive means used to avoid such an outcome, was accomplished easily: replace "Tuscany" with "Milan," especially since England had no regard for Milan's Habsburg Duke Philip, anyway.

This simple doctoring, even though it introduced a geographical blunder into the play, was so successful in England that it has been overlooked there, and elsewhere, ever since. The blunder has been tolerated and unquestioned throughout history because of the conviction that the playwright had never left England, and therefore, invented an "Italy" that was his alone.

≈

After sharing the lamentable family history with Miranda — who gets drowsy, then sleeps — Prospero summons Ariel, the other magic-worker on the island. He questions the airy spirit about the behavior of the people aboard the imperiled ship. Although we do not yet know

why (but soon will), it is apparent that Ariel is under some kind of ob-
ligation to Prospero. Listen, as Ariel gives his master an account of his
successful performance in Act I Scene 2:

Ariel: All hail, great master; grave sir, hail! I come
            To answer thy best pleasure, be't to fly,
            To swim, to dive into the fire, to ride
            On the curled clouds. To thy strong bidding, task
            Ariel and all his quality.

Prospero: Hast thou, spirit,
            Performed to point the tempest that I bade thee?

Ariel: To every article.
            I boarded the king's ship: now on the beak,
            Now on the waist, the deck, in every cabin
            I flamed amazement. Sometime I'd divide
            And burn in many places — on the topmast,[7]
            The yards and bowsprit would I flame distinctly
            Then meet and join. Jove's lightning, the precursors
            O'th' dreadful thunderclaps, more momentary ...
            fire and cracks
            Of sulphurous roaring, the most mighty Neptune
            Seem to besiege and make his bold waves tremble,
            Yea, his dread trident shake.

Prospero: My brave spirit,
            Who was so firm, so constant, that this coil
            Would not infect his reason?

Ariel: Not a soul ...
            All but mariners
            Plunged in the foaming brine and quit the vessel ...

Prospero: Why, that's my spirit!
            But was not this nigh the shore?

Ariel: Close by, my master.

Prospero: But are they, Ariel, safe?

Ariel: Not a hair perished;
                On their sustaining garments not a blemish,
                But fresher than before …

In affirmation of all this—gleaned both from Ariel and later, in Act II Scene 1, from Gonzalo—we know that King Alonso's voyage was to take him and his party from Tunis to Naples. As Ariel reports to Prospero:

> … And for the rest o'th' fleet,
> Which I dispersed, they all have met again,
> And are upon the Mediterranean flote (float),
> Bound sadly home for Naples,
> Supposing that they saw the King's ship wrecked
> And his great person perish.

And as Gonzalo says:

> Methinks our garments are now as fresh as
> when we put them on first in *Africa*, at the
> marriage of the King's fair daughter Claribel
> to the *King of Tunis*.[8]   (Emphasis mine)

Further, when Gonzalo turns to the king and says, "Sir, we were talking that our garments seem now as fresh[9] as when *we were at Tunis* (Emphasis mine) at the marriage of your daughter, who is now Queen," it is abundantly clear that the Neapolitan royal fleet has been in Tunis. The king and his party were celebrating the marriage of Alonso's daughter, Claribel, and it was on their journey home to Naples that the terrible tempest struck, and brought them to this island.

The most surprising fact about King Alonso's sea route[10] from Tunis to Naples is that this same route has appeared in literature before. It is *exactly* the route taken by Virgil's Aeneas fifteen centuries earlier, when Aeneas abandons his broken-hearted Queen Dido of Carthage, and sails for Rome. Through the banter among Sebastian, Gonzalo, Antonio, and Adrian in Act II Scene 1, the playwright informs us that the point of departure for both these voyages is the same city.

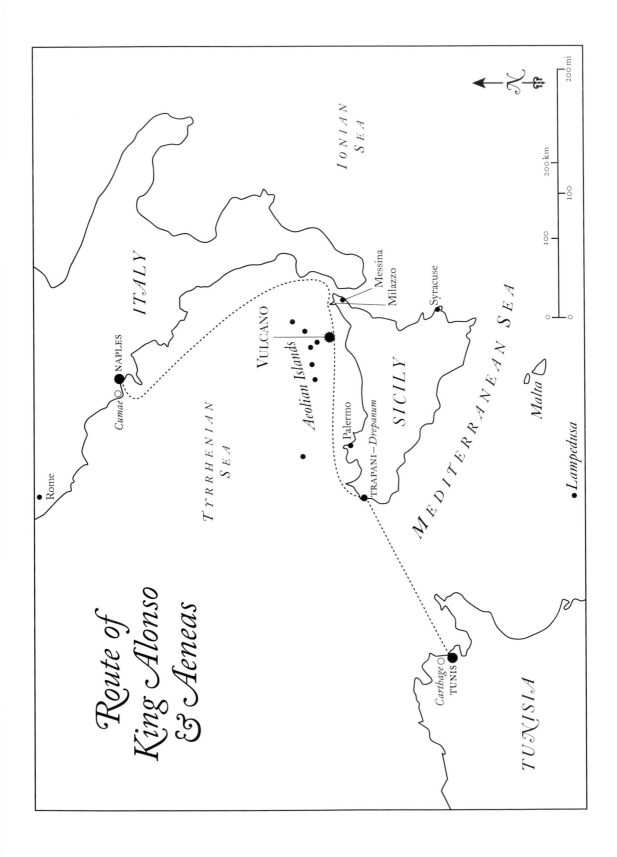

Route of
King Alonso
& Aeneas

ITALY

Rome

NAPLES
Cumae

TYRRHENIAN
SEA

Aeolian Islands

VULCANO

Palermo

TRAPANI—Drepanum

SICILY

Messina
Milazzo

Syracuse

IONIAN
SEA

MEDITERRANEAN SEA

Malta

Lampedusa

Carthage
TUNIS

TUNISIA

N

200 mi

200 km   100

100   0

> ... the motherland of storms, a womb that always teems with raving south winds. In his enormous cave King Aeolus restrains the wrestling winds, loud hurricanes; he tames and sways them with his chains and prison. They rage in indignation at their cages; the mountain answers with a mighty roar. Lord Aeolus sits in his high citadel ...
>
> ...
>
> Then, Juno, suppliant, appealed to him: "You, Aeolus — to whom the king of men and father of the gods has given this: to pacify the waves or, with the wind, to incite them — over the Tyrrhenian now sails my enemy ...
> ... Hammer your winds to fury and ruin their swamped ships, or scatter them and fling their crews piecemeal across the seas.

The playwright knew exactly where Virgil conceived those lines. It was at a spot where sudden, violent storms were notorious throughout history: the sea between the islands of Aeolus and the coast of Sicily. The next step for the playwright, having experienced the frightening truth of that Tunis-Italy sea route first hand — the very route described in *The Aeneid* — was to supplant the roles of Juno and Aeolus with those of Prospero and Ariel, in his play.

And there is another compelling parallel in *The Tempest*; it is a real-life individual of the playwright's time, someone he used as a model for his Prospero: the Grand Duke of Tuscany, Francesco I de' Medici (1541–1587).

*I*n the sixteenth century, the city-states of Italy were ruled by wealthy and powerful men, and members of their families. Cosimo I de' Medici (1514–1574), regarded by many as the reincarnation of Machiavelli's *Prince*, was one of the most ruthless. In 1564, toward the end of his reign, Cosimo I gave administrative powers of Florence to his eldest son, Francesco, and had his younger son, Ferdinand, made a cardinal.

The reclusive Francesco was odd and unstable. He was frequently reprimanded by his father for the amount of time he spent cloistered in his laboratory, obsessively studying alchemy and magic, and conducting experiments on how to turn base metals into gold. Francesco was known to take solitary walks in the city at night, and had secret passages and rooms in his residences constructed so he could move about unobserved. The unusual overhead passageway, part of which still crosses the Arno River above the famous Ponte Vecchio, enabled Francesco to pass from his palace outside the city, to one within it, without anyone knowing.

In December 1565, Francesco married Johanna (Giovanna), Archduchess of Austria. The marriage was not successful; Francesco was flagrantly unfaithful. Then, sometime around 1572, Francesco became utterly smitten with the strikingly beautiful Bianca Capello, daughter of a noble Venetian family,[14] who had eloped from Venice to Florence with a penniless Tuscan. Particular features of Bianca's stunning beauty were her penetrating blue eyes, which seemed nearly hypnotic. Because of her powerful enchantment of Francesco, some people were sure Bianca was a witch, capable of bending Francesco's will. Blue-eyed Bianca: a witch and a mindbender. Shortly after Francesco made Bianca his mistress, Bianca's young husband was found murdered in a Florence street; rumors flew that Francesco was involved.

With Cosimo I's death in 1574, power passed to Francesco, who, as Francesco I, ruled from 1574 until his own death in 1587. When the unhappy Grand Duchess Johanna died in childbirth in 1578,

Vulcano, Prospero's Island. Following an underwater eruption in 183 B.C., Vulcano emerged from the sea. The Italian vulcanologist Dr. Franco Italiano calls the island "an unimaginable world … (which) makes you respect and fear this place pulsating with life." [Aerial photo from Isole Eolie, Arte Photo Graphic Oreste Ragusi, Milazzo (Messina), *p. 57. Quote from* The Eolian Islands, Pearls of the Mediterranean, *Edizioni Affinita Elettive, Messina, Italy, 1997, p. 23]*

Francesco I immediately married Bianca Capello. But even before this latest outrage, Francesco's odd behavior had scandalized all of Florence. Not only was the duke despotic, secretive, and suspicious, he increasingly absented himself from public activities. When not with the mesmerizing Bianca, he devoted all his time to the secret arts.

Francesco's brother, Cardinal Ferdinand, who frequently visited the duke and his beautiful wife, was also alarmed. He, too, was concerned about Francesco's undignified conduct and strange dabblings; and now it came to his attention that Francesco and Bianca were making plans to adopt a child. Not only would a son extend Francesco's unpredictable rule, it would cut Ferdinand off from his inheritance and completely deny the more reasonable Ferdinand access to de' Medici power.

*A*t the beginning of October 1587, Cardinal Ferdinand was a houseguest at the ducal villa at Poggio a Caiano outside Florence. He dined with Francesco and Bianca. That evening, the royal couple became ill, apparently from the onset of malaria. By the next day, the two seemed to have recovered enough to dine again with Ferdinand. Later that night, however, the "malaria" worsened, and finally, Francesco succumbed. And in the first hours of the next morning, October 20, Bianca followed her husband to the grave.

Ferdinand, Francesco's successor as Ferdinand I, immediately took charge of all state affairs, swiftly ordering autopsies on both bodies. (Autopsies on princes and rulers were routine in Italy, but rarely were they performed on the wives.) The autopsies were accomplished with seemly dispatch, concluding that Francesco and Bianca had indeed died of malaria. However, suspicion that they may have been poisoned by Ferdinand never completely died out. The questions and gossip, and waves of shock, that spread far and wide could hardly have gone unnoticed by our playwright.

The deaths of Francesco I de' Medici, and the gorgeous Bianca Capello, have provided heated speculation in Italy for over 400 years. In 1857, their remains were exhumed, and reburied in the de' Medici crypt. In 1945, their bone fragments were studied. Nothing was resolved, and questions continued to swirl around their deaths.

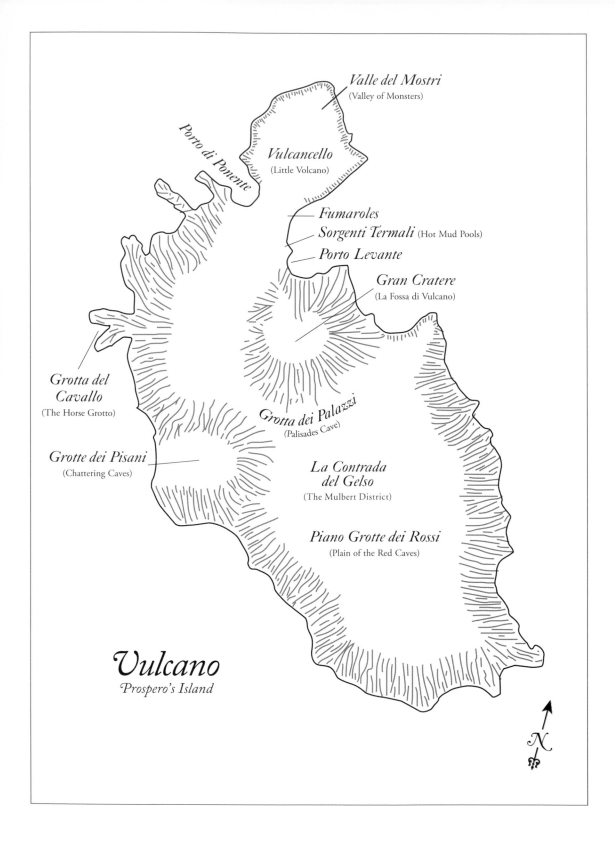

Valle del Mostri
(Valley of Monsters)

Porto di Ponente

Vulcancello
(Little Volcano)

Fumaroles
Sorgenti Termali (Hot Mud Pools)
Porto Levante

Gran Cratere
(La Fossa di Vulcano)

Grotta del Cavallo
(The Horse Grotto)

Grotta dei Palazzi
(Palisades Cave)

Grotte dei Pisani
(Chattering Caves)

La Contrada del Gelso
(The Mulbert District)

Piano Grotte dei Rossi
(Plain of the Red Caves)

Vulcano
Prospero's Island

N

At last, in 2007, another investigation was undertaken. Once again, the coffins of Francesco and Bianca were pried open, and complex tests by authorized experts were performed on their remains. No surprise to many—but for the first time in history scientifically determined—both Francesco and Bianca had been poisoned: high arsenic levels were found in their bones. At long last, the book on the so-called Medici Project could be closed; and today, the entire lurid story can be read by anyone on the Internet.

∾

King Alonso is now stranded, but safe, on an unusual island. In Book VIII of *The Aeneid*, Virgil calls it "Vulcania," and describes it in language which, even after two millennia, remains evocative and fresh:

> Close by that side of Sicily where lies Aeolian Lipare there rises high an island steep with smoking rocks. Beneath it a den with caves of Etna, hollowed out by forges of the Cyclops, roars; and pounding strokes echo, groaning, on those anvils; bars of Chalyb steel hiss through the caverns; fire pants in those furnaces; the house of Vulcan; and that land's name, Vulcania. The Lord of Fire from heaven's height descended here.

Roman "Vulcania," Italian "Vulcano," it is no surprise that the island is named for the Roman god of fire, forges and volcanoes.[15]

Like Stromboli, its sister island, Vulcano (the accent is on the first syllable) possesses an active volcano. It is the Gran Cratere, or La Fossa di Vulcano, and is especially noxious—and deadly; deadly to such a degree that although Vulcano is easily reached by small craft from mainland Sicily, twelve miles distant, and although people have sailed back and forth to the island for centuries, no one felt confident enough to live permanently on Vulcano until fairly recently.[16]

Out of the Gran Cratere's crater, and up through the crevices, cracks, and chimneys on its rim and sides, fumes, at high temperatures, are constantly vented. The fumes are combined steam, carbon dioxide, sulphur (both molten and bright yellow particulate sulphur), and sulphur dioxide gas. Sulphur dioxide is universally—and instantly—recognizable by its acrid, repellent odor of rotten eggs. That

Vulcano's hot mud pool … "the filthy-mantled pool … that foul lake," where the drunken Trinculo lost his bottles.
[*From* Isole Eolie, *Arte Photo Graphic Oreste Ragusi, Milazzo (Messina), p. 62*]

noxious combination of ingredients is also expelled through fissures, called "fumaroles," on the slopes of the volcano. The stinking, steaming, and spewing of the Gran Cratere is constant and dramatic — and always foul-smelling.

Forming a peninsula to Vulcano is Vulcanello, "Little Vulcano." It emerged from the sea as its own small body of land 183 B.C. and gradually grew, joining Vulcano to form one larger island. Vulcanello has two bays: one shallow called Porto di Ponente, with subsurface rocks where ships can run aground; and a larger, deeper, and safer one, called Porto Levante. In centuries past, vessels would anchor offshore at Porto Levante, and people would reach the island in smaller craft, beaching their boats on the shore. Only since the late nineteenth century has Porto Levante had a proper pier.

The best place to land at Porto Levante is near a large, variegated hillock. Immediately to the north of it are hot mud pools. The larger of these pools is especially impressive. Both carbon dioxide and sulphur dioxide effervesce through this pool's muddy mixture of mineral sludge. The brownish goo bubbles and steams, and stinks mightily. During certain months of the year, this hot mud pool is coated or "mantled," with a yellow layer of volcanic sulphur dust.

There are allusions to this hot mud pool in the parts of Act IV Scene 1, which concern the plot by Caliban, Stephano, and Trinculo to murder Prospero. At the end of a small theatrical performance in his honor, Prospero realizes that the trio's deadly deed is fast approaching. He summons Ariel to apprise him of the situation:

Prospero: Say again, where didst thou leave these vartlets?

Ariel: I told you, sir, they were red-hot with drinking …
           … Then I beat my tabor,
           At which like unbacked colts they pricked their ears,
           Advanced their eyelids, lifted up their noses
           As they smelt music, so I charmed their ears
           That calf-like they my lowing followed, through
           Toothed briars, sharp furzes, pricking gorse and
           thorns,[17]
           Which entered their frail shins. At last I left them
           I'th' filthy-mantled pool beyond your cell,
           There dancing up to their chins, that *the foul lake*
           O'er stunk their feet.   (Emphasis mine)

Soon, Caliban, Stephano and Trinculo enter this scene, soaked with the waters of "the filthy-mantled pool … the foul lake," and stinking to high heaven:

"Come unto these yellow sands" …
Even today, visitors to Vulcano are greeted by the yellow sands of which Ariel sings.

Left: Photo from Isole Eolie, Arte Photo Graphic Oreste Ragusi, Milazzo (Messina), p. 68.

Right: Photo from The Eolian Islands, Pearls of the Mediterranean, Edizioni Affinita Elettive, Messina, Italy, 1997, p. 22.

Fumaroles. *On land, gases violently escaping through small fractures in the earth's surface cause streams of vapors and loud hissing, while in swampy areas, mud is spit up in geysers. On the seabed, around rocks near the beaches, the underwater fumaroles create bursts of fizzing bubbles and a unique gurgling sound.*
Below: Photo from The Eolian Islands, Pearls of the Mediterranean, *Edizioni Affinità Elettive, Messina, Italy, 1997, p. 22.*

Trinculo: Monster, I do smell all horse piss, at which my nose is in great indignation.

Stephano: So is mine. Do you hear, monster?

And later, Trinculo drunkenly laments, "Ay, but to lose our bottles in the pool …" and indeed, it would be utterly impossible to see anything in the sludgy waters of the mud pool.

The setting portrayed through the words of Trinculo, Stephano, and Ariel—"foul lake," "horse piss," "filthy pool"—describe exactly the stinking, bubbling, hot mud pool of Vulcano. But what does Ariel mean when the spirit calls the mud pool "filthy-mantled?"

In our playwright's day, Vulcano's hot mud pool would have been "mantled," that is, covered by a floating crust of dry sulphur, and it would have been covered throughout the entire year. This curious natural phenomenon occurs when bright yellow particulate of sulphur, drifting down from the crater above, collects on the mud pool's surface. Today this coating of yellow dust is seen only during the mud pool's "off-season," that is, when the pool's surface has remained undisturbed by health-seeking tourists. But one can imagine

Photo from Isole
Eolie, *Arte Photo
Graphic Oreste
Ragusi, Milazzo
(Messina), p. 68.*

how it looked year-round — and across the centuries — from the yellow dust that remains untouched on much of the rim and slopes of the
Gran Cratere, as it did on the hot mud pool in the playwright's day.

Thus, toward the end of Act I Scene 2, when Ariel sings: "Come
unto these yellow sands ..." the playwright had seen this marvel.
Through the song of one of his characters in *The Tempest*, he described for his audience in faraway England one of the most singular characteristics of this one Aeolian island off the coast of Italy. The
airy spirit sings not of "sands," but of "*yellow* sands." And today, the
moment one lands at Porto Levante on the island of Vulcano, one can
still marvel at the startling yellow sands of which Ariel sings.

~

Along most of the wide beach of Porto Levante, both under the
sea and immediately adjacent to the shore, are hot springs and fumaroles, collectively called the *Sorgenti Termali*, the Surging Thermals.

Some of these hot springs are sulphurous, others are muddy, and still others exude that noxious-smelling sulphur dioxide. The carbon dioxide emitted by these underwater springs makes the sea water above them hot and bubbly — so hot, that people coming to the island for health baths and who plan to enter the water along certain parts of the shore are advised to wear protective footwear. Adding to nature's dramatic seaside features are the fumaroles along the beach, which, like geysers, violently spout steam and water.

At the beginning of Act I Scene 2, the playwright has given it to Miranda to describe the workings of Vulcano's undersea fumaroles, when she says:

> The sky, it seems, would pour down stinking pitch,
> But the sea, mounting to the welkin's cheek,[18]
> Dashes the fire out. ...

Observing fumaroles at the water's edge provides no little natural drama. When a fumarole erupts, it does so with violence, shooting high up into the air. Miranda describes the phenomenon correctly when she says the sea seems to be "mounting to the welkin's cheek," meaning to the edge of the clouds, or vault of heaven.

The undersea opening of a fumarole, filled with sea water when idle, soon takes on the look of a flaming geyser. When the searing molten sulphur spews upward, and comes in contact with air, the sulphur bursts into flame. The fire is almost immediately dashed out by hot seawater and steam. When the extinguished material falls back onto the beach, it looks like pitch — though stinks of sulphur dioxide. It is no wonder that Miranda was frightened.

∿

Visual spectacles aren't the island's only unique feature: there's the constant "music" — cracking, groaning, sighing and drumming. In Act III Scene 2, Caliban, the island's longest resident, who knows it well, describes this music to Stephano and Trinculo, saying:

> ... The isle is full of noises,
> Sounds and sweet airs that give delight and hurt not.
> Sometimes a thousand twangling instruments
> Will hum about mine ears, and sometimes voices ...

Prospero's Cave?
Vulcano is dotted with hundreds of caves, many of which are habitable. (Author's photo)

Virgil, too, long before Caliban, also mentioned Vulcano's groaning, hissing, pounding, and panting.

Caliban weaves many of Vulcano's unique features — its flora and fauna — into his lines in the play. In the opening of Act II Scene 2, for example, he complains about snakes, but especially about "urchin-shows:"

> ... hedgehogs which
> Lie tumbling in my barefoot way, and mount
> Their pricks at my footfall; ...

"Urchin" and "hedgehog" are different names for the same animal. Small nocturnal omnivores, about ten inches long, hedgehogs are found all over the Aeolian Islands. Residents of Vulcano today, especially those living in a small community on the far side of the island, bemoan the nightly invasion of their gardens by these spiny little creatures.

The notable characteristic of a hedgehog is its protective covering of hard, sharp, and elastic spines. When touched, or startled, urchins/hedgehogs roll into a ball with their spines — terribly painful when speared into flesh — sticking out in all directions. Prospero too, mentions them, threatening Caliban:

... urchins shall ...
exercise on thee;
thou shalt be pinched as thick as honeycomb,
each pinch more stinging than bees that made 'em.

Caliban also speaks about another resident on Vulcano, the "scamels." At the end of Act II Scene 2, he allies himself with Stephano and Trinculo, and enumerates the services he will provide. One service is the procurement of this island delicacy: "sometimes I'll get thee / Young scamels from the rock."

Scamels are bar-tailed godwits, a migratory marsh and shore bird, sometimes found along the Tyrrhenian and Ionian Seas of Italy and occasionally on beaches in England, or other northern climes. Young female scamels, not yet able to fly away, were considered a tasty source of protein.

Caliban also mentions Vulcano's berries. In Act I Scene 2, Caliban, complaining of Prospero's now-harsh treatment, says that at first Prospero had been kind to him:

Thou strokedst me, and madest much of me;
Wouldst give me
Water with berries in it; ...

The nature of those berries[19] has caused considerable speculation, although the berries of which Caliban speaks are clearly mulberries, a berry which proliferated in the wilds of Vulcano when the playwright visited the island. The seeds of the mulberry tree had been carried by birds from mainland Italy, where the trees had been imported in the fifteenth century when Italians first learned the secrets of making silk. Mulberry trees were an absolute requirement for the propagation of silkworms: the worms feed exclusively on the freshest and most tender leaves of the mulberry tree. Even today, an area on Vulcano is referred to locally as La Contrada del Gelso, The Mulberry District.

But who, or what, is this strange individual, Caliban, who knows so much about this island?

⌒

Throughout the Middle Ages and the Renaissance, the Catalans of Spain were regarded as the most skillful sailors on the

Mediterranean. Catalans were employed by the rulers of Spain, Sicily, and Naples, including the Holy Roman Emperor Charles V, Philip II of Spain, and his distinguished brother, Don John. An Elizabethan audience viewing *The Tempest* would have easily assumed that King Alonso's sailors were Catalans.

Catalonia, which consists of the northeasterly segment of the Iberian Peninsula and the Balearic Islands, corresponds, more or less, to the modern semi-autonomous province of Spain that still bears that name. Barcelona was, and still is, Catalonia's capital.[20]

The Catalan language is unique unto itself. Proudly spoken today by eight million people as their first language,[21] Catalan is not a Spanish dialect; it is a distinct Romance language, something akin to the Provençal dialect of southern France. Until 1609, Catalan was also an official language of Sicily. How much of this language the playwright learned in his southern travels can only be guessed. But what is clear from his *Tempest* is that he had enough association with Catalonians for him to have absorbed at least some of their distinct vocabulary. Catalans then still populated, and heavily so, the cities of Naples, Trapani, Messina, and Palermo, a notable fact which has been almost completely overlooked.

Countless books, articles, commentaries, and even dissertations, flatly assert that the name of the savage and deformed slave, Caliban, is some sort of variant of the word "cannibal." Cannibal worked its way into English from the Spanish word *Canibal*, sometime during the sixteenth century. *The Oxford English Dictionary* describes this word as "originally one of the forms of the ethnic name Carib or Caribes, a fierce nation of the West Indies whose members are recorded to have been anthropophagi" (eaters of human flesh).

In Act I Scene 3 of *Othello*, cannibal is used to mean a human flesh-eater, although one from some Far East or African place, not from the West Indies. No matter the origin of the word, however, the playwright seems not uncertain what a cannibal was — or did.

The Caliban of *The Tempest* demonstrates no interest in eating human flesh.[22] Caliban speaks of no such interest himself, nor do any of the other characters speak of him as having such an interest. If Caliban is neither a cannibal, nor an Amerind of the Carib nation, however, then what is he?

The Deep Nook, *the Grotta del Cavallo (Horse Grotto) where King Alonso's ship was hidden by Ariel.* [*From* Le Isole Eolie (The Aeolian Islands), *Carmelo Cavallaro- Vittorio Famularo,* SAMBUCETO *(Chieti), 1996, p. 61*]

W hile critics have overlooked Ariel's pointed refer- ence to the "deep nook," they have nevertheless, in Ariel's same speech, seized upon another word, "Bermoothes." For years, this word has been hotly debated among those interested in the works of Shakespeare. An entire fantasy has been spun around "Bermoothes."

In Ariel's litany of deeds well done in Act I Scene 2, we hear — only once — about the Bermoothes:

... in the deep nook, where once
Thou call'dst me up at midnight to fetch dew
From the still-vexed Bermoothes ...

Ariel was in the deep nook when Prospero ordered him to go to this place. It is clear, from Ariel's words, that it, the Bermoothes, is someplace *away from* the deep nook; it is another place entirely. For an airy spirit, however, it would not matter where it was; a spirit could get there and back in a flash. Ariel is revealing here something interesting. But what could the mischievous spirit possibly mean?

Some have contended that this Bermoothes is somewhere on the same *Tempest* island. Others insist that Prospero's island is one of the Bermuda islands in the Atlantic Ocean, having read somewhere in the literature of sixteenth- or seventeenth-century England that the Bermudas were also referred to as "the Bermoothes."[28] But why would Prospero want Ariel to go there — to those Bermudas many thousands of miles away — to collect some rapidly evaporating morning moisture, some "dew," and then bring it back to Vulcano in Italy?

He didn't. The playwright decided that here, at this exact point in his *Tempest*, Ariel should be given something clever and comical to say for the London audience. Here was a spot in the story for a moment of levity. Ariel should make a local joke, understood locally, and packed with local meaning.

For this moment of comic relief, the playwright selected the wretched haunt in London referred to as either the Bermudas, or the Bermoothes. This miserable London district consisted of about forty acres, roughly bounded by Carey Street on the north, The Strand on the south, Chancery Lane on the east, and Clement's Inn on the west. This quadrant was made up of narrow alleys and lanes, where dilapidated buildings encouraged prostitution, gambling, and the illegal manufacture of alcohol in the many hidden distilleries — "stills."

The London Bermoothes was teeming with ruffians, thieves, drunks, and bankrupt debtors, all seeking refuge there from poverty and despair, or arrest and imprisonment. It was *there*, to the London Bermoothes, that Prospero ordered Ariel to go. It was there that Ariel was sent at midnight to fetch that very different kind of "dew."

Just as "Bermoothes" or "Bermudas" could refer a Londoner to two very different places, "dew" also means two vastly different types of liquid. And illegal distilleries — stills — with their rough alcohol are a universal problem. Knowing such background, Ariel's puns are funny. Listen again:

> … Thou call'dst me up at midnight
> To fetch dew from the still-vexed Bermoothes …

In the sixteenth century, most, if not all, of the playwright's contemporary London audiences would get — and chuckle over — Ariel's little joke.[29] With time, however, all meaning of Ariel's words would be lost; and later English audiences, as audiences all over the world today attending *The Tempest*, would sit stone-faced, with Ariel's clever pun zooming right over their heads.

∾

No other place in the world possesses the unique combination of features described in *The Tempest,* and found together on the island of Vulcano: yellow sands, hot mud pools, volcanoes, springs, fumaroles, sulphur and acrid stink, pines, oaks, lings, Spanish broom, cliffs, caves, grottoes, mulberries, hedgehogs, and scamels. Indeed, everything mentioned by the characters in the play is readily seen, touched, felt — and smelled — by a visit to this one magical island off the coast of Sicily today.

The location of the playwright's dramatic tale, *The Tempest*, comes into focus as yet one more Italian setting for one of his plays. Not only does the island of Vulcano provide the framework for the playwright's story, his imaginative tale is pieced together from then-current Italian actualities engrafted onto an ancient Roman legend. Italy: country, history, and current events — font of the playwright's inspiration.

NOTES
1.   *A Midsummer Night's Dream.*
2.   "A small ship; in earlier times a general term for all sailing vessels of small size, e.g., fishing-smacks, xebecs, pinnaces; in modern use, applied poetically or rhetorically to any sailing vessel …" *Oxford English Dictionary.*

---

3. Literally, a "butt" is a great wooden cask or barrel to hold a quantity of wine for transport. It is used here as slang for a large and clumsy slow-moving boat.

4. "Hoist" is certainly the correct word. Prospero is saying here that this derelict boat or ship was without a proper gangplank. Sea-faring ships in those times had very high sides to inhibit pirates from boarding them.

5. The natural course of the Arno runs through the city of Pisa and thence to the Tyrrhenian Sea in a course too shallow to accommodate seagoing cargo vessels.

6. As Fernand Braudel wrote on page 62 in his *The Mediterranean*, there was a specific reason for the increase of trade with English merchantmen calling at the flourishing Tuscan port of Livorno: "... the return of the English to the Mediterranean appears above all to have been in reply to explicit invitations such as those of the Grand Duke of Tuscany ..."

7. Ariel seems to have described "St. Elmo's fire," a phenomenon which the playwright may have witnessed. Wondrously glowing, but harmless emanations are produced when static electricity is grounded to solid objects. The shimmering lights have been seen by Mediterranean sailors since seafaring began. They are named for the patron saint of mariners, St. Elmo, a shortened form of St. Erasmus. Erasmus was a bishop in a harbor city just north of Naples. He was martyred there in 304 A.D. Ariel's account to Prospero also speaks of the deadly lightning in the storm. When bolts of lightning split the air and electrify it, ozone is produced in abundance.

8. In light of the historical events that serve as the background to the thwarted Tunisian kingship ambitions of Don John of Austria, and the jealous vacillations of Philip II in *Much Ado About Nothing*, I see a mockery of them in this marriage of a "King of Tunis."

9. These unusual observations can be ascribed to the effect of the abundance of ozone created by the severe electrical storm at sea. Ozone is the third and most unstable of oxygen molecules, made up of three instead of two oxygen atoms. Acting upon the adverse odors in their clothes, the ozone would have restored a "freshness."

10. This route around Sicily was used by Cleomenes and Dion on returning from Greece in *The Winter's Tale*.

11. In the Punic Wars — the wars between Rome and Carthage in the third and second centuries B.C. — Carthage was made a ruin. The city of Tunis rose up about six miles from its barren site. Thus, both Adrian and the audience would learn a bit of ancient history.

12. Allen Mandelbaum translation, University of California Press, 1982.

13. Also called the Lipari Islands.

14. Bianca was the daughter of Bartolomeo Capello (or Cappello), a member of one of the richest and most noble Venetian families.

15. In ancient literature Vulcano has had other names: Thermessa for its hot mud and saline pools; Hiera or Iera, meaning sacred; and Therasia, meaning a hot land.

16. Pietro Boroli, *Sicilia Archeologica*, Istituto Geographico de Agostini, Novara, 1989.

17. Such thorny plants are typical of the heath on Vulcano. The most obnoxious plant, however, is the ubiquitous yellow broom, a plant referred to regularly in the play.

18. "Welkin" is an old synonym for "sky." "Cheek" in this context refers to a cloud or cloud formation.

19. There is another reference to these berries in Act II Scene 1.

20. There was a time when Catalonia was a separate state which also included adjacent lands to the north, which reached into what today is southern France.

21. The language is fiercely preserved, e.g., a thirteenth-century text written by Raimon Lull is generally understood by modern speakers of Catalan.

22. The idea of Caliban being a cannibal seems first to have been advanced in 1767, by a Cambridge scholar, a Dr. Farmer, in his *Essays on the Learning of Shakespeare*, as cited in the second edition of Samuel and George Steevens' treatment of *The Tempest* published in 1778. From that time forward, the Caliban anagram theory has been wrongly treated by Shakespeare scholars as though a true fact, upon which a continuous effort has been made to prove that the playwright had an interest in the Americas.

23. For centuries her name has been a subject of speculation, to which I add my own, that it is Greek: the first part a simplified "psycho-," meaning soul, spirit, mind, or mental process, coupled with "rax," a poisonous spider in Greece, or a version of "psychorrhax," to be translated as soul- or spirit- or mind-bender.

24. The sixteenth-century English way of saying Algiers.

25. Footnoted [226] in *The Arden Shakespeare — The Tempest*: "Debate over the 'one thing' has flourished. Charles Lamb quoted John Ogilvy's *Accurate Description of Africa* (1670) to argue that Shakespeare was drawing on the legend of an Algerian witch who saved the city when it was besieged by Charles V's navy in 1541; she put a curse on the fleet, raising a furious storm that drove the ships away." See Charles Lamb, *Critical Essays*, or Evangeline M. O'Connor, *Who's Who and What's What in Shakespeare*, for a detailed narration. In that story the witch

is not named. Whether she was named Sycorax by the playwright is an open question. Strangely, in any case, this event is not explained in the play, and rare is the scholar, let alone audience, who has indicated any interest in it.

26. *Caliban, m. mena de paria de los llegendes escoceses, Diccionari Enciclopedia de la Llengua Catalonia*, Vol. 1 (1930), p. 509. Barcelona, Salvat Editores, S.A.: *mena*: kind or sort; *paria*: an outcast, a pariah.

27. *Gran Diccionari de la Llengua Catalana*, Enciclopedia Catalana, S.A., Barcelona, 1997.

28. In that there were no dictionaries in those days, there was no uniformity in spelling. All sorts of words were spelled in different ways, with writers taking a stab at spelling how things sounded.

29. The joke might sound something like this to modern ears: "You woke me up at midnight to go get moonshine from those darn stills in the Bermoothes!"

EPILOGUE

*A*s we have seen in the foregoing chapters of this book, the "imaginary" settings for the ten Italian Plays of Shakespeare have presented both specific, and strikingly accurate, details about that country, as a result of dedicated sojourns within it by the playwright. The author's journeys took him from its Alpine slopes to the toe of its peninsula, across the length and breadth of its great island of Sicily, and included sailing trips on both the adjoining Adriatic and Tyrrhenian Seas. For the last four hundred years, nearly all of the playwright's descriptions of Italy's places and treasures have either gone unrecognized as being true, or have been dismissed as mistaken.

In researching and writing this book, it has been my goal to revisit these orthodox beliefs, and contrast them for their accuracy with the actual words of the English playwright.

BIBLIOGRAPHY

Acton, Harold, and Edward Chaney, eds. *Florence: A Traveler's Companion*. New York: Athenaeum, 1986.

Amphlett, Hilda. *Who Was Shakespeare?* London: William Heinemann Ltd., 1955.

Andrews, Mark Edwin. *Law Versus Equity in the Merchant of Venice*. Boulder: University of Colorado Press, 1965.

Attwater, Donald. *The Penguin Dictionary of Saints*. New York: Penguin Books, 1965, 1981.

Avery, Catherine B., ed. *The New Century Handbook of Classical Geography*. New York: Appleton-Century-Crofts Inc., 1972.

Azienda di Promozione Turistica del Montovano. *La Piccola Atene*.

Bacon, Delia. *The Philosophy of the Plays of Shakespeare Unfolded*. London: Groombridge and Sons, 1857.

Banchard, Paul. *Blue Guide Southern Italy: From Rome to Calabria*. 5th ed. London: Ernest Benn Ltd.; New York: W.W. Norton & Co., 1984.

Bandello, Matteo. *La Prima Parte de la Nouvelle del Bandello*. Lucca: 1554.

Barkan, Leonard. "'Living Sculptures': Ovid, Michelangelo and *The Winter's Tale*," *English Literary History*. Vol. 48, pp. 639–667, 1908.

Barron, Robert. *Decorative Maps*. New Jersey: Crescent Books, 1989.

Barzini, Luigi. *The Italians*. London: Hamish Hamilton Ltd., 1964.

Bate, Jonathan. *The Genius of Shakespeare*. Oxford: Oxford University Press, 1998.

———. *Shakespearean Constitutions: Politics, Theater, Criticism, 1730–1830*. Oxford: Clarendon Press, 1989.

Benson, P.J. *The Invention of the Renaissance Woman: The Challenge of Female Independence in the Literature and Thought of Italy and England*. State College: Penn State University Press, 1992.

Bergamo and Its Land. Bergamo: Publishers Bolis, 1970.

Bertrand, Louis. *The History of Spain (Part I)*. New York: Collier Books, Macmillan, 1971.

Bewes, Wyndham Anstis. *The Romance of the Law Merchant*. London: Sweet and Maxwell Ltd., 1923.

Biddulph, William. *The Travels of a Certaine Englishman*. 1609.

Black, C. E., et al. *Chronicles of the High Renaissance*. London: Angus Books, Ltd.

Boccaccio, Giovanni. *The Decameron*. 2nd ed. G. H. McWilliam, trans. London and New York: Penguin Books, 1995.

Bonomi, Sandro, et al. *Le Mura Ritrovate— Fortificazioni di Padova in Eta Comunale e Carrarese*. Panda Edizioni. Comitato Mura di Padova.

Irvine, Theodora. *How to Pronounce the Names in Shakespeare*. Detroit, Mi.: Omnigraphics, 1990.

Jackson, W.T.H. *The Literature of the Middle Ages*. New York: Columbia University Press, 1960.

Jeffery, Violet M. "Shakespeare's Venice," *The Modern Language Review*. Vol. 27, No. 1, pp. 24–35. London: Modern Humanities Research Assocation, 1932.

Johnson, Paul. *A History of Christianity*. New York: Athenaeum, 1977.

Jones, Charles W. *Medieval Literature in Translation*. New York: David McKay Company, Inc., 1970.

Kann, Robert A. *A History of the Habsburg Empire 1526–1918*. Berkley: University of California Press Ltd., 1974.

Kay, Richard. *The Broadview Book of Medieval Anecdotes*. Peterborough, Canada: Broadview Press, Ltd.

Kelly, Henry Ansgar. *The Matrimonial Trials of Henry VIII*. Stanford, Calif.: Stanford University Press, 1976.

Kelly, J.N.D. *The Oxford Dictionary of Popes*. Oxford: Oxford University Press, 1986.

Kendall, Alan. *Medieval Pilgrims*. London: Wayland Publishers, 1970.

King, Dean. *Harbors and High Seas*. 3rd ed. New York: Henry Holt and Company, 2000.

King, Ross. *Brunelleschi's Dome*. New York: Penguin Books, 2000.

Kinney, Arthur F. "Revisiting The Tempest," *Modern Philology*. 93, pp. 161–177, 1995.

Kittredge, George Lyman, ed. *The Complete Works of Shakespeare*. Ginn and Company, 1936.

Klein, Holger, and Michele Marrapodi, eds. *Shakespeare and Italy, Shakespeare Yearbook*. Vol. 10. Lewiston, N.Y.: The Edwin Mellen Press.

Klier, Walter. *Das Shakespeare—Komplott*. Gottingen: Steidlverlag, 1941.

La Duca, Rosario. *Il Castello a Mare di Palermo*. Palermo: Edizioni Popolari Siciliane, 1980.

Lambin, Georges. *Voyages de Shakespeare en France et en Italie*. Geneva: Librarie E. Droz, 1962.

Lane, Frederic Chapin. *Andrea Barbarigo, Merchant of Venice 1418-1499*. Baltimore: Johns Hopkins University Press, 1944.

———. *Venetian Ships and Shipbuilders of the Renaissance*. Baltimore: Johns Hopkins University Press, 1934.

Laughlin, Clara E. *So You're Going to Italy*. London: Methuen & Co. Ltd., 1925.

Laurence, Ray. *The Roads of Roman Italy*. London: Routledge, 1999.

Lawner, Lynne. *I Modi—The Sixteen Pleasures: An Erotic Album of the Sixteenth Century*. L. Lawner, trans. Northwestern University Press, 1988.

———. *Lives of the Courtesans: Portraits of the Renaissance*. New York: Rizzoli, 1987.

Lee, Sidney. *A Life of William Shakespeare*. 1898. Oracle Publishing Ltd., 1996.

———. *Great Englishmen of the Sixteenth Century*. London: 1904.

Levin, Michael J. *Agents of Empire: Spanish Ambassadors in Sixteenth-Century Italy*. Ithaca, N.Y.: Cornell University Press, 2005.

Levith, Murray J. *Shakespeare's Italian Settings and Plays*. New York: St. Martin's Press, 1989.

Liberati, Alfredo. *Accademia dei Rozzi in Siena (Ricordi e Memorie)*. Siena: U. Periccioli, 1966.

Lievsay, John L. *The Elizabethans' Image of Italy*. Ithaca, N.Y.: Cornell University Press—for the Folger Shakespeare Library, 1964.

Lister, Raymond. *Old Maps & Globes*. London: Bell & Hyman, 1965.

Logan, Oliver. *Culture and Society in Venice 1470–1790*. New York: Charles Scribner's Sons, 1972.

Looney, J. Thomas. *"Shakespeare" Identified, and the Poems of Edward de Vere*. Vols. 1 & 2. Ruth Loyd Miller, ed. Jennings, La.: Minos Publishing Co., 1975.

Lorenzetti, Giulio. *Venice and Its Lagoon*. John Guthrie, trans. Trieste: Edizione Lint, 1975.

Macadam, Alta. *Blue Guide Florence*. 4th ed. London: A & C Black; New York: W.W. Norton, 1988.

————. *Blue Guide Northern Italy: From the Alps to Rome*. 8th ed. London: A & C Black; New York: W.W. Norton, 1985.

————. *Blue Guide Rome and Environs*. 2nd ed. London: Ernest Benn Ltd.; USA: Rand McNally, 1975.

————. *Blue Guide Sicily*. 2nd ed. London: Ernest Benn Ltd.; USA: Rand McNally, 1981.

————. *Blue Guide Venice*. 4th ed. London: A & C Black.; New York: W.W. Norton, 1989.

Magi, Giovanna. *All Verona*. Florence: Bonechi Editore, 1990.

Magri, Gino. *Ostiglia Napoleonica*. Ostigilia: Stranieri Editore, 1982.

Magri, Noemi. "Places in Shakespeare: Belmont and Thereabouts," *The de Vere Society Newsletter*. June 2003.

————. "Italian Art in Shakespeare: Giulio Romano," *The de Vere Society Newsletter*. July 2000, p. 12.

Magris, Claudio. *Danube*. Patrick Creagh, trans. New York: Farrar, Straus and Giroux, 1989.

Makower, Joel, ed. *The Map Catalog*. New York: Tilden Press Book, Vintage Books, Random House, 1986.

Malynes, Gerard di (1586–1641). *Consuetudo, Vel, Lex Mercatorio or The Ancient Law Merchant*.

Marani, Ercolano. *Mantova—An Artistic and Illustrated Guide Book*. Milan: Moneta Editore.

Marlowe, Christopher. *The Famous Tragedy of the Rich Jew of Malta*. 1633.

Marqusee, Michael. *Venice—An Illustrated Anthology*. London: Conran Octopus, 1988.

Marrapodi, Michele, A.J. Hoenselaars, and L. Falzon Santucci, eds. *Shakespeare's Italy: Functions of Italian Locations in Renaissance Drama*. New York: St. Martin's Press, 1997.

Marsh, A.H. *The History of the Court of Chancery*. Toronto: Carswell & Co., 1890.

Matthew, Donald. *Atlas of Medieval Europe*. New York: Facts on File, Inc., 1984.

Maurer, Margaret. "Figure, Place, and the End of The Two Gentlemen," *Style*. Vol. 23, No. 3, pp. 405–429. Fall, 1989.

Maurice, C. Edmund. *The Story of Bohemia from the Earliest Times to the Fall of National Independence in 1620*. New York: Putnam; London: Fisher Unwin, 1908.

Mola, Luca. *The Silk Industry in Renaissance Venice*. Baltimore: Johns Hopkins University Press, 2000.

Montaigne, Michel de. *The Complete Essays*. M. A. Screech, trans. London: Penguin Books, 1991.

————. *The Diary of Montaigne's Journey to Italy*. E. J. Trechmann, trans. & notes. New York: Harcourt Brace & Company, 1929.

Montobbio, Luigi, et al. *Padova: Storia—Arte—Cultura*. Padova: Editoriale Programma, 1990.

Moreland, Carl, and David Bannister. *Antique Maps*. Oxford: Phaidon-Christies Limited, 1986.

Morris, Christopher. *The Tudors*. Fontana/Collins, 1955 (1982).

Morris, James. *The World of Venice*. New York: Harcourt Brace Jovanovich, 1960.

Morton, H. V. *A Traveler in Italy*. New York: Dodd Mead and Co., 1964.

Moryson, Fynes. *Itinerary*. 1617.

Moschini, Gianntonio. *Guida per la Città di Padova*. Venezia: Fratelli Gamba, 1817. Reprint, Arnaldo Forni Editore.

Muller, Adalbert. *Venice, Her Art-Treasures and Historical Associations, A Guide to the City and the Neighboring Islands*. Venice: H.F. & M. Munster, 1864.

Muraro, Michelangelo, and Paolo Marton. *Venetian Villas*. Peter Lauritzen, trans. Udine, Italy: Magnus Edizioni SpA., 1986.

Murray, Peter. *The Architecture of the Italian Renaissance*. New York: Schocken Books Inc., 1963.

Nagel's Encyclopedia Guide: French and Italian Riviera. Geneva, New York, Toronto, London: Nagel Publishers, 1964.

Nagel's Encyclopedia Guide: Italy. Geneva: Nagel Publishers, 1975.

Natkiel, Richard, and Antony Preston. *Atlas of Maritime History*. New York: Gallery Books, W.H. Smith, 1987.

Norwich, John Julius. *A History of Venice*. New York: Vintage Books, Random House, 1982.

Nutall, A. D. *A New Mimesis. Shakespeare and the Representation of Reality*. London: Methuen & Co., 1983.

O'Connor, Evangeline M. *Who's Who and What's What in Shakespeare*. New York: Avenel Books, 1978 reprint of 1887 edition.

Ogburn, Charlton. *The Mysterious William Shakespeare—The Myth and the Reality*. McLean, Va.: EPM Publications, Inc., 1984.

Ogburn, Dorothy, and Charlton Ogburn. *This Star of England*. New York: Coward-McCann, Inc., 1952.

Onions, C. T. *A Shakespeare Glossary*. Oxford: Clarendon Press, 1986.

Panthon, Patrick de. *Sicily*. Frommer's Touring Guides. Penelope Poulton, trans. New York: Prentice Hall, 1991.

Partridge, Eric. *A Dictionary of Slang and Unconventional English*. 7th ed. New York: Macmillan Publishing Co., Inc., 1976.

————. *Shakespeare's Bawdy*. 3rd ed. London: Routledge & Kegan Paul, 1968.

Peloubet, F. N., ed. *The International Bible Dictionary*. Philadelphia: John C. Winston, 1912.

Pereira, Anthony. *Naples, Pompeii & Southern Italy*. London: B.T. Batsford Ltd., 1977.

Petrie, Charles. *Don John of Austria*. New York: W.W. Norton & Co., 1967.

————. *The History of Spain*. Part II. New York: Collier Books, Macmillan, 1971.

Pevsner, Nikolaus. *An Outline of European Architecture*. London: Penguin Books, 1985.

Phillips-Watlington, Christine. *Bermuda's Botanical Wonderland*. London: Macmillan Education, Ltd., 1996.

Pignatti, Terisio. *The Golden Century of Venetian Painting*. Los Angeles County Museum of Art, 1979.

Plutarch. "Antony." *Plutarch's Lives*. New York: Modern Library Edition, Random House, 2001.

Pollard, Alfred W. *Shakespeare's Fight with the Pirates*. London: A. Moring, 1937.

Putnam, Robert. *Early Sea Charts*. New York: Abbeville Press, 1983.

Ragusi, Oreste, ed. *Isole Eolie*. Milan: Arte Photo Graphic Oreste Ragusi.

Renaissance, The. National Geographic Society Story of Man Library, 1970.

Renault, Mary. *The Mask of Apollo*. London: Longmans, Green and Co., Sceptre Edition, 1986.

Rorimer, James J. *The Cloisters*. New York: Metropolitan Museum of Art, 1963.

Rossiter, Stuart. *Blue Guide Greece*. 3rd ed. London: Ernest Benn Ltd.; USA: Rand McNally, 1980.

Roth, Cecil. *The Jews in the Renaissance*. Philadelphia, 1956.

Rowse, A. L. *William Shakespeare*. New York: Barnes & Noble Books, 1995.

Ruggiero, Guido. *The Boundaries of Eros: Sex Crime and Sexuality in Renaissance Venice*. Oxford: Oxford University Press, 1984.

Sammartino, Peter. *The Man Who Was William Shakespeare*. New York: Cornwall Books, 1990.

Sampieri, Placido. *Iconologia della Beata Vergine Maria Protettrice di Messina*. "Delle Imagini delle Madonna dell' Annunziata di Fiorenza nel Tempio di S. Giov. Battista detto de Fiorentini e Sua Origine." Lib. V., Chap. XXVII, pp. 622–624. Messina, 1644.

Saperstein, Marc. *Jewish Preaching 1200–1800*. New Haven: Yale University Press, 1989.

Schevill, Ferdinand. *Medieval and Renaissance Florence*. Vol. 1. New York: Harper & Row, 1961.

Schoenbaum, S. *William Shakespeare: A Compact Documentary Life*. Oxford: Oxford University Press, 1977.

Seragnoli, Daniele. *Il Teatro a Siena nel Cinquecento*. Roma: Bulzoni Editore, 1980.

Sereni, Emilio. *History of the Italian Agricultural Landscape*. R. Bruce Litchfield, trans. Princeton, N.J.: Princeton University Press, 1961.

Serra, Vittorio. *New Practical Guide of Milan.* Florence: Bonechi, 1990.

Shaheen, Naseeb. *Biblical References in Shakespeare's Plays.* Newark: University of Delaware Press, 1999.

Shakespeare, William. *Mr. William Shakespeare's Comedies, Histories & Tragedies—A Facsimile Edition Prepared by Helge Kokeritz—First Folio 1623.* Yale University Press, Oxford University Press, 1954.

Shewmaker, Eugene F. *Shakespeare's Language: A Glossary of Unfamiliar Words in Shakespeare's Plays and Poems.* New York: Facts On File, Inc., 1996.

Shulvass, Moses A. *Jews in the World of the Renaissance.* Chicago: Leiden, 1973.

Simeti, Mary Taylor. *On Persephone's Island.* New York: Vintage Books, Random House, 1986.

Simon, Kate. *Italy—The Places in Between.* New York: Harper & Row, 1970.

———. *A Renaissance Tapestry—The Gonzaga of Mantua.* New York: Harper & Row, 1988.

Sinsheimer, Hermann. *Shylock: The History of a Character or The Myth of The Jew. First Edition.* 1947.

Skeat, Walter W. *An Etymological Dictionary of the English Language.* Oxford: Clarendon Press, 1974.

Skempton, A. W. *A History of Technology.* Vol. III. *From the Renaissance to the Industrial Revolution c. 1500–1750.* Part IV. Chapter 17, "Canals and River Navigation Before 1750." Oxford: Clarendon Press, 1957.

Slater, Gilbert. *Seven Shakespeares.* London: Cecil Palmer, 1931.

Smith, Denis Mack. *A History of Sicily,* 2 Vols. *Medieval Sicily: 800–1713. Modern Sicily: After 1713.* New York: Dorset Press, 1968.

Società Editrice Affinita Elettive. *The Eolian Islands, Pearls of the Mediterranean.* Nicholas Whithorn, trans. Messina: Edizioni Affinita Elettive, 1997.

Spevack, Marvin. *The Harvard Concordance to Shakespeare.* Cambridge, Mass.: Belknap Press of the Harvard University Press, 1973.

Stanghellini, Enzo, and Gianni Ainardi. *Verona nei Secoli—A Stroll Through the Centuries.* Verona: Espro di E. Stanghellini & C.

Starr, Chester G. *A History of the Ancient World.* New York: Oxford University Press, 1965.

Stillinger, Jack. *Multiple Authorship and the Myth of Solitary Genius.* New York: Oxford University Press, 1991.

Stokes, Francis Griffin. *Who's Who in Shakespeare.* Avenel, N.J.: Crescent Books, 1989.

Storti, Amedeo, ed. *You in Venice.* 1967–68.

Strode, Hudson. *The Story of Bermuda.* New York: Harcourt Brace & Company, 1946.

Stuard, Susan Mosher. *A State of Deference: Ragusa-Dubrovnik in the Medieval Centuries.* Philadelphia: University of Pennsylvania Press, 1992.

Sugden, Edward H. *A Topographical Dictionary to the Works of Shakespeare and His Fellow Dramatists.* Manchester University Press, 1925.

Sullivan, Edward. "Shakespeare and Italy," *The Nineteenth Century and After.* Jan. 1918, pp. 138–153.

———. "Shakespeare and Italy II," *The Nineteenth Century and After.* Feb. 1918, pp. 323–339.

———. "Shakespeare and the Waterways of Northern Italy," *The Nineteenth Century and After.* Aug. 1908, pp. 215–232.

Sutherland, John, and Cedric Watts. *Henry V, War Criminal? and Other Shakespeare Puzzles.* Oxford: Oxford University Press, 2000.

Sweet, George Elliot. *Shake-Speare: The Mystery.* New York: Vantage Press, 1956, 1985 edition.

Symonds, John Addington. *Renaissance in Italy.* New York: The Modern Library.

Sypher, Wylie. *Four Stages of Renaissance Style.* New York: Doubleday & Company, 1956.

Talvacchia, Bette. "Giulio Romano's Hall of Troy," *Journal of the Warburg and Courtauld Institutes.* Vol. 51, pp. 235-242. 1988.

Tenenti, Alberto. *Naufrages, Corsaires, et Assurances Maritimi a Venise 1592–1609.* Paris: S.E.V.P.E.N., 1959.

Thomas, Keith. *Religion and the Decline of Magic.* New York: Charles Scribner's Sons, 1971.

Ticknor, George. *History of Spanish Literature.* Vol. 1, p. 252. New York: Harper and Brothers, 1854.

Tieto, Paolo. *Riviera del Brenta.* Padova: Panda Edizioni, 1987.

Tooley, R. V. *Maps & Map-Makers.* London: B.T. Batsford Ltd., 1978.

Tooley, R. V., and Charles Bricker. *Landmarks of Mapmaking.* Dorset Press, 1976, 1989.

Treharne, R. F., and Harold Fullard. *Muir's Atlas of Ancient and Classical History.* 6th ed. George Philip and Son, Ltd.

Treves, Sir Frederick. *The Riviera of the Corniche Road.* London: Cassell and Company, Ltd., 1923.

Turnbull, Patrick. *Provence.* London: B.T. Batsford Ltd., 1972.

Van de Gohm, Richard. *Antique Maps.* London: The Macmillan Company, 1972.

Van Dorn, William G. *Oceanography and Seamanship.* New York: Dodd, Mead & Company, 1974.

Vickers, Robert H. *History of Bohemia.* Chicago: Charles H. Sergel Co., 1894.

Virgil. *The Aeneid.* Robert Fitzgerald, trans. New York: Random House, 1981 and 1990.

———. *The Aeneid.* Allen Mandelbaum, trans. Berkeley: University of California Press, 1971–1981.

———. *The Aeneid of Virgil.* Rolfe Humphries, trans. New York: Charles Scribner's Sons, 1951.

———. *The Aeneid, Ecologues, Georgics.* J. W. Mackail, trans. New York: The Modern Library, Random House, 1934.

Viviani, Giuseppe Franco. *Verona—Guide to the City.* Udine: Magnus Edizioni, 1990.

Viviani, Lorenzo. *A Day In Verona.* Florence: Bonechi Edizioni, 1969.

Waern, Cecilia. *Medieval Sicily, Aspects of Life and Art in the Middle Ages.* London: Duckworth & Co., 1910.

Ward, Bernard Mordaunt. *Introduction to "A Hundreth Sundrie Flowers."* Ruth Loyd Miller, ed. Jennings, La.: Minos Publishing Co.

Ward, W. H. *The Architecture of the Renaissance in France.* Vol. 1. *The Early Renaissance (1475–1640).* New York: Charles Scribner's Sons, 1911.

Watt, Homer, Karl V. Holzknecht and Raymond Ross. *Outlines of Shakespeare's Plays.* New York: Barnes & Noble, 1941.

Webb, Judge. *The Mystery of William Shakespeare.* London: Longmans, Green and Co., 1902.

Webbe, Edward. *Edward Webbe, Chief Master Gunner, His Travails 1590.* English Reprints. Edward Asher, ed. London: Alex Murray and Son, 1869.

———. *The Rare and Most Wonderful Things Which Edward Webbe an Englishman Borne, Hath Seen and Passed in His Troublesome Travails.* 1590.

Webster, John. *The White Devil.* Lincoln: University of Nebraska Press, 1969.

Wells, Stanley, and Gary Taylor. *Modernizing Shakespeare's Spelling.* Oxford: Clarendon Press, 1979.

Whalen, Richard F. *Shakespeare: Who Was He? The Oxford Challenge to the Bard of Avon.* Westport, Conn.: Praeger, 1994.

Wheatcroft, Andrew. *The Habsburgs: Embodying Empire.* London: Penguin Books, 1995.

Wilford, John Noble. *The Mapmakers.* New York: Alfred A. Knopf, 1981.

Yates, Frances Amelia. *Charles V and the Idea of Empire, Astrea: The Imperial Theme in the Sixteenth Century.* London: 1975.

———. *John Florio.* Cambridge: Cambridge University Press, 1934.

———. *The Occult Philosophy in the Elizabethan Age.* London: Ark Paperbacks, Routledge & Kegan Paul, 1983.

Young, Alan. *Tudor and Jacobean Tournaments.* Dobbs Ferry, N.Y.: Sheridan House, 1987.

Yriarte, Charles. *Florence.* Philadelphia: The John C. Winston Co., 1897.

Zenfell, Martha Ellen, ed. *Insight Guides.* "Bermuda." Singapore: Apa Publications, 1991.

Zoppe, Leandro. *Itinerari Gonzagheschi*. Milano: Itinera Edizioni, 1988.

Zorzi, Alvise. *La Repubblica del Leone*. "Cronologia Veneziana." Milan: Rusconi Libri, SpA., 1979.

Zucchini, M. *Bonifica Padana*. "Notizie Storiche." Rovigo Istituto Padano de Arte Grafiche, 1967.